Colección Támesis

SERIE A: MONOGRAFÍAS, 278

TRAFFICKING KNOWLEDGE IN EARLY TWENTIETH-CENTURY SPAIN

CENTRES OF EXCHANGE AND CULTURAL IMAGINARIES

This study makes an original contribution to scholarship by tracking and evaluating the significance of the various individuals and (particularly) institutions responsible for the traffic of ideas both between Spain and the outside world, and also between Madrid and the interior. This has not been attempted before, and it is a necessary supplement to the usual focus on individual authors and texts, allowing us to appreciate the importance of setting the latter in the context of the circuits of knowledge functioning in Spain in their time. It looks in breadth and in detail at the nature of Spain's cultural and intellectual exchanges with Europe in the early decades of the twentieth century.

Three features make it original in its approach. It focuses on a broad range of institutions, including publishing houses and journals, as "centres of exchange", and looks at how they promoted and facilitated Spain's contact with Europe. The second feature is that it foregrounds the idea of "cultural imaginaries" as the driving force behind Spain's exchanges with Europe. Thirdly, in terms of territory, it departs from a Franco/German-centred concept of Europe, paying particular attention to a Europe of the margins, in the form of England and Russia, as two countries that held particular attractions for the Spanish mind. While being centred on Madrid for its case-studies, it also pays specific attention to issues of internal dissemination.

ALISON SINCLAIR is Professor of Spanish at the University of Cambridge.

ALISON SINCLAIR

TRAFFICKING KNOWLEDGE IN EARLY TWENTIETH-CENTURY SPAIN

CENTRES OF EXCHANGE AND CULTURAL IMAGINARIES

TAMESIS

First published 2009 by Tamesis, Woodbridge

ISBN 978–1–85566–190–5

Tamesis is an imprint of Boydell & Brewer Ltd
PO Box 9, Woodbridge, Suffolk IP12 3DF, UK
and of Boydell & Brewer Inc.
668 Mt Hope Avenue, Rochester, NY 14620, USA
website: www.boydellandbrewer.com

The publisher has no responsibility for the continued existence or accuracy of
URLs for external or third-party internet websites referred to in this book,
and does not guarantee that any content on such websites is,
or will remain, accurate or appropriate

A CIP catalogue record for this book is available
from the British Library

This publication is printed on acid-free paper

Printed in Great Britain by
CPI Antony Rowe, Chippenham and Eastbourne

CONTENTS

FIGURES

ACKNOWLEDGEMENTS

None of this book would have been possible without a great deal of openness and support on the part of others. Most significant was the generous funding from the British Academy that provided me with research leave for 2001–2003. The tardiness of completing this project is in part related to other research opportunities that presented themselves in that period, and which without doubt enriched the initial intentions of the project. My involvement, thanks to the intervention of Jo Labanyi, with Luisa Passerini's *Europe in Love* project at the KWI in Essen took place during this research period, and enabled much fruitful contact with other scholars from Europe working on the early twentieth century. Two publications emerged from that project that reappear in revised form in this work, the chapter on Russia, and the part of Chapter 4 that deals with the *Revista de Occidente*. I also continued to collaborate with Richard Cleminson on eugenics and sexual reform in early twentieth-century Spain. This area of interest had been sparked by contact with Tom Glick, who had generously shared with me a wealth of information about Hildegart Rodríguez. I had intended to have a chapter in this study on the trafficking of knowledge about sexuality and draw on it partially for Chapter 9. This work, however, came out in much-expanded form in a book on Hildegart, *Sex and Society in Early Twentieth-Century Spain* (University of Wales Press 2007). I was also able to explore various themes of this study in symposia kindly supported in Cambridge by CRASSH (Centre for Research in Arts, Social Sciences and Humanities): conferences on the World League for Sexual Reform (2000), on Alternative Discourses in Early Twentieth-Century Spain: Intellectuals, Dissent and Subcultures of Mind and Body (2002), an international workshop on Heredity, Degeneration and Eugenics (2006), and an international conference on Eugenics, Sex and the State (2007). I am grateful also to other venues where I was able to present sections of this year: conferences in Stirling, Swansea and Cambridge, and seminars in Nottingham, Aberdeen, Sheffield, London and Essen.

I am grateful to Taylor & Francis for permission to draw on three of my articles for sections of this book: 'Spain's Love Affair with Russia: The Attraction of Exotic (Br)Others', *European Review of History* 11(2): 207–24; '"Telling it like it was?" The "Residencia de Estudiantes" and its image', *Bulletin of Spanish Studies* 81(6): 739–63; 'On a Mission: Travelling with a Purpose in Spain in the 1930s', *Journal of Iberian and Latin American Studies* 12 (2–3) (Aug/Dec 2006), 189–201, special double issue edited by Claire Lindsay and Montserrat Lunati (see the website for these journals at http://www.informaworld.com).

Archival work for this project centred on Madrid, the Biblioteca Nacional, the Hemeroteca Municipal in the Casa del Conde-Duque, the Archivo General de Administración at Alcalá de Henares, the Residencia de Estudiantes, the Ateneo de Madrid, and the archive of the Duque de Alba in the Palacio de Liria in Madrid, and I am grateful to the numerous members of staff who were friendly and helpful to me. If this book has been much concerned with networking, doing the work was an ongoing example of how important it is, and I am in debt to all of those who gave their time to what was sometimes a rather open-ended line of enquiry. I was able to consult the archival holdings of Ricardo Baeza generously made available to me by his daughter-in-law Mari Baeza, both in Madrid and at the amazing library at Montblanc. I would also like to thank Diego Hidalgo for making his father's papers available to me in Madrid, and José Álvarez Junco for his advice. In the UK I was able to use the resources of the British Library (where I would like to thank Barry Taylor and Geoff West), and the Wellcome Institute, where Lesley Hall was particularly helpful. But none of this work would have been possible without the ongoing friendly support of the staff at the University Library, Cambridge, particularly that of Neil Hudson in the periodicals section of the West Room, and Sonia Morcillo. Nor would completion of the book have been possible without the encouragement of Stephen Hart and Ellie Ferguson at Boydell & Brewer.

It would be hard to thank all of those who helped this book on its way, and through whose conversations, contacts and support it was possible for it to come into being. They include, besides those already mentioned: Carmen Aguilera, Josefina Aldecoa, Andrew Anderson, Karen Arrandale, Michael Aronna, Julia Biggane, Jean François Botrel, Stuart Davis, Nigel Dennis, Manuel Durán, Sally Faulkner, Simon Grayson, Clara Herrera, Diego Hidalgo, Belén Jiménez, Tony Kapcia, Neil Kenny, Tess Knighton, Jo Labanyi, Kurt Lipstein, Anja Louis, Asensi Madinaveitia, Anaí Martínez, Ruth Mas, Jordana Mendelson, Álvaro Ribagorda, Mike Richards, Stephen Roberts, Lorna Sinclair, Sarah Wright.

Lastly, I owe a special debt of gratitude to Maruja Rincón for her friendship and hospitality, and to my family, particularly Stewart, without whose ongoing support no books (nor much else!) would get finished.

ABBREVIATIONS

AGA	Archivo general de la Administración (Alcalá de Henares)
BILE	*Boletín de la Institución Libre de Enseñanza*
BIRS	*Boletín del Instituto de Reformas Sociales*
CHI	Comité Hispano-Inglés
CIAP	Compañía Ibero-Americana de Publicaciones
ILE	Institución Libre de Enseñanza
JAE	Junta para Ampliación de Estudios
JIAL	Junta de Intercambio y Adquisición de Libros
Liria	archive of the Palacio de Liria, Madrid
RO	*Revista de Occidente*
SCC	Sociedad de Cursos y Conferencias
WLSR	World League for Sexual Reform

ORIENTATION

1 Maps for Cultural Trafficking[*]

The activity of trafficking is inevitably and rightly associated with business (and with busyness). It is about the to and fro of exchanges, about barters, bargains, happenstance, opportunism. These characteristics constitute not only the activity of commerce, but are the vital part of cultural exchange. This book sets out to look at cultural trafficking in Spain, and in particular to look for what is dynamic, lively and imaginative in it. Spain in the early decades of the twentieth century engaged in dynamic and extremely complex types of cultural exchange with elsewhere. Its great (and obvious) trading 'partner' is Europe, yet Europe is not a single entity. In concentrating, as I shall, on Europe, I am conscious that there are at least two major other significant trading areas for Spain: Latin America and the United States. Both of them will figure from time to time in these pages, but both merit their own separate treatment.

In addition to this, regretfully, it has not been possible to provide an extensive consideration of the part played by Catalonia. A great deal of the emphasis of the first sections of the book is upon urban activity, and with a prime emphasis on Madrid. The reason for this has been partly strategic, and partly determined by beliefs about the effective centrality of Madrid in the trafficking of culture. Martínez Rus (2003: 209, 222) refers to some 276 publishers existing in Spain in 1935, 120 of whom were based in Madrid and 98 in Barcelona, a feature of the cultural profile that bears out the importance of Madrid, but also signals the significance of Barcelona. I have set aside, with regret, a detailed discussion of the case of Catalonia, and specifically Barcelona and Valencia, major cities that have long been recognized as significant in cultural trafficking. The publishing activities of Sempere, for example, stand as an iconic and emblematic representation of what was achieved outside Madrid, while the *Cuadernos de Cultura* published by Marín Civera Martínez (Valencia 1930–3) serve as a major example of a socialist

[*]   I would like to acknowledge the generous support of the British Academy whose funding of a Research Readership made the research for this book possible.

organ of transmission of information in the fields of politics, medicine and
sexuality (see Sinclair 2007: 220).

Trading is more than an activity: it arises out of relationship (curiosity,
desire, necessity) and forms a further relationship (importer, exporter, middle-
man), with consequences such as prosperity, diversity of available materials,
the cultivation of taste and fashion. 'Trafficking' as a concept applied to
knowledge (including cultural practice) therefore informs us about cultural
relations, at the same time as it sheds a light on the nature of both sides in a
trading relationship. And just as our personal relationships are founded not
on objective realities but on desires, projections, idealizations, identifications
and prejudices, even on paranoias, so we can think of cultural relations as
driven by and nuanced by, cultural imaginaries.

This is the perspective from which this book sets out. It seeks to examine
Spain's cultural relations with Europe, looking in detail at a wide spectrum of
routes by which knowledge, customs, education and attitudes related loosely
to Europe, or more specifically to different countries within Europe, came
to Spain. It views the process not as one of simple delivery of these 'objects
of exchange', but rather one in which the reception of such objects resulted
from a desire, and that desire was predicated on a series of cultural imaginaries that pertained both to Spain itself and to other European countries.
Nor should we think of 'objects of exchange' as stable or unchanged by their
passage over borders. At the simplest level, books in translation are famously
mistranslated, abridged (this is the case of various editions of the Bible in
Spanish in the nineteenth century), plays in translation will be adapted for
local audiences, travelling exhibitions will contain selections that relate both
to the proposed viewing public and to the exhibitor's perspective. 'Objects of
exchange' are also 'boundary objects'. As Golinski summarizes,

> Boundary objects are things that link together different social groups, who
> may view and use them in quite different ways. [...] These objects exist in
> distinct 'social worlds', to the extent that they are understood differently
> and used to advance different aims by the communities involved.
>
> (Golinski 1998: 44)

'Objects of exchange', in cultural terms, do not have a single point of
entry to a country. The capital is not the province, and in the case of Spain
there are significant regional activities related to cultural exchange. Cities of
the periphery above all, such as Barcelona, Valencia, Seville, had their own
distinct functioning in relation to cultural exchange. In addition to this, there
is the fascinating (and unexplored) dynamic between the cultural importations through the regions, and cultural importations through Madrid. But this
study is characterized by both its particularity and its limitation, in that my
focus has been on cultural activity of reception and propagation related to

Madrid. I have tried nonetheless to retain a focus on the specificity of the centre in my discussions of cultural exchange, and an awareness of activity that was not associated with the centre. Some of the ideas of propagation of cultural knowledge, particularly those explored in the section on 'Spreading the Word', emanated from the centre, with the sort of 'centralist' and colonial conviction that accompanies such enterprises, however worthy in intention.

In the chapters that follow politics has a part, but it is deliberately placed on the margins of my discussion, as a sort of counter-balance to those histories that privilege public and political life to the detriment of detail at the level of the social and untidy. Unlike other studies on cultural and social life of the early twentieth century in Spain what follows here does not therefore take a specific focus upon political event (though political event is ever present as stimulus, restriction, complication), nor even on the life of the mind that is in conversation with political event, social context and cultural aspiration. Rather it holds as its central focus the mechanics and processes that permitted ideas to circulate. The background assumption of this study is that our view of Spain in the early decades of the twentieth century has been retrospectively simplified, resulting in part from the cultural and intellectual shut-down in the Franco regime. This simplification brought in its wake a cultural amnesia, so that knowledge of the vitality and variety of cultural and intellectual life in Spain 1900–1939 has been lost (Glick 1982: 535, 569–71). Numerous '1898' commemoration conferences held in 1998 highlighted this loss and need for re-writing. Conspicuous in what has been lost is the understanding of how far Spain was interested in what was beyond its boundaries, and, in practical terms, how it was enabled to have concepts of the world beyond its boundaries. The lack of intellectual and cultural traffic caused by Spain's isolation in the Franco years has led us to lose sight of its lively curiosity about things foreign to itself that was so evident in the period before Franco.

Much of the production of this amnesia can be traced to the Civil War and its aftermath, and the subsequent re-writing of Spain's culture and history from a perspective of Nationalist domination. This has affected scholars within Spain, but also those from outside. As Roberts (2007) indicates, there is not a lack of scholarship in the area of intellectual history *per se*, but it has its own traditions and reactions to those traditions. Initially we might be led to interpret the trends of scholarship in terms of the political context in which it took place. In the wake of 'generation' criticism, of which the offerings of Ortega (1942) and Marías (1961) are the most significant, a mode of criticism that explained events in terms of a collective cultural context (which could, of course, be presented in a reduced and highly selective mode), much of the emphasis has been on the emergence of the figure of the intellectual. Notwithstanding, and with some logical link to the preceding theory on generations, there has been some concern with context, in a manner that broadened out the sense of the circumstances in which individual intellectuals lived and thought. Crucially Mainer (1972) spoke of intellectuals as part of a class, and his view that they constitute a 'pequeña burguesía en crisis' (1972: 84), gave rise to a new wave of scholarship. Consequently critics such as Inman Fox (1976) and Villacorta Baños (1980) extended this view of the class placing of the intellectual, and, yet more usefully, broadened their vision to include the function of institutions such as the Ateneo and the role of the press in the emergence of the intellectual as a force to be reckoned with.

Yet the intellectual does not sit easily or naturally within a class, as is observed by a number of commentators. Specifically, and in the Hispanic situation, Santos Juliá sees the intellectual as standing apart, with some horror, from the masses: 've la multitud, la masa, le produce horror y se percibe entonces a sí mismo como un ser aparte, con una misión específica ante la masa y frente al Estado' (1998: 4), an attitude that was embodied with full force by Ortega in 1930 with *La rebelión de las masas*.

This *esbozo* of the dynamic between the intellectual and the masses is, of course, one that will emerge with more nuancing and detail in the course of the following chapters, and the ambiguous positioning of the intellectual and the institutions associated with the intellectual, cross-hatched with various institutional and class lines, will be returned to with some frequency. For the moment let it suffice to observe that the view of the operational complexity of Spanish society is one that has been approached with caution, and with a regard on the one hand to the belief that 'Spain is different', while believing also that taking models drawn from other European countries is instructive.

The movement in scholarship noted above by Roberts is not confined to Spain, but belongs to a general pattern in the practice of history, and the issues associated with the writing of intellectual history are nicely clarified by Wickberg (2001). Nonetheless, putting his ideas into practice by applying them to the topic of this study throws up a number of problems. Wickberg traces a movement through the 1960s and 1970s that has altered the understanding of the practice of 'intellectual history'. He distinguishes between 'intellectual history' as that which is concerned with the history of thought, and 'social history' as that which is concerned with the social history of intellectuals, having a focus on 'intellectual biography, histories of institutions (universities, salons, reading groups, professional organizations), publishing, authorship and reading' (2001: 383–4). All this would seem to indicate in relatively unproblematic manner that the academic home of this present study should lie within social history rather than in intellectual history. Wickberg's further comment, however, that the historian of thought is interested in ideas while the social historian is interested in persons (384), and that the emphasis of historians in the 1960s and 1970s on 'demography, geography and economy, rather than mind, psychology and culture' (386), is all too sweeping, and makes 'social history' a less than obvious academic home for this study. He finally pins his colours to the mast, and declares, that

> We ought to abandon our sentimental attachment to intellectuals, whether as 'role models' of critical social activity or as professional problem solvers or as authors of texts we happen to find interesting; that attachment stands in the way of a clear understanding of the role of thought in history.
>
> (Wickberg 2001: 393)

In response to this, then perhaps I too should pin my colours to the mast. I am aware of the pitfalls that attend the treatment of elites in a study that is concerned with intellectual and cultural exchange. I am aware also of the degree to which a study that is concerned with elites only would render the idea of 'centres of exchange' all too restricted. But I cannot ignore the fact that much of what I shall deal with will fall naturally into the concept of an elite culture, albeit one that is understood in far broader terms than is habitual. Following this line, the appropriate adoptive home of this study would seem to be 'intellectual history', given the degree to which it deals with elite and their ideas, though never at the expense of the perception of the Other, in the form of non-elite groups. Wickberg offers a final rider:

> taking an appropriate lesson from social history, we should turn toward what we might call the ideational history of the social, an examination of the conceptual underpinnings of the social order. We should take the documents and subject matter of the social historian and subject it to the methods and insights of the historian of thought. (Wickberg 2001: 393)

This demonstrates the degree to which even in this radical re-thinking, there is inevitably (and thankfully) a reluctance to abandon a focus on the intellectual, even if it is through using the intellectual's capacity for critique to survey the materials considered by the social historian.

One way to frame the questions involved here is to return to a Hispanic conceptualization. Unamuno (1895) posited the notion of *intrahistoria* that would stand in counterpoint to the 'facts' of history, and the recounting of the surface events of political happenings. My contention is that there is an interest in the middle ground, where the ongoing (*intrahistoria*) interacts with the here-and-now, where ideas and culture are taken in (and therefore, logically, have been promoted or broadcast) so that what results is neither *intrahistoria* nor *historia* but something much richer. Most of all, the interest lies in just how this interaction takes place, rather than simply with what the content of the interaction might be. Just as medium cannot be separated from message so the study of centres of exchange cannot be separated from those 'goods' that were exchanged, even though such goods consisted in ideas, texts, cultural concepts. I would suggest further that the promotion and broadcasting (with the implicit operation of selection, censorship and limitations on what is to be received) is the more significant operation (in terms of intellectual history) when compared with the actual taking in, or at the least it has so far been underestimated. This is because propagation (marketing) is laden with intent (benevolent and enlightenment-oriented, or controlling and propaganda-driven), an intent that tells us not about the information in itself but of those who would be information suppliers, and mediators. At the same time, there is the elusive element of desire: what is it that assures a publisher that there is a market for a type of publication? What encourages a library to collect translations of books from English rather than from German? The collecting activity of the library fuels in part the publisher who decides to bring out translations, and yet, as the chapter on publishing houses will demonstrate, many more rogue factors enter into the equation.

But just as I moved from a sketch of the developments in the writing of history within the Spanish context to a broader approach to such developments, so too it is pertinent to move from the Hispanic *intrahistoria* opposition to *historia*, and to look outside Spain, and outside the period of the material of this study for possible sources of conceptualization. There is no single answer, and in thinking about models for this study, for the framing of questions, I have had recourse to a number of thinkers, although I do not propose to adopt any single theoretical approach at the expense of others. The complexity of the material to be covered in a study such as this makes the adoption of simple models attractive, but one that calls equally for some resistance. This is because of the difficulties that arise, for example, in the application of some of Wickberg's initial distinctions, and attested to in the way that Wickberg himself counsels caution in separating off definitively the arena of the intellectual historian from that of the social historian. The scene of cultural reception is in all respects an interactive one, and there are interactions not just of reception (the taking-in) but also interactions of promotion. That is, there is an active dynamic to be observed between centres of exchange as ideas catch on, and there is the vital question of how the authority of individual intellectuals, functioning within a centre, comes to be validated by others (Collini 2006: 55). We can distinguish, moreover, between the active work of promotion carried out by Ortega in his editorial policy and his notes to the reader of the *Revista de Occidente*, and the more neutral, but fascinating information that can be gleaned from the borrowing rates of library books listed in the *Boletín del Instituto de Reformas Sociales*. More than this, there is the intervention of chance, of individual entrepreneurial activity, of commercial pressure and opportunity. The whole contributes to the cultural capital eventually attaching to a specific import.

One productive model is Michel de Certeau's *strategy* (the operations of major institutions and organizations that carve out their space of operation, and exist physically at identifiable addresses) as distinct from the activity of *tactics* of those who move outside or around those institutions providing the more dynamic picture of cultural life. The way that Certeau defines these two ideas instantly puts them forward as positional rather than fundamental, and it is clear that he regards more warmly those who in alternative and oppositional manner engage in *tactics*. Thus for *strategy*, he notes:

> I call a *strategy* the calculation (or manipulation) of power relationships that becomes possible as soon as a subject with will and power (a business, an army, a city, a scientific institution) can be isolated. It postulates a *place* that can be delimited as its *own* and serve as the base from which relations with an *exteriority* composed of targets of threats can be managed.
>
> (Certeau 1984: 35–6)

This makes evident the degree to which strategy is a state either attained to (or perhaps inevitably is fallen into) as soon as an institution or an individual is isolated and can defend their territory, although Certeau does not seem to see this mobility between the two options, or that one is – perhaps inevitably – followed by, or combined with the other. By contrast with *strategy*, a *tactic* is

> a calculated action determined by the absence of a proper locus. ... A tactic has no place but that of the other. Thus it must play on and with a terrain imposed on it and organized by the law of a foreign power. ... It is a manoeuvre 'within the enemy's field of vision', as von Bülow put it, and within enemy territory. (Certeau 1984: 36–7)

These distinguishing definitions that Certeau presents as opposites in fact throw up the likelihood that social and public relations are always, as it were, in play, always dancing and fencing in relation to one another. Using the concepts, but remembering that they are positions, not necessarily final, alerts us to the dynamics of power, ambition, defensiveness and desire for stability that exist within institutions and those that move inside them and on the margins. Most of all it opens up the possibility of seeing how interactive the relations are. What we see through these models is, as it were, guerilla warfare, the ambushing of the stability of the strategic place, opportunistic movement around the possibility of what is seen to be resistant and stable (and hence a limitation). Certeau observes how those interpreting and critiquing society are naturally drawn to the sorts of discourse that most closely resemble their own. This is clearly limiting and counter-productive. As Ahearne summarizes the division that cultural elites make of texts, it is one that

> presents a small section of society which is mentally and linguistically proficient, and whose productions are worthy of serious consideration. On

the other hand, it presupposes that the 'productions' of the vast majority of the population are hardly worth the name, and that their mental, linguistic and practical activity is inevitably derivative, inculcated, superstitious, recalcitrant or passive. (Ahearne 1995: 19)

Yet this sort of trenchant division (not dissimilar to that of Wickberg) is misleading as a view of Certeau, whose favoured images in fact reveal how his desire is to concentrate on the cross-hatchings (see Revel 1991 in Ahearne 1995: 26). Revel's concepts of 'crossroads, networks, places of transit, limit markers' lend themselves with particular felicity to the concerns of this study.

The complexities of Certeau's attitude to Bourdieu are instructive in indicating the degree of nuance that it is appropriate to have in mind when considering centres of exchange and their subtle and interactive existence with one another, and with the culture that they traffic. They also indicate the degree to which institutions will strive towards stability rather than rupture or discontinuity. Certeau drew on and yet drew away from Bourdieu, whose concepts of both cultural capital and *habitus* have a bearing on his delineations. The reason for Certeau's degree of disengagement with Bourdieu here has affinity with his reservations about Foucault. The drawback of Foucault (for Certeau) is in the former's mirage of a society that is all-controlling, all-disciplinary and all-disciplined (Ahearne 1995: 146–7), and his objection is to its rigidity, its lack of loopholes for creativity and avoidance. Similarly with Bourdieu, he finds that his concepts and divisions, while initially appealing, are ultimately too restrictive, too inclined to sweep away the ingenuities of man and the vicissitudes of history and society. The appeal of Bourdieu's *habitus* for Certeau no doubt lies partially in the non-conscious elements involved, the unchartability of that which goes to make up the context in which we are defined, but this is area that Certeau is inclined to extend.

One of the ways in which Certeau thinks about the activities of institutions is in relation to *place*, so that he allows us to think how institutions engage in strategies that cordon off a place (whether this be in the metaphorical place they occupy in the culture or in the actual geography of a country). The result is that those who are thus excluded are necessarily in a place not their own, and thus obliged (as visiting traders are) to operate in a place not their own. Curiously too, and again revealing what could be a source of appeal for Certeau, Bourdieu's *habitus* reveals a level of affiliation with Unamuno's *intrahistoria*. It is 'the active presence of the whole past of which it is the product', and he concludes from this that 'As such, it is what gives practices their relative autonomy with respect to external determinations of the immediate present' (Bourdieu 1992 [1980]: 56). In these words we can recognize the conservative nature and defensiveness of the 'habitus' ('the *habitus* tends to protect itself from crises and critical challenges by providing itself with a milieu to which it is as pre-adapted as possible' [Bourdieu 1992: 61]). This in its turn relates to the process of *strategy* formation that Certeau perceives as a natural, indeed an inevitable stage. Moreover, in the places where Bourdieu observes dynamic action, it is one with a motion towards stability, or one that has to struggle within the static to have its new formation accepted, as illustrated by his comment that 'every group is the site of a struggle to impose a legitimate principle of group construction' (Bourdieu 1991: 130). The *habitus*, moreover, is as much formed by ways of being and actual habits not consciously learned as it is by any formal structures.

Should these warnings of factors which affect us and which may not be consciously perceived not be enough to alert us to problems in the understanding of social strata and individuals, we have the danger of the simple, the self-evident. For Gramsci, 'common-sense' consists in a rag-bag of 'conceptions of the world', many of which are 'imposed and absorbed passively from outside, or from the past, and are accepted and lived uncritically' (Forgacs 1988: 421). The problem is that some of the common-sense has elements of truth, and while it may induce us to accept situations as inevitable, it may also be the means of encouraging rebellion against them. The notion of common-sense is further problematized by Bourdieu, who presents dominant individuals in need of a discourse that will give them the upper hand, and again 'common sense' appears to join forces with the motion to retain stability. That is, their desire is not to move towards entropy, but to effect some work of consolidation. As he observes:

> Finding nothing for which to reproach the social world as it stands, they endeavour to impose universally, through a discourse permeated by the simplicity and transparency of common sense, the feeling of obviousness and necessity which this world imposes on them; having an interest in leaving things as they are, they attempt to undermine politics in a depoliticized political discourse, produced through a process of neutralization or, even better, of negation, which seeks to restore the doxa to its original state of innocence and which, being oriented towards the naturalization of the social order, always borrows the language of nature. (Bourdieu 1991: 131)

We can illustrate briefly some of the above in terms of the Spanish cultural scene of 1900–1936, looking at the activities of the Junta para Ampliación de Estudios (JAE), the Residencia de Estudiantes and journals such as the *Revista de Occidente*, where we can see the recurrence of a move towards stability. Contrary to the second law of thermodynamics, and contrary to the motion of interactivity that Certeau's models suggest, it would appear that a society in motion has certain inbuilt tendencies that make it desire stability, rather than (or perhaps because of) the entropy that it fears might occur. On a detailed scale, we can see some of the institutions of Spain as engaging in what could be understood as Certeau's *strategy*. They are institutional, in that they have the form, ethos and self-defensiveness of institutions, and yet in relation to the State, they are alternative, set up in opposition. The result is that they look as though they belong to the world of tactics, rather than strategy. Like the Institución Libre de Enseñanza (ILE), founded in 1876 by Francisco Giner de los Ríos, and forming their originary genealogical point, these institutions, or centres of exchange, are non-establishment, existing on the margins and deliberately so, both for the purposes of survival and to facilitate their outward looking. The JAE, while eventually becoming official and a recognized organ of the State, began on the margins, and the struggle of the initial year of its existence attests to the difficulties of gaining recognition, and hence authority. The marginality of position of origin of these centres both explains their institutionalization of themselves and their defended setting aside of others from within their boundaries. It also complicates their relation with the State and its institutions, since it is not obvious that they differ fundamentally from it, at least in their structures.

Meanwhile, those engaged in *tactics* might, in the terms of this study, be represented by a whole range of bodies and persons. Paul Julian Smith has placed the figure of the gypsy in the position of *tactics* (Smith 2000: 36). In the context of this study, there are, as it were, equivalents of the gypsy. They are, however, removed from the position of *tactics* through the manner in which they are presented to others by occupants of *strategy* as being marginalized players present on a stage that is commanded by strategy. Most famously there are the peasants visited by the Misiones Pedagógicas, and the inhabitants of Las Hurdes) (see Chapter 8).

What is more striking is the sense in which even the institutions of the centres are themselves tactical. This is because, as in the case of the ILE mentioned above, and its offshoots, they are set up in opposition to a perceived established mainstream. This relates in conceptual terms to the way in which, as I shall explore presently, the consensus on the intellectual is that s/he is one who observes from the position of the margins, rather than from the position of one fully committed to an establishment stance. But if we take heed of my point above, namely that the alternative institutions of this period, the JAE, the Residencia and their parent organization, the ILE, are *de facto* cast in the self-defining framework that Certeau associates with *strategy*, then *tactics* belongs elsewhere. The question is whether the place(lessness) of *tactics* is for those excluded from these institutions, whether it is the place of the broader audience they indirectly seek to communicate with (those sharing an intellectual level in the form of lecture audiences, those who attended schools staffed by beneficiaries of JAE grants, and those regarded more hierarchically as is the case of members of *pueblos* visited by the Misiones Pedagógicas). This leaves the question of whether readers of books and articles that come through the centres of exchange, with their tastes, desires, capacity to buy or reject, those who (within Certeau's concept of reading as a device of tactics) *tactically* engage with the cultural strategies and structures of others. Or does the area of *tactics* most appositely refer to the complex worlds that surround, for example, the production of newspapers, the world of publishers, editors and translators, all in constant flux, neediness, each with different, clashing and occasionally overlapping agendas?

Certeau has a sense of those tendencies that will restrict the activities and creativity of members of the society, deriving from their own demarcation of their role as special. This in its turn is something that had been made particular to the intellectual in Mannheim's views on the nature (and limitations) of the 'intelligentsia' (Mannheim 1956: 100–63). For Mannheim, the intelligentsia is a group that necessarily comes to self-knowledge through experience that is gained at second-hand. The member of the intelligentsia is furthermore impeded by the very diversity of the origins of his group (and here Mannheim adds in the degree to which the intellectual is disconcerted in the face of the social norms and certitudes of the proletariat) (102). More than this, the diversity of origins conspires to make it difficult for the intellectual to act in concert with others (104). Yet here the detached position and the isolation of the intellectual come into fruitful combination, since it is arguably because of that isolation that they will seek to meet in informal groupings, salons, *tertulias* in Spain, small meeting points and places (Simmel's *rendezvous* [Frisby 1985: 77]) where individuals come and go (see Chapter 9). Mannheim's vignette of the nineteenth-century intellectual is one that can be re-applied to the intellectual in early twentieth-century Spain. He

> occurs in many intersecting groupings, and it is this multiple affiliation which produces the differentiated personality of the early nineteenth century. He has avenues of escape, for he can withdraw from one group to another and his stakes in any one are limited. (Mannheim 1956: 141)

What Mannheim's vignette does not highlight is the greatly valued element of freedom, movement and the advantages of being unattached. This is powerfully outlined by David Castillejo, son of José Castillejo, secretary of the JAE, in a way that will resonate as much with academics and intellectuals of today as it did in early twentieth-century Spain when the State hand in education was heavy, obstructive and time-consuming:

> Lo más sagrado para el intelectual son sus libertades: su libertad de *movimiento*, su derecho a manejar su propio *tiempo*, su derecho a escoger y ordenar sus temas de *trabajo e investigación*, su derecho a escoger su *equipo y colegas*; la libertad de distribuir el dinero que se le adjudica según su parecer; y su liberación de todo trámite y *papeleo oficial* que destruye su alma. (D Castillejo 1997: 20)

Whether the separate positioning of the intellectual is seen as the source of his strength or the weakness of the intellectual depends on the view taken of his potential usefulness. Mannheim stresses all the discouraging features of the intellectual: distancing, lack of confidence. Nonetheless he is aware that the intellectual 'can more easily change his point of view', adding that 'he is less rigidly committed to one side of the context, for he is capable of experiencing concomitantly several conflicting approaches to the same thing' (105). The intellectual as a member of crossroads meetings, as a multi-participator in a diversity of different social strata and professional occupations (characteristic of many figures that will be prominent in this study) is – when not grouping with others in a defensive organization – at least free to think and observe, even if there will be a probable lack of consistency in his utterances and occupations.

Jo Labanyi observes (1999) that we might need particular models to talk about the phenomena of Hispanic society, and she suggests Gramsci. The appropriateness of Gramsci's models for Spain is anticipated by Villacorta Baños (1985) who comments on how Gramsci has awareness of the intellectuals' potential for being seduced or coerced into those structures from which they would make themselves distinct, something that comes about through their role as mediating functionaries (Villacorta Baños 1985: 48, commenting on Gramsci 1973: 31). For Villacorta Baños, the tendency for the intellectual in Spain is to be drawn into taking shelter in the public domain, which paralyzes him. But the very diversity of the world in which he finds himself, 'sus retribuciones, las demandas sociales de actividad cultural a través de la prensa, las conferencias, las instituciones privadas, las editoriales, etc., las vías de ascenso profesional, son algunos de los aspectos más patentes que pone en movimiento la ruptura de la homogeneidad de los grupos intelectuales', is one that arguably sets up a counterpoint of fragmentation, and thereby of more productive possibilities (Villacorta Baños 1985: 48). It also flags up the importance of the centres of exchange, however fluctuating, for their support of the individual. Villacorta Baños also has recourse to Mannheim in support of his perception of 'el tránsito desde una inteligencia relativamente homogénea que parte de posiciones de clase privilegiadas y actúa como agente transmisor directo del sistema social hasta otra fuertemente vertebrada que actúa en círculos institucionales y sociales relativos', which clearly views the shift from a boundaried elite to one in a state of fragmentation as one that might nonetheless be productive (73).

At this point, we could observe that, with luck, the intellectual might move into the role Gramsci articulates as that of the 'entrepreneur' (Gramsci 1988: 301) who has to move and organize others. Gramsci refers to this as a 'sort of technical capacity', and adds that they have to be able to engage in this entrepreneurial activity: the entrepreneur must be an organizer of masses of men; he must be an organizer of the 'confidence of investors in his business, of the customers for his product, etc.' and adds that

If not all entrepreneurs, at least an elite amongst them must have the capacity to be an organizer of society in general, including all its complex organism of services, right up to the state organism, because of the need to create the conditions most favourable to the expansion of their own class.

(Gramsci 1988: 301)

But then we could speculate about what happens when – within this system – the intellectual gets paralyzed, albeit within a microcosm. For Gramsci the second sort of intellectual is the traditional one, who may well be the organic one who can get fixed into the same position in the State, losing mobility. With Gramsci's model in mind we can review the units in Spain's intellectual activity in this period. While there are individuals and groups running counter to State institutions, and thus operating 'organically', in their activity designed to promote their own existence and ethos, they inevitably become involved in a type of definition and self-definition that will work against their own creative independence.

In relation to the individual intellectual and the centres of exchange within which he or she might operate, the characteristics of the intellectual offered by Collini are particularly helpful. His study of intellectuals in Britain emphasizes the sheer variety of ways in which the term 'intellectual' has been used, by turns in a tone of admiration or – more interestingly – as a term of disparagement and dismissiveness. Collini proposes four characteristics of the intellectual that qualify him to be considered as such, and his emphasis is on the dynamic relationship of the intellectual with his society. First, the intellectual has a 'qualifying activity' (performance), and secondly this implies some medium of expression that allows a relationship with the 'public' (both medium and public being flexible and variable notions). A third characteristic is that he pronounces on topics in general, rather than from the position of any specialization that he may have (that is, his knowledge and his performance take him across intellectual borders of discipline), and fourthly, his reputation, based upon his performance, is something that has to be recurrent, not based upon a single piece of academic or intellectual production (Collini 2006: 52–6). As Collini summarizes (56), it is the intersection of these four characteristics that will determine the 'cultural authority' of the individual. He also notes the differentials that will need to be borne in mind when thinking of the 'public', in that there is a direct public that is addressed (by an article in a review, by a lecture, by other forms of statement), but there is a special sector of the public that will actually confer authority. Thus, 'the public for whom a particular figure may possess some standing to act as an intellectual will always be partly different from, and usually broader than, the audience at whom the activity which earns that standing is directed' (Collini 2006: 55).

All too easily, elite institutions tend to dominate studies of Spain's relations with the outside world. Yet we need to bear in mind the perceptions just outlined of the intellectual as one who is apart, of uncertain class origin, and who may, despite the detachment that comes with the occupation of the intellectual, ultimately tend towards attitudes that are, if not actually conservative, then at least self-preserving. The preservation of freedom (of intellect) arguably comes at a price. That price could be judged to consist in the construction of elites and elite groups. This study will continue to err to some degree on the side of looking at elite bodies and their productions. But my hope is to rectify the imbalance thus produced in part by placing conscious emphasis on the degree to which some institutions were indeed elitist, operated with elite assumptions and agendas, and demonstrate the degree to which they treated those at the receiving end of some of their activities as unenlightened Others. In addition, my intention is to look at areas of exchange we could regard as 'mixed' (not necessarily intended for an elite circle) such as the press, the activities of large publishing houses, publishers of popular novelettes who included elite figures among authors of non-elite orientation. By discussing how elite and non-elite institutions co-existed, and occasionally overlapped in either personnel or interest, a more complex model of Spain's cultural and intellectual exchanges with those outside its borders should emerge.

At the same time as the line of scholarship on intellectuals and the course of intellectual history has developed within Spain itself, we find that in works of scholarship in the 'European' field, Spain is habitually conspicuous by its absence. Studies on comparative literature, history or culture that purport to discuss 'Europe' frequently lack a treatment of the Hispanic dimension. A double form of absence thus obtains. On the one hand Spain is absent from the European picture given that there is an inadequate sense of the degree to which Spain received and reacted to cultural and intellectual trends from outside its boundaries. On the other there is a lack of understanding about what it was within Spain that enabled contact with non-Hispanic source, influence and inspirations. There was a considerable exchange of cultural ideas in the period under discussion, but our view of what permitted such trafficking in cultural ideas to take place has tended to be focused on a collection of usual suspects, institutions such as the ILE, the Residencia, individuals such as Ortega and Unamuno, and I shall inevitably re-visit them. These institutions and figures had, without doubt, a considerable role in cultural trafficking, but they did not operate in isolation. This study takes as its starting point, therefore, the centres of exchange themselves, their conservative or liberal nature, the degree to which they fostered exchange, or may alternatively have resisted it. Within the structures and details of the centres we can see the activity of individuals, but they are, as it were, perhaps less omnipotent than they might seem when viewed in individualistic isolation. I do not propose, however, to embark on histories of these major institutions: they already exist (see, for example, Cacho Viu 1962 and Jiménez-Landí Martínez 1973, 1987 on the ILE, Sáenz de la Calzada 1986 and Jiménez Fraud 1972 and 1989 on the Residencia, and Sánchez Ron 1988 on the JAE). My intention is rather to re-focus upon them, sometimes in passing, and to view their activities not as iconic cultural centres and repositories, but as part of the mobile and jostling world in which they actually had their being. My interest is thus in relation to institutional centres to look at the nature of their activity, the sources of motivation, and the means by which their activity was taken forward. It will be observed that I return with frequency to the ILE (though leaving any formal history of the ILE to be pursued in other sources), and I am aware that in so doing I run the risk of appearing to follow in the lines of traditional histories of this period. But singling out the ILE as central to the concept of Spain's exchanges with outside does not in fact constitute a dutiful nod in the direction of conventional intellectual histories of the period. What stands out of the material to be covered here is the degree to which the ILE, whether by direct influence or as example to be emulated, permeates the history of Spain looking out across its boundaries. The ILE is central, but what is most significant is that it is marginal in its own deliberate positioning. In this it is characteristic not just of Spain, but indeed of the functioning of those insti-gating change and exchange, whether from an elite position or otherwise.

Similarly, related to the amnesia mentioned at the start of this introduc-tion, my intention is to take to task a number of *idées reçues*. The Residencia de Estudiantes, for example, has the reputation of being one of the major conduits for ideas to reach Spain from outside. Yet the Residencia, as demon-strated in Chapter 5, has a history and a structure that is elitist, Anglophone and aristocratic, with clear consequences for its activities. The JAE rightly has fame for stimulating and enabling study abroad, but is the more inter-esting when seen in the light of who its prime movers and decision-makers were, and what the cultural imaginaries were that impelled their activity.

One of the areas of prime interest for this study is the world of publishing, both in the form of books, and of newspapers. I have adopted an approach not of universal coverage, but of sampling, to give examples not only of what could happen, but of what did happen. Looking at the catalogues of major (and not so major) publishers of the years of the project throws up a profile of their activity, their expectations in relation to their readership, and in relation to their own economic survival. It also enables us to envision them as establishing – in whatever deliberate or non-deliberate way – a canon of literature, whether national or foreign. My prime interest has been in the foreign imports, but it is also of interest to see the national context in which, in terms of the book trade, these exotic objects are to be found.

Canon is, of course, central to the institutions engaged in cultural diffusion, in that the mindset of the institution will provide its demarcation, its attitude to what is to be taken in, and indeed to what is to be sought out. Examina-tion of the catalogues of publishing houses provides one sense of canon, as does a survey of some library holdings (whether institutional in the case of the Ateneo de Madrid, or personal in the case of Ricardo Baeza or Miguel de Unamuno). But canon as a concept is also present in the activities of the Sociedad de Cursos y Conferencias in the Residencia de Estudiantes, and yet more so in the activities of the Misiones Pedagógicas that sprang out of the Residencia. In their mission to 'take culture to the people', the Misiones, and in the more expansive form that preceded them, the project of the Bibliotecas Populares, propagated a canon, whether of art forms (the travelling Museo) or the book lists for the use of those setting up popular libraries. If the canon 'embodies the kinds of knowledge a society perceives as important to retain from its past in order to construct its future' (Lauter 1991: 249), then it is instrumental in a project of nation formation, whether political or (merely) cultural or spiritual. Lauter further alerts us to the limiting sense of canon: it is 'a process by which a society generates and maintains a necessary level of unity' (Lauter 1991: 165). As Davis reminds us, a constant with the canon is that 'however else it may be defined, [it] is based upon a centre and margins definition, within an inclusion/exclusion dialectic, and that it finds its most important stronghold in the educational institution' (Davis 2001: 139). Consequentially when we look at the imposition, or creation, of a canon in the importation of ideas we meet a double and paradoxical action: in the activity of curiosity and exploration there is the idea of control of that outward-reaching movement. Canons vary across the chronological and social spectrum in Spain in this period, with publishing houses arguably more adventurous than academic institutions, albeit limited by their sense of what might be economically viable or productive. And as canons are provided for those perceived to be lower down the scale of cultural sophistication so they are the more restricted and carefully constructed. Certain small publishing ventures, short-lived, show an extreme sense of canon as they target their reader from particular angles.

It is also through the canons and through publishers' lists that we can, in part, perceive major cultural concepts, frequently in the form of cultural 'imaginaries' (rather than realities). What is 'Europe' for Spain? What offerings in cultural or intellectual terms did France make to Spain (or was thought to be able to make), or Germany? The truism, not completely devoid of substance, is that France offered literature and/or culture, while Germany offered science, *Wissenschaft*, method, training, but also the culture of academic endeavour.

I have not opted as a general procedure to devote specific chapters to specific European countries. The major omissions are of specific chapters on France and Germany. Both of these countries figure prominently in the activities of the JAE. Both have, as noted, offerings traditionally associated with Spain's intellectual and cultural imports. In Chapter 3, which looks at the activity of publishers, I explore the degree to which specifics of those countries are adopted via the centres of exchange, and place them in contrast with one another. It will also be evident, when working through the activities of publishers, and those of institutions, when scanning through the contents of journals and perusing the contents of libraries, that both France and Germany figure prominently in the cultural trafficking of Spain's institutions. I have given prominence, however, to Spain's sometimes real, sometimes imagined cultural relationships with two different countries, and the section on 'Cultural Attachments' (Chapters 5 and 6) examines the significance of *concepts* of different European countries, and proposes that at least two 'love-affairs' can be discerned, one with England and one with Russia. These two 'love-affairs', different and yet arguably complementary in nature, stand themselves in some counterpoint to the precise relations with individual European countries and with the concept of European culture itself. Other 'love-affairs' could no doubt also be sketched: the two here are examples of conceptual desire.

The inclusion/exclusion dialectic, remarked upon by Davis, is revealed or flagged up partly in the ethos of institutions. Related to the cultural imaginaries that attend the majority of cultural exchanges, there is the ethos of the receiving institution, and that of the imagined donor institution. The ILE is – both in its founding and the memory it retrospectively creates – an institution above all of attitude, that of its individualistic, self-marginalized founder Francisco Giner de los Ríos. His disciples (a word that picks up the charismatic influence of the founder, one exerted long into the history of the JAE and the Residencia de Estudiantes in which he was implicated, inspirationally if not practically) carry forward the ethos. One of the chief standard-bearers in this is José Castillejo, and equally so, Alberto Jiménez Fraud, the director of the Residencia at its inception in 1910. The ethos created and then propagated is one of individual self-reliance, voluntary marginality combined with independent outreach to a world beyond the perceived academic restrictions of Spain in 1876 when the ILE was founded.

As the title of this study indicates, my primary concern is not with the *content* of exchange (what was imported to Spain), but rather with the activity and nature of those 'centres' that facilitated such importation. Perhaps even more than this, my interest is in the degree to which there is contact between centres: through overlap of membership, through professional networks, through activity in a third centre. To produce a full coverage of all the centres that could be identified as important in this period would require a more extensive piece of work. One example of how detailed the work can be is Rhian Davies's excellent in-depth study of *La España Moderna* (2000). There are, in addition, studies that highlight overarching movements and developments of the press, such as the collection edited by Jesús Timoteo Álvarez (1989a). They provide a backcloth of information, but necessarily with less detail on individual publishing houses and enterprises than that provided by

Davies. Faced by the alternatives of the zoom lens and wide-angled panoramic view, my choice has been predominantly to present a series of snapshots and case-studies that allow us to see not simply the nature and functioning of individual centres, but to see their interrelationship. In some instances, as with the *Revista de Occidente* 1923–36, it has been possible to take an uninterrupted longitudinal view, but one that itself constitutes a sort of selective snapshot, since its focus is upon cultural exchange. In others, I have chosen to sample data at (roughly) ten-year intervals. This has enabled, for example, some comparison between the 'European scene' reflected by the *Boletín de la Institución Libre de Enseñanza* with the *Boletín del Instituto de Reformas Sociales*, and in turn with the view of Europe that emerges from the *Revista de Occidente*. Given that the ILE, according to its canonical historian, stands for 'el más coherente y sostenido intento de configurar la vida de este país según los principios de la cultura europea moderna' (Cacho Viu 1962: 5), the comparison allows for a series of 'established' views of Europe. In their turn we can see how they differ from the sense of Europe gained in other fields.

What has mainly struck me is the complexity of the fabric related to the dissemination of ideas, and yet the existence of specific movers and shakers who were crucial to such dissemination. A number of focal points of reference will recur with regularity. To take just one example, in the case of Russia and the interest so clearly evident in both pre- and post-revolutionary Russia, the points of relevant reference are myriad, and we find here and elsewhere that not only do the same individuals operate in a variety of distinct but crucial areas, but that groups of them combine and re-combine in different ways. For this reason, the final chapter, 'Wheels within Wheels' will take a further and final look at the phenomena of contact, cross-fertilization and networking that have become evident in the course of preceding chapters, and that could be considered to be the most significant element in Spain's engagement in cultural exchange.

Part, if not all, of the networking derives from the position of the intellectual: a marginal figure, marginalized, moving between groups, and free to engage in a variety of pursuits and sets of ideas. The intellectual is the one who thinks, on the margins. Roberts (2007: 26) refers us to Varela (1999: 150) for the question of what critics have considered in trying to understand the intellectual, and has called 'las experiencias, los intereses, las formas, las ideas de un grupo humano, que se desenvuelve en un espacio temporal y social común'. This overarching view of the domain of the intellectual, which could be extended to a community as a whole, is one we might adopt for a holistic, if rather undifferentiated, view of Spanish society. Yet to adopt such a blanket coverage allows for a merging of concepts of cultural and intellectual, and places on one side what one can periodically discern as the stratospheric interests of the intellectual (interests appealed to in Residencia lectures on current trends in physics, represented for example by the Duc de Broglie and Professor Fabry in the 1929–30 session [pamphlet of *Sociedad de cursos y conferencias* 1929–30, in Residencia library]). If Spain was open to currents from abroad, these were 'cultural' (aesthetic and literary) as much as 'intellectual' (encompassing academic disciplines of science, philosophy, history, archaeology). But there were also the channels of intellectual exchange that came through professional organizations, such as international bodies concerned with medicine. Arguably these might be seen as less diffuse in their communications, less bound to ethos and cultural imaginaries, although whether this was in fact the case is something that would have to be tested by a series of in-depth studies. In terms of the vision of the activities of international professional organizations as clear potential channels of exchange, the history of Spain's participation, such as can be pieced together from the remaining documentation in the Archivo General de la Administración (AGA) in Alcalá de Henares, is patchy and sad rather than heartening.

I have not proceeded in chronological order, nor is there even-handedness in the space allotted to particular periods. All the information on publishers is dated after 1913, with an emphasis on the 1920s and 1930s. And it should be added that, as with all boundary dates, those adopted for this project are necessarily approximate. Taking 1900 allows us in a sense to start with a clean slate (after the disaster of 1898), though with much of the writing associated with the '98 still to come. Inevitably, however, periodic reference needs to be made to at least the last three decades of the nineteenth century, given the long genealogical lines that attach the twentieth century to its predecessor, most notably but not exclusively with the founding of the Institución Libre de Enseñanza (ILE) in 1876, and the nature and activities of the Ateneo de Madrid in the late nineteenth century. Moreover some of the traditions of the press as a vehicle for both elite and popular exchanges are established well before 1900, although this study will have its principal attention fixed upon productions of the twentieth century only. It is possible also that the *modus operandi* of printing houses, particularly in relation to the selection of works to be translated, is something established in the late nineteenth century and simply continued, or slightly modified in the twentieth century, even in the case of those printing houses set up in the twentieth century.

The end-date adopted for this study is 1936, marking the onset of the Civil War, is a point at which the slate was, if not cleared, radically altered. Yet activities continued beyond 1936: the Misiones Pedagógicas would continue their work until well into 1937; Biblioteca Nueva, one of the major publishing houses to be considered, survived the war and the postwar period albeit with measures of survival rather than of the outreach and expansion that mark its activity in the 1920s and 1930s.

2   What and Where is Europe?

> I have used the term cultural experience as an extension of the idea of transitional phenomena and of play without being certain that I can define the word 'culture'. The accent indeed is on experience. In using the word culture I am thinking of the inherited tradition. I am thinking of something that is in the common pool of humanity, into which individuals and groups of people may contribute, and from which we may all draw *if we have somewhere to put what we find*. (Winnicott, 'The location of cultural experience', in *Playing and Reality*, 1971)

'Europe is elsewhere,' notes Luisa Passerini (1999: 10–11), in relation to England's attitude to the continent to which it belongs. The model she proposes of Europe is imaginative: it consists in a civilized culture based upon the assumptions and practices of courtly love. In her persuasive and vigorous study of England's attitude to Europe in the interwar years, she details the varied aspects of this style of civilization. Subsequent writings on the topic have confirmed Passerini's hypothesis, but, in the case of Spain, have also commented on difference (Sinclair 2010 forthcoming; Labanyi 2010 forthcoming). For Spain, Europe is a place not belonged to, and yet comes to be a buzz-word for 'foreign', 'modern', 'development', 'adventure' (or indeed, as experienced also in the English context, as 'liaison', 'flirtation with the exotic and sophisticated').

In the official mind above all, 'Europe' for Spain of the early twentieth century is of unclear meaning. The efforts of the JAE, from its inception in 1907, were directed towards making Europe (or at least specific sections of it) more accessible to educated Spaniards. In like manner, the Residencia de Estudiantes (founded 1910) would open windows to the world beyond the Pyrenees, albeit with rather selective and a (modern) canonical view. Yet Spain's relationship with Europe, whether desired or repudiated, had been clearly active before these organized motions of outreach, and alongside these institutional aspirations there would be meditations offered from intellectuals on the margins. The precise desires of the JAE and the Residencia were largely predicated on the aspirations of the ILE, which, under the leadership of Giner, set its gaze not just on the mountains and plains beyond

Madrid, where he would take his students on excursions to walk the hills, but on the vistas of European culture beyond the Pyrenees.

The complication of 'Europe' for modern Spain is the degree to which it does not denote a reality but a cultural idea of otherness. This is because for a substantial proportion of the population it was not a place regularly travelled to, or whose living conditions were experienced. Indeed, the experience of 'Europe' could only be in the world of the imagination or the imaginary, since 'Europe' is not a place as such, but a collective of distinct countries. Europe existed as 'other', a place to be desired, or perhaps identified with, a place whose *mores* might be of interest to Spain. It would inevitably be contrasted with less desirable Others. In the spirit of Passerini's perception, Europe for Spain represented an aspiration to the civilized, contrasting with perceptions of Spain's own state, and also with less acceptable forms of Other, associated with degeneration, elements to be excluded (Arabs, Jews, gypsies).

The early twentieth century is a heyday for cultural generalizations about nationhood, and specifically in relation to the expanded (or contradictory) nature of nationhood posited by Europe. A nice tension exists between the delineation of nation, so prevalent in Spain for a good two centuries, with all its gendered and affective baggage such as the 'Mater dolorosa' (Álvarez Junco 2001), and the concept of Europe. Madariaga's essays, *Carácter y destino en Europa: Ingleses, franceses, españoles* (1928), provide an example of how a concept of Europe as such is avoided, rather characterized by an idiosyncratic selection of nations, based on personal experience. He aligns Spain with soul and passion, thus contrasting it with the characteristics of logic, practicality and action associated with the other two nations. His *Bosquejo de Europa* would not appear until 1951, and continues to work on cultural concepts of individual nations, placed in contrastive dyads with one another. In general 'membership' of Europe, in cultural terms, was something to which some of Spain aspired, and later chapters in this book will trace the routes towards that membership, and the acquisition of necessary elements.

In the discussion of Spain's view of Europe (a concept that is already overstretched in its generalization) we need to be aware of varying time-lines and place-lines. Looking to the north of the Pyrenees, it is impossible to think of Europe without the major cataclysm of the First World War, in which the physical horrors of the battlefield left France scarred territorially, and inflicted a loss of population across the continent. It would mark indelibly both the cultural memory of individual countries and the concept of Europe as a whole. When Europe is viewed from the other side of the Pyrenees, its vicissitudes in themselves are partially understood, but they are inevitably in play with the desires that Spain has for Europe as its Other. Spain had had its own cataclysm in the Cuban war of 1898, the final stage of the loss of imperial identity. The effect of this war, to be followed by further disastrous military activity in North Africa, was to occupy its thoughts much more directly than the World War in which it did not participate. Apart from discussions in the press about whether Spain should support the Allies or Germany, reactions to the war were sparse. Valle-Inclán's short piece, *La media noche* (1917) brings a curious reportage from the front, where the horrors of trench warfare were cast within a highly *modernista* and aestheticized framework.

We could posit, therefore, a number of plateaux in the development of Europe as perceived by Spain. Europe was an 'elsewhere' that was viewed in divers ways by the generation of 1898. In the succeeding generation, that of Ortega, it would come to be the place of 'knowledge' and above all of 'science'. But as Europe emerged from the war, and – visibly – was not the Europe it had been, inevitably new currents were provoked in the Spanish reaction to it. Just three sample titles of works produced through the 1920s attest to the degree of affective charge that would continue to obtain in Spain's relation to Europe. Adolfo Agorio's somewhat apprehensive title of *La sombra de Europa: transformación de los sentimientos y de las ideas* (1920) would be followed by Clotilde de Arvelo, *Visiones de Europa* (1928) and Ricardo León, *Europa trágica* (1929).

Two obvious cases present themselves as examples of one-man centres of cultural exchange, Unamuno and Ortega. Equal but different, both in the public perception that there was of them (see Roberts 2007 on the problems in coming to terms with Unamuno as an intellectual in a post-Ortega world), and in the way they operated, they encompass in intellectual terms, if not in artistic terms, some of Spain's relation to, and reaction to Europe.

In *En torno al casticismo* (1902) there is little doubt that Unamuno took the view that Spain in its isolation was faring badly. After four chapters in which his line was to focus in on Spanish qualities, his fifth chapter, 'Sobre el marasmo actual', speaks of a state that is far from self-sufficient: it is desperately in need of contact with elsewhere.

> No hay corrientes vivas internas en nuestra vida intelectual y moral; esto es un pantano de agua estancada, no corriente de manantial. Alguna que otra pedrada agita su superficie tan sólo, y a lo sumo revuelve el légamo del fondo y enturbia con fango el pozo. Bajo una atmósfera soporífera se extiende un páramo espiritual de una aridez que espanta. No hay frescura ni espontaneidad, no hay juventud. (Unamuno 1902a: 860)

The task in hand is centred, however, more on Spain's own self-knowledge than on its contact with the outside world. It is with the eyes of the outsider that it will come to know itself. Whatever Unamuno means at this point by 'Europe', he is convinced that it is an essential part in the equation of self-learning: 'España está por descubrir, y sólo la descubrirán españoles europeizados' (Unamuno 1902a: 866). In this case, Europe is not envisaged as a value in itself, but as some part of a cultural process that will re-vitalize

Spain. In his famous combination of the simultaneous knowledge of outer and inner, he finishes this chapter with a paradox based on a European experience that is enlivening, but (at this stage) completely imprecise:

> que sólo abriendo las ventanas a vientos europeos, empapándonos en el ambiente continental, teniendo fe en que no perderemos nuestra personalidad al hacerlo, europeizándonos para hacer España y chapuzándonos en pueblo, regeneraremos esta estepa moral. Con el aire de fuera regenero *mi sangre*, no respirando el que exhalo. (Unamuno 1902a: 869)

The process that Unamuno passes over briefly at this point, that of the rude immersion in the *pueblo*, is one to which others will return, in different guises, in the following decades (see Chapters 7 and 8). But it is a process about which he was to feel rather more hesitant some four years later in 'Sobre la europeización'. In this essay the nature of 'Europe' is still unclear. He couples it with 'modernity', observing that this latter term is even less clear than that of Europe, though both are being required, or recommended, of Spain. While what he says seems to be typical of his playing with terminology, it is nonetheless symptomatic of the sheer vagueness (his term) of what is meant by 'Europe', let alone by the process of engaging with it:

> El término *europeo* expresa una idea vaga, muy vaga, excesivament vaga; pero es mucho más vaga la idea que se expresa con el término *moderno*. Y si las juntamos, parece como que dos vaguedades deben concretarse y limitarse mutuamente, y que la expresión 'europeo moderno' ha de ser más clara que cualquiera de los dos términos que la componen; pero acaso sea en el fondo más vaga que ellas. (Unamuno 1906: 925)

The vagueness associated with the idea of Europe is, of course, consonant with what Passerini identifies as the utopian concept of Europe as an 'elsewhere'. And, as is the case with all utopias, Europe is somewhere that we are not, and that we can only perceive from another place:

> in most cases consciously European feelings do not arise until after the experience of living elsewhere. It is only when placed in this position that many people suddenly see, as they did not before, the continental affinities which go beyond national and regional differences. (Passerini 1999: 11)

But Unamuno, widely read (Sinclair 2001) and highly civilized though he is, in 1906 has not reached that position of detachment from which an engagement with the concept of Europe, in Passerini's terms, might take place. Indeed, we can see him in retreat, and his later experience of exile in 1924 does not increase his feelings of being European, although it does sharpen his sense of what being a Spaniard entails. Much of this is touchingly expressed in terms of loss or absence in *Cómo se hace una novela* (1927), his most modernist of fictional writings, on the edge of tolerance between auto-documentary and fantasy (Sinclair 2001: 212, 222–4).

If Europe for Spain is always already elsewhere, a fact accentuated not only by a history of the Inquisition and isolationism (tragically to be reinforced after the Civil War) but simply and massively by geography, Europe is also always already imbued with desire or intention. From the 1898 crisis onwards, it came to be inflected more acutely by Spain's internal feelings of loss, figuring as the place or the object that might fill the void, make up the deficiency. Spain, in Costa's view, in his speech on 'Reconstitución y europeización de España' (1898), had erred in its choices (a recurrent theme for the writers of 1898):

> Todo lo que era progreso, riqueza y contento de la vida, todo lo que era aumento del bienestar, de vigor, de salud, de vida media, de población, de cultura, de aproximación a Europa, de porvenir en la historia del mundo, lo hemos disipado, ¡locos criminales!, en pólvora y en humo. (Costa 1898)

Thus for Costa, the equation between Spain's desire for regeneration was completed with the process of Spain being 'europeanized', moving back to that place it had turned its back on. This for Costa was put in strongly practical terms, and it is interesting to see how Ortega, recalling Costa's position in 1910, generalizes and almost make it more abstract:

> Regeneración es inseparable de europeización; por eso apenas se sintió la emoción reconstructiva, la angustia, la vergüenza y el anhelo, se pensó la idea europeizadora. Regeneración es el deseo; europeización es el medio de satisfacerlo. Verdaderamente se vió claro desde un principio que España era el problema y Europa la solución. (Ortega 1910a: 521, commenting on Costa's essay, *Reconstitución y europeización de España* (1898))

For regenerationists, exemplified here by Costa, Europe was not so much an object of desire, or even perhaps curiosity, in itself, but rather a remedy. It was a tool for Spain to pull itself back from its position of despair. But in this manner Europe, though the ideal and miraculous tool for Spain's problems, is diminished by being simply a tool. In his practical approach, which distantly envisioned Spain as agent and Europe as a means to regeneration, Costa was arguably presenting an attitude that would be expressed rather more sharply by Unamuno in 1902 in his speech at the Juegos Florales of Cartagena. Here, midway between his views on Europe in *En torno al casticismo*, and those in 'Sobre la europeización', Unamuno responds to the idea that Spain should 'europeanize' by the assertion that Europe is in fact too small for that: 'europeizarnos, no, que Europa nos es pequeña' (Unamuno 1902b:

725). Spain needs to become universal, and Europe is in fact too small for Spain's aspirations.

Ortega and Europe

What we can see in these early attitudes to Europe as a concept is almost a knee-jerk reaction to the idea that Spain might be deficient, or not sufficient enough for itself, and a need to defend some idea of self-worth at all costs. Some of the anxiety underlying this can be seen in minor ways. Thus the Sección de Literatura in the Ateneo de Madrid in the winter of 1903–4 would discuss the question '¿Influyen en los intelectuales contemporáneos los autores extranjeros más que los nacionales?' (Villacorta Baños 1985: 312). When Europe then comes into public discourse in the early decades of the twentieth century, the method used by Ortega, and building on what had been done by the JAE, is to give 'Europe' greater precision. It is redeemed by a confirmation that what Europe has to offer is not a culture that would threaten that of Spain, but rather a knowledge of science that would contribute to its well-being. Thus there is a conversion. If Passerini equates Europe with a sense of civilization based upon amorous decorum, in this second wave of thoughts about Spain, Europe comes to be associated more simply, and arguably less problematically, with knowledge, in the sense that this is knowledge that 'other people' have.

The crucial distinction here is that 'knowledge' (and, with it, method and educational discipline) is something that can be acquired, indeed that can be packaged and propagated (as indeed it will be on a number of different fronts). It can thus be distinguished from 'culture', a concept that in this early twentieth-century discussion all too readily gets to be associated with a concept of Spain's 'nature'. The distinction between nature and culture in this period is, we might recall, far from being either absolute or clear, giving rise, not least, to the reaction of those who, like Unamuno, felt that 'Spanishness' might be threatened by the cultural input from Europe. The blurring of the terms is a confusion that we find in contemporary writing of eugenicists in Spain and elsewhere. The very degree of blurring, whether in discussion of the degeneration of the body, or the race, or in the deficiencies (or values) of culture, is characteristic of the period, and arguably leads to some of the more extreme statements, prompted by an acute need for clarification (Pick 1989: 8–9).

We can see how Ortega picks his way through a sense of muddle in 1908, a date by which he continues to subscribe to Europe as a *concept*. In an offering that presages his lament about the particularity of influence in Spain, he declares:

> Para unos Europa es el ferrocarril y la buena policía; para otros es la parte
> del mundo donde hay mejores hoteles; para aquéllos el Estado que goza
> de empleados más leales y expertos; para otros el conjunto de pueblos que
> exportan más e importan menos. Todas estas imágenes de Europa coin-
> ciden en un error de perspectiva; toman lo que se ve en un viaje rápido,
> lo que salta a los ojos y, sobre todo, la apariencia externa de la Europa de
> hoy, por la Europa verdadera y perenne. (Ortega 1908b: 100)

His solution is again to equate Europe with science. But he recognizes that
this will lead to feelings of inferiority:

> Si creemos que Europa es 'ciencia', habremos de simbolizar a España en
> la 'inconsciencia', terrible enfermedad secreta que cuando infecciona a un
> pueblo suele convertirlo en uno de los barrios bajos del mundo.
>   (Ortega 1908b: 104)

This shuddering reaction to what equating Europe with science might mean
for Spain's national selfhood would be skirted in different, more affirmative
manner by Unamuno in his 1909 articles in *The Englishwoman* (the place
of publication a casual sign of his familiar international wandering and his
epistolary contact with Royall Tyler: see Ribbans 1991: 383–4; Ouimette
1997: 165 n2; Sinclair 2001: 66). In these articles Unamuno defended against
the inferiority that would result from going to Europe for scientific culture,
declaring that Spain was simply not inclined naturally that way, its citizens
being more interested in topics such as death (Unamuno 1909: 87–8). By
Baroja's intervention in this area two things had happened: the approach was
less passionate, less suffused with emotion and a sense of nation bound to the
spirit. He speaks of Spain 'collaborating', and not with Europe, in the area
of science, at university level, but with the 'pueblos' of Europe (both more
particular, and yet adroitly avoiding a sense of a current dynamic between
nations). But secondly, Baroja defines himself as an organicist with the absurd
claim that physically Spaniards are different. Their distinctiveness is based
not on culture (as Unamuno and Ortega would readily concede), but on the
fact that 'nosotros tenemos la retina, los bronquios, el estómago, el hígado,
la piel, diferentes a un alemán, a un inglés o a un ruso, y no podemos sentir
igual que ellos' (Baroja 1917: 67).

By 1909 at least, then, there is the reassuring perception that what Europe
had to offer Spain was 'knowledge', although such reassurance is not unproblematic. Ortega continues to predicate that 'Europa es ciencia antes que
nada', implying that Spain by contrast is the territory that lacks this 'ciencia',
Spain thus being diminished (Ortega 1909a: 118). One month before this,
however, Ortega had taken another angle on the way in which Spain was
diminished, imagining how Europe might – on looking over the Pyrenees at

Spain – be 'recorriendo con sus ojos severos la desnudez de nuestras carnes señaladas por todos los vicios' (Ortega 1909b: 129). This gripping image of a national sense of shame resulting from a sense of primeval nakedness reveals the concept of Spain as visceral.

Whether 'ciencia' is understood as 'science' or 'knowledge' is arguably immaterial in this context, since Ortega's emphasis in general is on systematized knowledge, something available to be taught and transmitted, and contrasting with other areas of the mind such as instinct or 'sabiduría' (wisdom). If Ortega has little space to give to wisdom, he thereby proclaims himself of the world of modernity. We need to note, however, that when Ortega makes his famous statement 'Europe es ciencia antes que nada' it is not in a context of recommending the sort of activity in which the JAE was already engaging, in funding young Spanish scholars to study science abroad, particularly in Germany. The context is in fact one of political education. What Spain has been lacking is a sense of political awareness, says Ortega, an awareness that would lead in its turn to 'conciencia de libertad'. Europe may be 'ciencia', but his distinction is one that separates Europe as a mystical concept from one that is now pledged to practical action.

Ortega was patently sensitive to the problematic nature of 'Europe' for Spain. Writing in 1910 on what was to be a short-lived review, *Europa*, in which he was briefly a contributor (Gómez Aparicio 1974: 538), Ortega is outspoken about how the suggestion of Europe would produce strong reaction in the very sectors of society that should have been prepared to embrace it, and he uses the review as a platform to rehearse a bracing vision of Europe:

> Decir Europa es gritar a los organismos universitarios españoles que son moldes trogloditicos para perpetuar la barbarie, para empujar los restos de una antigua raza enérgica a todos los extremos de la desespiritualización.
>
> (Ortega 1910b: 142)

His solution is, in a sense, to *revert* to Europe as a concept, a quasi-mystical one, a concept that is to transcend relationships with individual member countries. Thus while there was a real ground-level activity already in Spain by this date to set up cultural and educational contacts with parts of Europe, Ortega is here still cautious about the implications, solving them by having recourse not to a higher authority, but to a 'higher goal'. The new review has an aim of attacking methodically and energetically what he refers to as the 'achabacanamiento nacional'. Europeanization is the tool to be used, he says, but the goal is to go beyond the thoughtless attachment to individual countries. He laments the fact that 'Hoy estamos afrancesados, anglizados, alemanizados: trozos exánimes de otras civilizaciones van siendo traídos a nuestro cuerpo por un fatal aluvión de inconsciencia.' The danger, moreover, is Spain's passivity. In a conclusion that disturbingly echoes Unamuno, yet avoids repeating it completely, he concludes 'Somos cisterna y debiéramos ser manantial' (Ortega 1910b: 145). Clearly the notorious aridity of central Spain leads its thinkers to cast regeneration in terms of watering. The interest here is the shift from the sense of the 'cisterna' (man-made storage for water), and the 'manantial' (the spring that would come spontaneously from the bedrock of Spain).

Ortega's pledge to action would become more concrete in 1914, with the foundation of the Liga de Educación Política. Speaking of the mission of this Liga, he anticipates what would be the commitment of the Misiones Pedagógicas. The action envisaged is, moreover, in relation to Europe in that it is to run *parallel* to similar movements. This is a moment for Spain to join in, and become part of a European and cultured group:

> Todo español lleva dentro, como un hombre muerto, un hombre que pudo nacer y no nació, y claro está que vendrá un día, no nos importa cuál, en que esos hombres muertos escogerán una hora para levantarse e ir a pediros cuenta sañudamente de ese vuestro innumerable asesinato.
>
> (Ortega 1914: 284)

In announcing the planned activity of the Liga in Spain, he highlights how it is in train with liberal movements elsewhere in Europe, motivated not by 'utopías más o menos remozadas, sino el ideal de la eficacia' (Ortega 1914: 286). Yet Ortega's discourse carries more of the rhetoric of regeneration (with its connotations of enlightenment and enlivening) that will characterize the Republican educational drives of the 1930s than is implied by his appeal to practicality and what is 'eficaz':

> Vamos a inundar con nuestra curiosidad y nuestro entusiasmo los últimos rincones de España: vamos a ver España y a sembrarla de amor y de indignación. Vamos a recorrer los campos en apostólica algarada, a vivir en las aldeas, a escuchar las quejas desesperadas allí donde manan; vamos a ser primero amigos de quienes luego vamos a ser conductores. Vamos a crear entre ellos fuertes lazos de socialidad – cooperativas, círculos de mutua educación, centros de observación y de protesta. Vamos a impulsar hacia un imperioso levantamiento espiritual los hombres mejores de cada capital, que hoy están prisioneros del gravamen terrible de la España oficial, más pesado en provincias que en Madrid. Vamos a hacerles saber a esos espíritus fraternos, perdidos en la inercia provincial, que tienen en nosotros auxiliares y defensores. Vamos a tender una red de nudos de esfuerzo por todos los ámbitos españoles, red que a la vez será órgano de propaganda y órgano de estudio del hecho nacional; red, en fin, que forme un sistema nervioso por el que corran vitales oleadas de sensibilidad y automáticas, poderosas corrientes de protesta. (Ortega 1914: 286)

The mission of culture that will be taken on by the Republic (with its roots in the Bibliotecas Populares movement) will be discussed in Chapters 7 and 8, but it is patent that it has its roots in a moment of political conviction about the need for civic education. Ortega uses a vocabulary that links him to the '98 ('apostólica algarada', 'levantamiento espiritual' 'espíritus fraternos'). It will equally link him to movements such as the Liga de Campesinos (see Chapter 8). Yet it is clear that his impulse of brotherly support with his 'espíritus fraternos' is set in a hierarchy that for him is inevitable. As he declares, 'vamos a ser primero amigos de quienes luego vamos a ser conductores', he is being more pragmatic than the Misiones will be in the first instance. His attitude here is also more alive to the political and social problems of the *pueblo* he seeks to enlighten than is the case of Cossío's statement of mission for the Misiones Pedagógicas some sixteen year later. And in his mention of the intention of spreading 'una red de nudos de esfuerzo por todos los ámbitos españoles ... red ... que forme un sistema nervioso por el que corran vitales oleadas de sensibilidad y automáticas, poderosas corrientes de protesta' we can see that for him the idea of networking between groups is seen as an aim, rather than something that results by happenstance. This aim will be realized in part by the *Revista de Occidente* (and is certainly part of what it sets out to do). But at this stage it is a comment of its time in the way it envisages the network as a vital nervous system, thus picking up on the organicist analyses of Spain as a body in need of regeneration. At the same time, in more modern mode, it anticipates (without formulating how this will come into being) the interrelationships between groups that will develop in Spain (see Chapter 9).

1914, however, marks the opening of the First World War. With it comes a set of consequences for Spain. First, it will focalize those who are pro-Europe (or indeed those who are not pro-Europe) into supporting either Germany or the Allies. And second, it will present problems in that the war will make heavy inroads into the concept of Europe as 'civilization'. In taking sides, Spaniards were making cultural and sociological choices. Those supporting the cause of Germany did so because of perceived values of the monarchy, discipline, religion and a sense of hierarchy, while supporters of the Allies were perceptibly in favour of trans-national values. Thus opting for France was 'opting for a future Europeanised, secular and democratic Spain' (Hess 2001: 61; Romero Salvadó in Mar-Molinaro and Smith 1996: 119–32; Villacorta Baños 1980: 128–32). On 9 July 1915 *España* published a manifesto proclaiming support for the Allies. The signatories included prominent figures from literature, history, science, painting and music: Unamuno, Américo Castro, Marañón, Menéndez Pidal, Fernando de los Ríos, Ortega y Gasset, Ramón Casas, Santiago Rusiñol, Zuloaga, Valle-Inclán, Pérez Galdós, Pérez de Ayala, Azorín, Antonio Machado, Ramiro de

Maeztu, Gregorio Martínez Sierra, Azaña, Gustavo Pittaluga (see Hess 2001: 61; Díaz Plaja 1973: 26–8).

España provides us in fact with a noteworthy example, despite the suggestions of its name, of an attempt to engage with Europe in the years of the First World War. It counted Ortega, Baroja, Pérez de Ayala, Eugenio d'Ors, Gregorio Martínez Sierra, Araquistain and Ramiro de Maeztu among its contributors. Ortega was its first director, and was followed in early January 1916 by Luis Araquistain (Gómez Aparicio 1974: 541). An indication of its profile of European (and extra-European awareness) can be seen from some of the biographical vignettes it offered in 1915, offering a context of European awareness for the manifesto mentioned above. Subjects of the vignettes included Aristide Briand, Hollweg (the German Chancellor), Ellen Key, Emile Verhaeren, Henri Bergson, Hauptmann, G K Chesterton, H G Wells, Ivan Mestrovic, Clemenceau, Rodó, Keir Hardie, the Empress Eugénie, Lloyd George, Lord Kitchener, Maeterlinck, Rabridranath Tagore, Rémy de Gourmont, Theodore Roosevelt, Winston Churchill and Woodrow Wilson. Politics walks alongside philosophy, sociology alongside literature. Yet *España*, as evidenced by the manifesto, did not wish Spain to be interested in Europe while remaining at a distance. Spain's detached form of neutrality vis-à-vis the war was lamented by Araquistain in *España*'s pages. It was a neutrality that inspired indifference rather than interest, an indifference that Araquistain had deemed to be derived from Spain's apparent own indifference.

> La indiferencia del mundo por nosotros se basa en el supuesto de que él nos es indiferente. Tiene que partir de nosotros la iniciativa, ya que somos los que menos podemos ofrecer en el intercambio, renunciando a soberbias tan injustificadas como estériles. (Araquistain, 19 February 1915)

Thus Spain's becoming interested in the world beyond the Pyrenees would be the key to its being found of interest to others.

Supporting the Allies or Germany immediately put into question the nature of 'Europe', the problematic nature of which had been signalled by Ortega in his perception of 'Las dos Alemanias'. He had distinguished between the Germany that had contributed to international culture through its philosophy and the Germany that could be met with at ground level. In a surprising preview of the attack on the 'hombre-masa' that would be made in 1930 in *La rebelión de las masas*, he compared Spain and Germany, alleging that 'no conocemos en España nada que asemeje a la incultura, a la vulgaridad de espíritu, a la pobreza de energías de la Alemania filistea' (Ortega 1908: 24). Significantly, then, he retains his aspirations for contact with Europe, in the form of Germany in this case, to the field of literary and cultural production, rather than engage with the hands-on realities of German life. His conclusion from the latter is that 'el hombre alemán es el europeo de menos valor' (1908:

24), a judgement that confirms his concept of 'Europe' as cultural ideal rather than social and political reality.

Trend would comment in 1921 how Spain after the First World War was somehow more Europe than Europe itself: it had come to be a preservation of that civilization that Spaniards had aspired to:

> The Spaniards of to-day have done a real service to Europe. By remaining neutral they have not only saved their country, but they have preserved more of the European spirit – or what we used to believe was the European spirit – than any other of the belligerent peoples. Travel and conversation with men of very different classes in very different provinces shows convincingly that the European view of life and its values – that mixture of idealism, humanity and common sense with other ingredients not so easily described – is more alive to-day in Spain than in most other countries.
>
> (Trend 1921: 1)

In a further comment he indicated what would be one of the cultural aspirations of Spain, at least as experienced by Giner, Castillejo and their acquaintance: 'Listening to Spaniards I have often felt that they are expressing a point of view which is very "English"' (Trend 1921: 1–2).

Trend spoke as a friend of Spain, a major cultural bridge. His view of Spaniards as those who had preserved European values would have been impossible without his intimate knowledge of the country, and his enthusiasm for its people. But for others there was the strong conviction that while Europe might exist for Spain, Spain lay outside the curiosity of Europe. Marcelino Domingo commented, in a lecture reported by *La Voz* on 17 August 1920,

> La primera impresión que se recibe al salir de España es que España no existe para el extranjero. Ninguno de nuestros problemas representa una inquietud fuera de España; ningún conflicto nuestro interesa fuera de aquí; España no existe para Europa. (Anon 1920: 7)

But for others, in the wake of the war, Europe – as a political entity – had been damaged, so that, converse to earlier perceptions of it, neediness was the keynote. As the comments of Julio González in the *Revista de Filosofía* founded by the Argentine José Ingenieros indicate, it was as if the tables had been turned (although there is a difference here in that Europe was being perceived from Latin America, not from its closely aspirant neighbour, Spain):

> ¿De dónde puede llegar entonces la luz que necesita el abismo de Europa, cada vez más negro y tenebroso a medida que los tratados van surtiendo su efecto, y sus dirigentes dejándose caer por el plano inclinado que los está lanzando al fondo de todas las tiranías y despotismos? (González 1924: 87)

Another outsider, Paul Valéry, also noted that the First World War had caused Europe to lose its way (Valéry 1927). No longer was Europe unilaterally downgraded by a Spain enveloped in a sense of its own decadence, but what had been the creation of a desperate bid not to lose national pride now seemed to be a reality.

Ortega, we recall, was a strong champion of Europe, so the question of how Europe was presented in the *Revista de Occidente* was crucial. Consistently through its pages we find evidence of Ortega's intention of producing an educated and cultured population by exposure to the 'best' ideas from Europe and elsewhere. But *dirigiste* as his attitude was to this publication, which bore strong traces of his leadership and indeed his agenda (see Chapter 4), some of the articles in it shared the view that Europe in the postwar period was not what it had been. As Waldo Frank declared, Europe, not just as it had been but as it had been known, had come to an end:

> Europa, el conjunto cultural, ordenado en formas sociales y espirituales, y en el cual los hombres eran como células de un cuerpo, ya no existe. La quiebra de sus órganos jerárquicos ha significado la muerte del cuerpo.
>
> (Frank 1929: 354)

Furthermore, through this period, the question of what Europe consisted of (in terms of nations) was explored. Ortega, for example, in 1930, came to a series of complex conclusions. Europe was both its member nations, and not its member nations. On the one hand there was a sense of Europe as a reality, with its own customs:

> los pueblos europeos son desde hace mucho tiempo una sociedad, una colectividad, en el mismo sentido que tienen estas palabras aplicadas a cada una de las naciones que integran aquélla. Esa sociedad manifiesta todos los atributos de tal: hay costumbres europeas, usos europeos, opinión pública europea, derecho europeo, poder público europeo.

But at the same time this 'reality' of Europe was, as it were, in an infant state compared with that of its constituent parts, and

> todos estos fenómenos sociales se dan en la forma adecuada al estado de evolución en que se encuentra la sociedad europea, que no es, claro está, tan avanzado como el de sus miembros componentes, las naciones.
>
> (Ortega 1930: 118)

Much later in this essay, however, in which one of the disturbing common factors between the countries of Europe is the existence of the 'hombre-masa', he asserts that for most Europe was perceived as the big three: France, England and Germany (a view taken by numerous works subsequently in comparative studies). But having said earlier that Europe was less advanced than the countries that composed it, he now asserts that being a member of one of the constituent nations was equivalent to being *provincial*.

This practical, and narrow, view of Europe contrasted with the view of Keyserling who, with some prescience, and with some intuition for what would prove attractive to Spain, had posited that Europe needed to deal with its margins. Spain and Russia stood at its extremities. Both were 'países esencialmente no europeos', and in their shared standing aside observed by Keyserling, we can see some of the roots of Spain's fascination with Russia (as explored in Chapter 6). In characteristically conservative mode, Keyserling suggested that Spain's significance to Europe was based on its difference from it:

> España sólo podrá tener importancia en ella en tanto que sea diferente de otros países y haga sonar un tono especial de la vida, singularmente puro y convincente, que se escuche en la vida toda. (Keyserling 1926: 138)

There is no way, then, that 'Europe' can be understood as a fixed entity in the Spanish mind, not even in the sense that it is part of the Spanish national imaginary. Events from without and from within impacted on the perception of this significant geographical territory that had come to be associated with high levels of culture and civilization. The previous chapter explored models of understanding intellectual and cultural interactions, not least those involving leadership and authority. So what is interesting is to explore how far what Europe represents for Spain in this period has a relationship with those interactions.

The following chapters in this study look at specifics of how Spain related to Europe. The chapters comprising the section 'Centres of Exchange and Bodies of Print' (3 and 4) look at the diversity of ways in which Spain related to different European countries, with due attention to the expected Franco-German emphasis in the expected canon, and looking at both outreach and responsiveness in the importations Spain made from Europe. But the chapters in the section 'Cultural Imaginaries and Special Attachments' (5 and 6) show the degree to which outreach was predetermined by a degree of commitment in terms of the imagination. Significantly those two love-affairs are with the extremities of Europe. Russia is clearly on the margins, and England, though included by Ortega in his concept of the 'big three', is paradigmatically that country for which Europe is 'elsewhere'.

The two love-affairs, dealing as they do with elements of the national imaginary, run contemporaneously with the other much more down-to-earth forms of interaction between Spain and Europe in the section on 'Centres of Exchange and Bodies of Print'. What I have outlined in this chapter is a series of reactions that are grounded in a sense of Spain as a national entity, a cultural phenomenon, that compares itself unfavourably with Europe (the 'elsewhere' with the greater territory, and perceived greater level of economic or political success). Clearly the sense that Spain was in some sense inferior to 'Europe' (a sense defended against more or less strongly as we have seen) had a logical consequence. If Spain was lacking in cultural or intellectual areas, then its solution was to seek them elsewhere, to enter into the market of cultural exchange. That figures such as Unamuno proposed the exchange not to be solely with Spain as purchaser, but as vendor of its own values and qualities, is not surprising. But whatever the debates about exchange, the need for it, the potential for it, that I have outlined here, there were real and practical moves related to Spain entering into cultural trafficking with Europe.

Running parallel with the elements of debate I have alluded to, and in a number of ways consequent upon them, we find a strong educational drive, which inevitably has a relationship with Spain's attitude to Europe. This can be characterized as a sustained and dramatic programme of liberal educational reform stemming from the setting up of the ILE in 1876. Its offspring would include significant other educational institutions, not only the Residencia de Estudiantes but the Residencia de Señoritas, founded in 1915 and the Instituto-Escuela founded in 1918 (Zulueta and Moreno 1993). Central to the idea of educational reform were two ideas: one, that education needed to be released from a deadening strait-jacket of curriculum, and a framework of examination that did little, if anything, to develop the mind and interests of the student; the other, that if Spain was to advance in this area, it needed to learn from abroad. The first idea is embodied in all the practices of the institutions I have named. The second is embodied in the powerful JAE, which organized and co-ordinated educational visits abroad. In the course of twenty-nine years, from its inception in 1910, it received 9,000 applications for grants, and awarded 1,500 (Zulueta and Moreno 1993: 32). It is important to bear in mind the degree to which these educational developments, crucial for the intellectual life in Spain at this period, were not officially promoted by the government, and indeed ran counter to government aims and policy. The uneasy co-existence of public and private sectors is seen most noticeably in the travails of the JAE, outlined in painful detail in the letters of Castillejo, its secretary (D Castillejo 1997, 1998, 1999). Not only was the government obstructive in 1907 when the JAE was set up, but became intrusive and difficult during the dictatorship years.

These institutions provide a real basis for a set of cultural and intellectual contacts between Spain and the rest of Europe. The two countries highest on Spain's list of interests within these institutions were England and Germany. France, while being regarded as a regular source for intellectual inspiration, does not, however, hold the privileged place of the other countries I have mentioned, although the evidence of the interest of publishing houses tells a rather different story.

In the chapters that follow it is my endeavour to give the flavour of the many-faceted nature of Spain's exchanges with Europe. I have focused more on unofficial channels than on official ones, on free enterprise rather than on organization, on individual curiosity (or the expectation of profit in sensing a market for materials) rather than on a designed programme. In Certeau's terms, my interests are more with the tactician than with the strategist, with the mosaic of enterprise rather than with the grand plan. On the front-line (of publishers, newspapers and journals) there is much variation, individual activity. In a second wave of activity, concerned with the diffusion within Spain of knowledge acquired, we find more emphasis on the strategic, with a sense of canon conveyed through both the Bibliotecas Populares movement and the Misiones Pedagógicas. But even these areas of strategy carry all the hallmarks of the tactician who has to do what he can, where he can, move where it is possible (literally so, in the activity of taking culture, imported or local, beyond centres of urban development in Spain). Cultural trafficking is not, in the final analysis, something that can be designed by government, but rather comes from individual energy and curiosity. At every turn we can see how, in national rhetoric, Europe was desired, posited as a model for iden-tification (or a model to be rejected), but curiously was made anonymous in the urge for cultural contact. At the same time the heterogeneity of 'Europe' in practice (contrasting with the mythical and utopian unity of 'Europe' at the level of national rhetoric) enlivens the vision of Spain's engagement with its elsewhere. It plays havoc with the generalizations of those arguing for an idea of simple reception of influence from outside.

3   Publishers, Power and Canonicity

In the broad scheme of things, publishing books as a way of spreading culture is arguably much less cost-effective, or indeed in any way effective, than other mass media of culture. Jordana Mendelson's work on the work of the *periódico mural*, for example, illustrates the immediacy and effect of print culture in a non-standard situation (Mendelson 2007). If you engage in propaganda, then, as Carmelo Garitaonandía points out, non-book publishing is likely to be far more effective than what can be achieved by engagement in the book trade (Garitaonandía 1989: 166). Not only posters on walls, but the radio and newsprint are all going to reach a wider public at greater speed. So when we look at the activity of the book trade, we are automatically into a territory of elites and minorities. Furthermore, in a country that, according to *El Sol* in 1918, had a level of illiteracy in the population of 50.2 per cent (a level that rose to 60 per cent in rural areas, with 48 per cent in urban centres) (Álvarez 1989b: 83), then the idea of 'cultural dissemination' is necessarily automatically curtailed. The issues of how to transfer knowledge to the people, a large proportion of whom had to be assumed as either illiterate, or barely literate, is taken up in Chapter 7, 'Taking the Knowledge to the People', where the propagation of specific canons is examined in detail. In the interim, we can see a spectrum of activity in publishing houses as centres of exchange. Some houses, particularly in the production of specific collections, suggest a canon that – if not implied as definitive – is at least indicative, and with some feeling of authority about it. But even specific collections are variable in their aspect and claim to authority. At the other end of the spectrum some houses appear to have been more fluid in their operations, perhaps opportunistic, and where the direction of publication has been influenced less by any editorial policy than by the suggestions of individuals. The variation along the spectrum relates, at its extremes, to Certeau's axis of strategy and tactics.

As Collini has somewhat disturbingly (but aptly) observed, 'Professions, like clubs, are about excluding people' (Collini 1991: 237). The production of an elite journal, supported by its own publishing house, is closely aligned to the (virtual) creation of a club. Membership is by subscription to the journal and purchase of the books in the collection. It is a self-perpetuating exercise, in which knowledge is amassed, and built upon. Collini has likened the experience of the periodical to that of Anderson's imagined community:

> More than many other forms of writing, the periodical essay is an *excerpt whose full intelligibility depends on a fairly intimate acquaintance with the larger cultural conversation from which it is taken.* To adapt a phrase from a quite other context, it may be helpful to speak of the 'imagined community' of a journal's readers. The notion of such an imagined community can be posited as a kind of transcendental deduction from the very act of writing for periodicals: more specific inferences can be made from noting which topics are assumed to be of interest, or identifying which allusions and references a writer does or does not feel called upon to explain, and so on. (Collini 1991: 56, emphasis mine)

This concept of an 'imagined community' is central to the activities of centres of exchange, one that allows for the creation of a body of readers or participants, and one that produces (and subsequently speaks to) its own closed circle of informed and initiated members.

What the activities of a publishing house allow for, by contrast with those of a journal, is a more flexible concept of the 'imagined community', although flexibility is variable over time and between publishing houses. I shall move therefore from the highly defined to the less defined, beginning with the Revista de Occidente publishing enterprise on the basis of its being an exceptionally well-defined one, and where there is the clear evidence of complementarity between the activity of the publishing house and that of the journal. The journal as such, with one of its main lines of development, is discussed in greater detail in the following chapter. Nonetheless, briefly but necessarily anticipating the concerns of the following chapter, it is important to step across to look at the journal to see how the two enterprises coincide in meeting specific aims of Ortega, and primarily that of creating a body of people with whom he could converse.

This chapter looks at publishers and publishing houses as centres of exchange, with a focus on the ways in which and the degree to which they promoted or reflected areas of interest. My assumption is that their operation was not neutral, and that it responded to a variety of impulses: economic, educational, the politics of survival (in publishing), the driving power of editors and, at a lower level, journalists and translators. It is impossible to map the publishing activity of a country over three and a half decades in the space of one chapter. Instead I shall take a number of cases in order to illustrate the ways in which publishers mediated, directed or promoted cultural exchange.

The information available for the publishers discussed is uneven, and does not necessarily match the respective importance of the houses concerned. Publishing was marked by the existence of relatively small enterprises, a significant number of them operating as family firms (Martínez Martín and Martínez Rus 2004: 21–2). There are, however, three large enterprises where it is possible to draw on relatively detailed sources: the Revista de Occidente (the publishing house attached to the journal of that name), Espasa Calpe and Biblioteca Nueva. The degree to which they were clearly led from the top varies, with the strong direction given (perhaps imposed is a more accurate word) to Revista de Occidente by Ortega contrasting with the more fluid dealings and enterprises of Espasa Calpe and Biblioteca Nueva. Of these giants, Biblioteca Nueva came first, founded in 1910 on the dissolution of the Biblioteca Renacimiento, which had been founded by Ruiz-Castillo's father, a 'socio capitalista' and Gregorio Martínez Sierra (Ruiz-Castillo 1979: 83). Calpe was founded in 1919, when it launched La Colección Universal (López Campillo 1972: 51), and was joined by Espasa in 1925 (see Castellano 2000: 40–8, 72–95).

These large publishing houses are, of course, not the only ones of significance, and I am conscious of having left on one side the Compañía Ibero-Americana de Publicaciones (CIAP), which took over a number of smaller enterprises, including Renacimiento, Mundo Latino, Fe, Estrella, Biblioteca Corona, Atlántica, Mercurio, and, among reviews, *Cosmópolis*, *La Raza*, *El perro, el ratón y el gato*, *La Gaceta Literaria* and *Comercio* (Santonja 1989: 15). I make brief mention of a number of these smaller enterprises, some of them offshoots from the main stem and arguably just as important in the landscape of cultural trafficking and prominent particularly through the 1920s and the Second Republic. Santonja, in his study of Cénit, Ulises and Fénix (1989), amply demonstrates the general contribution of such publishing houses and their specific contribution to the availability of foreign texts in Spain. We might also note the case of Morata, well known for its publication of scientific and medical work, and significant for the considerations of Chapter 9 on networking and cross-hatching. In terms of the framework of Michel de Certeau, the nature of the Revista de Occidente enterprise, while offering itself as an importer of the innovative (and arguably thus as non-establishment), operates very much in the sense of 'strategy'. The strong linkage between the review, the publishing house and the figure of Ortega himself, means that the sense of boundaries and internal integrity is overwhelming. By contrast, Espasa Calpe and Biblioteca Nueva, both of them more extensive operations than Revista de Occidente, are, by their sprawling nature and varied publications, open to a wider number of avenues, to the speculative and at times idiosyncratic publishing patterns that one could ascribe to tactics. In the discussion to follow it is also worth noting the growth of the publishing industry itself. Some 2,500 works in print in 1928 rose to 4,000 by 1933 (Santonja 1989: 9), a level of activity, patchy and unpredictable, and partially indicated in the activities of the Ferias del Libro, that provided support for the enterprise of setting up public libraries in Spain, particularly in the first two years of the Republic (Santonja 1989: 31).

Revista de Occidente

The Revista de Occidente, as the publishing arm of the review of that name (subsequently referred to as *RO*), cannot be ignored in a consideration of Spain's centres of exchange. Founded and directed by Ortega, the journal had from its inception in 1923 the reputation of being the flagship of intellectual advance in modern Spain, and of forming a major conduit for ideas from abroad to reach Spain. Specifically engaged in the education of the intellectual, and the formation of a readership, it was deliberately and explicitly non-political. The detail of the breadth of that education and formation indicates the degree to which there was a definite (or even a definitive) sense of canon, in both the journal and the publishing house, a canon that can be argued to be as restrictive as it was expansive.

Founded in 1923, the journal was unashamedly committed to the education of the intellectual, and the formation of a special readership. Like the press of the same name, and as suggested by its title, *RO* set out to put its readership in contact with cultural preoccupations, ideas and trends in Europe, and to some (markedly select) degree with the United States. 'Occidente' indicates not geography but attitude, a look towards the Western world that associates the West with civilization and progress: in geographical terms Germany is of course to the east of Spain, as is much of France. But the joint enterprises had a clear and boundaried idea of what this cultural contact, and indeed cultural content, should consist of. If we regard what the publishing house provided as the 'library' of the reader educated by Ortega, and the review *RO* as the passing enlightenment or updating of that reader, then the cultural view propagated is a menu of philosophy (predominantly German), sociology (again, predominantly German), with side-dishes of 'new' disciplines such as philosophical anthropology, patho-genealogy (Nóvoa Santos), and new entrées of cosmology, phenomenology and physics. Offerings of literature occur on a regular basis, and in appreciable individual portions. They are predominantly avant-garde, and come, curiously, without a surrounding of comment or interpretation. The inference is that the educated reader (particularly the reader well versed in Ortega's aesthetics from the 1925 essays on the *Deshumanización del arte* and the *Ideas sobre la novela*) will know how to deal with them, something that itself implies the nature of the club that the *Revista de Occidente* has formed.

Between 1924 and 1936, the Revista de Occidente press produced some 253 titles. The chronology of the collections provides its own partial reflection of the public events of Spain in that period. It flags up, for example, the commemoration (indeed the celebration of, and creation of the public cultural figure of, Góngora). Yet, just as is the case with *Revista de Occidente*, the journal, it largely eschews politics. The 'collections' of 'Libros de Política' and 'Cuadernos de Política', of June and October 1931 respectively, are notably underpopulated. There is the interesting oddity, moreover, that in the account given of these collections by López Campillo (1972), neither of the two items of 'Libros de política', and only one of the four items of 'Cuadernos de política' appear in her original list of works of the press in the chronological order in which they appeared. They are not the only omitted items. The list of 'Manuales de filosofía' contains two items not in the original list, as does 'Nova novorum'. What is striking in the political sections is the fact that the omitted items account for nearly all of the production.

The sections, wide-ranging and with apparently clear agendas, appeared as regular new enterprises, and were: 'Obras de José Ortega y Gasset', October 1924; 'Musas lejanas', March 1925; 'Nuevos hechos, nuevas ideas', May 1925; 'Los grandes pensadores', July 1925; 'Historia de la Filosofía', November 1925; 'Historia breve', December 1925; 'Hoy y mañana', March 1926; 'Nova novorum', May 1926; 'Colección centenario de Góngora', April 1927; 'Biblioteca de Historiología', April 1928; 'Los poetas', December 1928; 'Manuales de Filosofía', December 1928; 'Los filósofos', April 1930; 'Estudios sociológicos', December 1930; 'Libros de Política', June 1931; 'Los libros románticos', March 1932; 'Textos filosóficos', October 1934; and 'Libros del siglo XIX', June 1935.

Clearly some of the collections have as their objective the transmission of a European culture to Spain. The nature of that European culture, while to some degree eclectic, is also strongly Germanic, a feature that is not surprising given the role of Ortega in the collections (see Orringer 1979). López Campillo is at pains to argue against the view that the journal *RO* published predominantly German items. She points out that the number of German authors is just under the total of the other non-Spanish contributors, and that the contributions of the German authors is five times less than that of Spanish ones (López Campillo 1972: 71–2). Nonetheless her calculations demonstrate with admirable clarity the degree to which the 'outside' was not just Nordic, but largely Germanic. Meanwhile, the character of the 'outside' as we can perceive it in the collections of the Revista de Occidente is overwhelmingly Germanic. Not only does it provide an overview of major works in philosophy, sociology and (accessible) science that were produced in Germany, but – what is more significant – much of the world of the outside is mediated through German writing. A significant proportion of the works that treat of the culture of the world outside Spain thus come through Germany, with the inevitable input of that lens of mediation, its choices and emphases.

Some of the collections begin, as it were, further back, presenting a backcloth to that culture, or what might be viewed as a background to the European culture that is imported. This is the case of the collection 'Musas lejanas', a fanciful title, with the subtitle of 'Mitos. Cuentos. Leyendas', and which constitutes an early canon of distant items suggested by the Revista de Occidente. There are few attributions indicating the sources of the items, but it is possible to speculate that the greater part of the fourteen-volume collection may have come via German, given that the two main translators (known also for their reviews in the *Revista de Occidente* journal) are J R Pérez Bances (whose work is mainly through German) and R M Tenreiro (whose work spans French and German). With the exception of the *Cuentos malayos* these 'distant' muses are predominantly either Oriental (in the broad sense) or medieval (in a narrow European sense). One possibility for the origin of the Malayan tales is that they could have come via an English translation, 'Malayan literature; comprising romantic tales, epic poetry and royal chronicles / translated into English for the first time, with a special introduction by Chauncey C. Starkweather' (New York: Colonial Press), in a series labelled, appositely for the purpose of the Revista de Occidente collections, 'The World's Great Classics. Colonial Edition'. Whether or not this is the case, the contents of the World's Great Classics series itself, which includes Chinese, Arabian, Hindu, Persian, Babylonian, Assyrian, Armenian, Egyptian, Hebrew, Moorish and Turkish literature, as well as Malayan, typifies a concept of the exotic world that existed more generally outside Spain. The interest in the Orient expressed, or arguably propounded in the 'Musas lejanas' series, links to the nature of the lectures run at the Residencia de Estudiantes, and to the areas of interest of the Centro para Estudios Históricos. Its phrasing makes it less historical, more literary, more *evocative*, than a simple 'Literaturas extranjeras' collection, proposing its exoticism, and suggesting in advance a level of reverent acceptance of this distant canon. Launched merely two months before the aggressively modern 'Nuevos hechos, nuevas ideas', this backcloth of ancient and oriental texts arguably also sets a type of tone to the collections. It suggests that if one is to have a type of 'cultural coverage' of the modern world, a grasp of culture at large, then that has to include major legends, folk-tales. It implies, though does not state, that this is more crucial than publication of a series of individual 'great works'. Indeed, what is striking about the Revista de Occidente collections is the way in which they eschew the concept of 'great works', at least in literary terms. Canons of literary 'great works' will appear elsewhere, but are not the main content of Ortega's educational drive.

What then does drive the collections? It is difficult to avoid the conclusion that the aim of the collections is not simply or merely to produce a Europe-wide panorama of cultural and intellectual life. It is far more precise, and reflects to a degree that verges on parody Ortega's belief in the centrality of German academic production to the Europeanization of Spain. The collection 'Nuevos hechos, nuevas ideas' is dominated by German titles, in a proportion of some 86 per cent. Some of the volumes are clearly Germanic productions in totality, and evidence of Ortega's preferences in philosophy and sociology (Simmel's sociology represented in six volumes 1927, and Scheler on knowledge and culture, resentment and morality and, to cap it all, man's position in the cosmos [1926, 1927, 1929, 1936]). Others are in the nature of a 'Germanic view' of more general issues. Thus we find the introduction by Grundler to a philosophy of religion (1926), Landsberg on the Platonic Academy (1926), and Haeberlin on the foundations of psycho-analysis (1928). Science is represented well through Germany, with Weyl on matter (1925), Kramers and Holst on atomic structure (1925), and Driesch (1927) combining the theory of relativity and philosophy (see Glick 1988 and 1987). There are no French or Italian items in this collection, and only four that come from English: Stoddard (1927) on the rebellion against civilization, and three scientific items by Eddington (1928), Bertrand Russell (1929) and Raymond Allen on technocracy. Of these, Eddington published in *Residencia* III (1), on 'Universo estelar', and both he and Russell are relatively promi-nent in *RO*: they are part of the established canon of the *RO*/Residencia axis.

The collection 'Los grandes pensadores', with nine items, does not fore-ground German philosophers in terms of bulk, although Leibnitz, Kant, Fichte, Hegel, Schopenhauer and Nietzsche feature in three collective volumes , and Hegel, Fichte and Wundt are unsurprisingly featured in 'Los filósofos'. But this latter collection, as is the case with 'Historia de la filosofía' (a collection entirely consisting of works by August Messer), and 'Manuales de filosofía', is dominated by German authors, so that the *view* presented to the reader comes via the German academic system. 'Textos filosóficos' again bears a Germanic weight.

Two further features of selection deserve comment. A significant propor-tion of works in German and written on philosophy came from the collec-tion Frommanns Klasiker der Philosophie. Of the list for this collection in 1909, nine titles out of twenty would re-appear in the Revista de Occidente collections, while in 1924 eight out of the twenty-two listed are in Revista de Occidente. In terms of an accepted European philosophical canon of philoso-phers there is no obvious reason for the selections made or rejected. Why should Hobbes be chosen and not Plato, why Rousseau and Kierkegaard yet not Descartes? The implication might be that if Ortega made specific choices it was not just on account of topics covered but on the basis of the reputa-tion of the critics writing (Tönnies on Hobbes, Høffding on Kierkegaard and Rousseau).

Another instance where a specific foreign collection was drawn upon in order to make a selection for Revista de Occidente was 'Today and tomorrow' by the English publisher Kegan Paul, forming part of 'Hoy y mañana'. Here the selections made are striking and interesting, revealing the conservative

bent of Ortega's canon. The list for the series 'Today and tomorrow' published
in the 1925 edition of Ludovici's *Lysistrata* (one of the works selected for
Ortega's collection) is as follows:

> J B S Haldane, *Daedalus: or Science of the future* (appears in *RO*)
>
> Bertrand Russell, *Icarus: or the Future of Science* (appears in *RO*)
>
> F G Crookshank, *The Mongol in our Midst* (neither in *RO* nor published
> in RO)
>
> A M Low, *Wireless Possibilities* (neither in *RO* nor published in RO)
>
> Gerald Heard, *Narcissus: or the Anatomy of Clothes* (neither in *RO* nor
> published in RO)
>
> F C S Schiller, *Tantalus: or the Future of Man* (in RO editorial)
>
> C J Patten, *The Passing of the Phantoms* (neither in *RO* nor published in
> RO)
>
> H F Scott Stokes, *Perseus: of Dragons* (neither in *RO* nor published in RO)

This is a clearly English/American list (Schiller, in this case, being Ferdinand Canning Scott Schiller, born in 1864 in the US, and later moving to
Oxford). On this basis, it would appear that Anthony Ludovici has been put
on a plane with Haldane, Russell and Schiller. The stridently conservative
and anti-feminist nature of *Lysistrata* as part of the Revista de Occidente
collection comes as a surprise, but not when one takes into account the profile
of publications on gender that appear in *RO* (see Chapter 4), and the apparent admiration for German culture held by Ludocivi. In his ideas on gender,
Ludovici is also syntonic with a number of contemporary eugenicists, and
we could note in passing that eugenics is a keynote of both the Schiller and
the Haldane items here (though Haldane would later become a fierce critic of
eugenics). This perspective is not one that we might automatically associate
with Ortega, but it does profoundly reinforce the conservative drive of works
such as *La rebelión de las masas*, published and re-published by the Revista
de Occidente with insistence. This last work initially looks like an example
of Ortega's local success. The most common size of run for works published
by the Revista de Occidente was 2,000 copies. *La rebelión de las masas* came
out in runs of 3,000 in its first edition of 1930, second edition of 1930 and
third edition of 1931. This, however, was still not as remarkable as some of
the other runs for Ortega's works, such as *La redención de las provincias* of
1931, which had a run of 6,000.

Not only did Ortega have clear views on what he would publish, but also
had clear limits on what he would take of contemporary culture. He thus
operated as a one-man example of strategy, deciding for himself what would
be central and what peripheral. Interestingly, however, he would espouse
Jung via a number of articles in *RO* including those on 'Tipos psicológicos' in
1925, and 'El hombre arcaico' in 1931, and included *Lo inconsciente* by Jung

in 'Nuevos hechos, nuevas ideas' in 1927. But he drew the line at Frazer's *Golden Bough*. A letter to Ricardo Baeza, c.1924, states not hesitation but conviction that Frazer is inappropriate for the Biblioteca Siglo XX:

> Estoy en tratos para incluir en la 'Bibl. de S. XX' algunas cosas inglesas y no necesito decirle que para ellas contaba *in mente con Ud*. Pero el 'Golden Bough' y, en general, toda la obra de Frazer me parece lo menos siglo XX del mundo y verdaderamente desastroso. Por el camino de Frazer no se sale a parte ninguna y la prueba de ello es que desde su publicación sobre el totemismo y exogamia andan estos problemas más confusos que antes.

He does, nonetheless, offer a possibility, but only if it proves to be economic, and one that is somewhat detached from the Revista de Occidente. He refers to publishing it in the 'Biblioteca de la Revista':

> En cambio, podíamos publicar el 'Golden Bough' en la biblioteca de la 'Revista' siempre que no nos costasen mucho los derechos. ¿Quiere Ud. escribir al autor sobre el asunto? Cualquiera que sea mi juicio personal sobre los métodos de Frazer su obra me parece, claro está, un buen magasin de hechos, sobre todo en este resumen nuevo que conozco.

The same collection of letters contains one from Frazer's wife, Mrs Lilly Frazer, who on 29 February 1924 indicates that other places might be interested in the *Golden Bough* even if the Revista de Occidente is not. Given that the work never appeared in the Revista de Occidente it would appear that the money for 'derechos' Baeza has offered (at Ortega's suggestion) was not sufficient. Mrs Frazer's letter makes it clear she has a sense of the work's value that presumably was not matched.

> As you are the best judge of what you can afford to pay for the 'outright of authorization' (to quote you), will you make me a proposal and I will then reply at once. I may add that we both know Spanish *very well* and that my husband's works are in great demand in S. America – therefore the appeal for the Spanish reading public ought to be fairly extensive.

The reference to publishing Frazer in the 'Biblioteca' is unclear. There is a 'Biblioteca de Ideas del Siglo XX', directed by Ortega, and published in the Calpe catalogue of 1923, and the Espasa Calpe catalogue of 1926. The remit of this collection was to include 'los libros maestros de Europa y América' of the last twenty years. Its intention seems therefore to be in line with the collection of 'Nuevos hechos, nuevas ideas', since these works 'inician nuevas maneras de pensar en filosofía como en política, en crítica artística como en biología, en ciencias sociales como en física'. The nine authors listed in 1923, with the exception of Bonola on non-Euclidean geometry, originally published in Italian in 1906, are all German, and span the sciences, philosophy, sociology, and culture – the typical Revista de Occidente mix: Ricker, *Ciencia cultural y ciencia natural*; Born, *La teoría de la relatividad de Einstein*; Üxküll, *Ideas para una concepción biológica del mundo*; Driesch, *Filosofía del organismo*; Worringer, *El espíritu del arte gótico*; Wöfflin, *Conceptos fundamentales en historia del arte*; Spengler, *La decadencia de occidente*; Hertwig, *La evolución de los organismos*. The 1926 catalogue adds to this collection Keyserling's *Diario de viaje de un filósofo*.

A different aspect of the particularity of the canon/s of the Revista de Occidente is to be seen in its collections involving Spanish literary production. On the one hand there is its publication of literary works, in the series 'Nova novorum', devoted to prose works, and 'Los poetas'. While the latter, featuring Guillén, *Cántico*, Salinas, *Seguro azar*, Alberti, *Cal y canto* and Lorca, *Romancero Gitano*, appears to have predicted what would become the standard canon of poetry of the 1920s, the prose collection – its novelty and non-standard nature apparent from the title of the collection – seems so quirky as to be a deliberate stand on avant-garde writing. It includes Álvarez, *¡Tararí!* (1929); Espina *El pájaro pinto* (1927) and *Luna de copas* (1929); Jarnés *El profesor inútil* (1926) and *Paula y Paulita* (1929); Salinas (1926) *Víspera del gozo* (1929). This approach to national literature is not mirrored in a display of the literatures of other European countries, the only exception being Revista de Occidente's participation in the showcasing of Russian works, in 'La Rusia actual'. As is evident, however, when we see this collection alongside the Russian items selected by other publishing houses, the works selected are far from constituting an agreed canon.

One might imagine that the regular subscriber to the journal *RO* would be a prime consumer of the various collections alluded to above. One subscriber, however, suggests that this is not the case. Ricardo Baeza, translator, journalist and owner of one of the most extensive private libraries in Spain (of some 40,000 volumes), took the journal *Revista de Occidente* from 1923 to 1936 (virtually its prewar entirety), but desisted from purchasing its volumes, with the exception of Keyserling's *El mundo que nace* (1926). Baeza was a voracious reader of foreign works, literary, historical, philosophical and scientific, but is perhaps an example of the reader who was well ahead of the canon being offered by the Revista de Occidente.

In the event, the Biblioteca de Ideas del Siglo XX, as it was advertised in *Residencia* 1 (2), May–August 1926, and in successive issues until 1931, did not look like the context in which Frazer might obviously have appeared. The contents in the advert for the collection display, with one exception (Bonola) a still heavily Germanic view of science, sociology and aesthetics. The translators of five of these works from German, García Morente (translator of Ricker, Born and Spengler), Tenreiro (translator of Üxküll), and Moreno Villa (translator of Wöfflin), industrious and prolific to a degree, figure widely in *RO* the journal, and in *Residencia*. Gutiérrez del Arroyo (brought in for Italian) appears as translator of two French works in the Colección Universal of Espasa Calpe. As part of an inner circle of translators and reviewers, they are arguably as responsible as anyone else for the selections and publication of these collections.

Espasa Calpe

The major publishing house that would be Espasa Calpe was formed in 1925 by the joining of two separate and successful enterprises. As the introduction to the 1926 catalogue summarizes, Espasa was well established and well known, not least for its *Enciclopedia*, which it presents as being 'suma del humano saber y alarde del adelanto de las Artes gráficas' (see Castellano 2000). Calpe, by contrast, was the more recent venture, based on the book trade, and 'dotada de las nuevas formas de expansion de nuestro espíritu', and formed the aspect of modernity in the joint venture. Calpe's name itself, as it appears at the head of the *Catálogo general* of 1923, reveals the broad base of its operations, being an acronym for Compañía Anónima de Librería, Publicaciones y Ediciones. Its catholicity of activity, range of interests represented in the collections and sheer vitality make it a strong competitor to the Revista de Occidente house in terms of a centre of exchange that will make a difference to a broad population.

While the Revista de Occidente collection looks impressive in its entirety, and contains some 254 items, the Calpe collection of 1923 is of another order of magnitude, consisting of 1,141 volumes in 66 collections. When Espasa joins Calpe in 1925, this gives rise to a much-expanded catalogue in 1926 with 104 collections in it. The expansion is across the board, and to some degree reflects the encyclopaedic interests and activity of Espasa before the merger. Possible reflections of the fact that the 1926 catalogue comes from the middle of Primo de Rivera's regime are collections of an explicitly moral or religious nature: 'Literatura moral recreativa', 'Episodios milagrosos de Nuestra Señora de Lourdes', 'Vida de León XIII' and 'Historia eclesiástica'.

Placed at the head of the 1923 catalogue, and with justification, is the Colección Universal, a collection that had been initiated in 1919. The 740 volumes of this catalogue will rise to 1,000 in the 1926 catalogue, although they do not represent the same number of discrete published works (the collection in the two catalogues consists of 307 and 414 titles respectively). The division of the works according to the original language of publication reveals a profile quite distinct from that of the Revista de Occidente in that it has a significantly prominent French input. In the 1926 catalogue, works translated from French represent 37.7 per cent, followed by the relatively even paired groups of English at 15.3 per cent, Spanish at 14.75 per cent, followed by German at 11.48 per cent and Russian at 10.4 per cent. The tail comes in with Italian at 4.9 per cent, Greek at 2.7 per cent, Latin at 1.3 per cent, Hungarian at 1.09 per cent and Polish at 0.3 per cent.

The Colección Universal is recalled by Spaniards who remember it from their youth as one that was a major channel for foreign works to enter Spain. The publicity for the collection in the 1926 Espasa Calpe *Catálogo general* includes words of praise from a careful selection of representatives from the sciences and the humanities: Ramón y Cajal (histologist), Rodríguez Carracido (chemist), Menéndez Pidal (philologist), Benavente (playwright). The collection is then proclaimed to be an instrument of self-education, given that it is 'una *selección metódica de las mejores obras del ingenio humano* en todos los ordenes' (emphasis as in original). It promises the reader only first-class books, which (in the tradition of Lope and Cervantes, one might note) will offer pleasure, and contribute to his 'cultura y progreso'. The collection promises accessibility ('pone al *alcance de todos*' [emphasis as in original]) of the most famous works of the world, and yet which are not always easy to obtain. From the list that follows (Lope de Vega, Fray Luis de León, Shakespeare, Goethe, Cicero, Cervantes, Leibnitz, Goldsmith, Alarcón, Prévost, Eliot, Andreiev, Musset, Dostoiewski, Caesar, Tacitus, Beaumarchais, Dante, Austen, Molière, Plutarch, Thackeray, Victor Hugo, Quevedo and 'others'), the concept of the world is not only Eurocentric but reflects the Europe of well-established countries (Espasa Calpe 1926: 22). It contrasts in this with the 'geographical' Europe of the 'Geografía y viajes' collection of J Dantín Cereceda, which is promised to be modern and scientific, and in a spirit of inclusiveness lists in its Eurasia section the new nations of Europe: the Baltic States, Yugoslavia, the Free State of Danzig, Finland, the Ukraine, Poland (Espasa Calpe 1926: 85). This broad and adventurous concept of Europe stands out alongside the narrow mainline one habitually obtaining at this period in Spain, and particularly with the imaginary of Europe that dominates in cultural imports. It also contrasts favourably with the catalogue of Renacimiento (included at the back of Rafael López de Haro, *El pais de los medianos (novela)* [1913]). Here Anatole France is copiously represented, and the Classical collection gives good space to Greek, Latin and Spanish classics, but English, German, Italian and French are represented by five entries each or fewer. Its profile contrasts, incidentally, with that of Cénit, which was dominated by German and Russian authors (Santonja 1989: 61).

This 'universal' collection is clearly one that was selective, with striking inclusions and lacunae. The most (geographically) exotic item included is perhaps *La joven siberiana* by Javier de Maistre, an exoticism undermined by the fact that it was translated from French by Ceferino Palencia Tubau. In addition to its geographical boundaries, the collection limits its field chronologically, so that in terms of contemporary cultural outreach, it opts distinctly for modern writing, leaving classics of Greek and Latin very much in a minority. Latin texts are represented by Apuleius, Caesar, Cicero, Tacitus and Vives (one work of each), with Greek appearing as Plutarch only (with the various volumes of the *Vidas paralelas*). This will compare (if it is a fair comparison) with nineteen titles in the recommendations for Bibliotecas Populares (discussed in Chapter 7), which additionally offer three solid background texts. This is the difference, arguably, between selecting texts for the well-read literate person, and the library foundation offered in popular libraries. Nonetheless one might eventually conclude that the Bibliotecas Populares recommendations, in terms of educational provision, served their clientele well.

Looking at contemporary European languages, we can see French at a predicted lead, confirming the belief that what Germany was expected to provide 'solid' information, science and philosophy while France would be the source of literature, the sense of canon is less than adventurous. What it does mark out are a number of differences between what was anticipated to be popular or attractive to readers then, and what we might consider canonical now.

The profile of the French texts is resoundingly canonical, with the seventeenth and nineteenth centuries well represented, but with more Musset than Molière, more Mérimée than Montesquieu, more Nodier than Nerval, more Sand than Stendhal, Taine weighing in heavily, Voltaire rather less so. The little-remembered Sandeau of the nineteenth century is (slightly) more prominent than Mme de Staël, or Sainte-Beuve. Gobineau is selected for five volumes of the *Novelas asiáticas*, consonant with the 'Musas lejanas' collection produced by the Revista de Occidente. If Balzac is reasonably included with a total of eight novels (though without the dark tones of *Cousin Pons*, *Cousine Bette* or *Les Illusions perdues*), Zola is perhaps not surprisingly absent, entailing the omission of cornerstones of naturalism such as *Germinal*, *La terre*, *La bête humaine* or *L'assomoir*. Realism is acceptable, naturalism is forbidden territory, and Zola is elusive through a whole range of catalogues, demonstrating the degree to which catholic taste exists in somewhat tense opposition to what is ratified by Catholic approval. Meanwhile the inclusion of nineteenth-century Edmond About, absent from modern canons, is nonetheless reasonably so given the degree to which he appeared in English translation as well as in Spanish.

The English selections suggest that an operation of mirroring has taken place. The works of Shakespeare, for example, are numerous – some sixteen plays, reflecting the Golden Age world of the *comedia* in which issues of kingship, succession and good governance would be to the fore. Yet two things are noticeable. A number of the history plays get re-labelled as tragedies (*Richard II*, the little-remembered *Henry VIII*, the even less remembered *King John*), and there are noticeable gaps in the tragedies: *King Lear*, *Othello*, although an advert in the 1923 catalogue for an edition of Shakespeare's plays includes *King Lear* and announces that *Othello* will be forthcoming.

Dickens is given a decidedly lightweight profile that represents his early works: for this collection he is the writer of *Pickwick Papers*, *The Cricket on the Hearth* (now habitually classified as 'minor') and the less than canonical *Master Humphrey's Clock*. Entirely missing are the major novels such as *Bleak House*, *Dombey and Son*, *Great Expectations* or *Our Mutual Friend*, but the unthreatening *David Copperfield* is included. Dickens is thus associated with the jolly, England as the place of Christmas japes, pleasant and comforting entertainment, while Dickens as the novelist of sinister intentions, crime and tragedy is absent. Possibly the major later novels of Dickens are omitted from the canon of the Colección Universal for reasons related (though not on any transparent basis) to the selection that excludes Zola. George Eliot makes a surprisingly brief appearance with *Silas Marner* (no broad panorama as in *Middlemarch*, nor treatment of the Jewish question as in *Daniel Deronda*), and while Thackeray is included, *Vanity Fair* is not. Contemporary writing is present solely in the form of Wilde's *Lady Windermere's Fan* and *The Importance of Being Ernest*. It is difficult to conclude definitely what this selection tells us, but there is the impression that the stronger meat and more disturbing texts that could have been included are being avoided. At the same time Darwin's *Origin of Species* and Hume's *Treatise on Human Nature* provide some balance in the intellectual weight of the selection.

The German part of the collection, meanwhile, follows two routes. One is that of the English items (and in part the French ones), in which the underlying criterion for choice seems to be readability and the provision of lightweight matter. Hence the number of 'tales' that are included (a full nine volumes of Hoffmann's Tales, and four volumes of Keller's *Men of Sedwyla*). Travel is clearly (as so often) intuited as harmless entertainment, and hence the seven volumes of Heine's travel literature. But the German selection also reflects the idea that what Germany has to offer is solid philosophy: four volumes of Kant, a little ('opúsculos') Leibnitz, and aesthetics made amenable (following in the line of amenable entertainment set up by a canon of tales and travels) in Schiller's volume *La educación estética del hombre en una serie de cartas*. Goethe is well represented, and backed up by three volumes of Eckermann's conversations with him. There is, then, some sense in which German culture is intuited as offering substantial intellectual fodder as well as what will go down easily.

What is striking, however, is that what Germany has to 'offer' according to this collection is quite distinct from what it has to 'offer' when seen from the point of view of the Revista de Occidente. German literature was notably absent from that smaller collection, and there is perhaps an absence of a sense of what the German literary canon might be. To some degree in the case of Espasa Calpe this is balanced, although not entirely, by the Colección Contemporánea.

The Colección Contemporánea of contemporary novels is explicitly outward-looking, its aim being to produce the 'obras más selectas de cuantos hoy ejercen el reinado literario en sus respectivos países', and its introduction adds that the translations have been made directly from the language of the originals. The 1923 collection published by Calpe has thirty-five titles, a small handful of which are double titles. The figures are small here for statistical purposes, but French titles run at 40 per cent, with German and English equally at 14.28 per cent, leaving a strong tail to Italian with 11.42 per cent, with Portuguese taking a lead (8.57 per cent) over both Russian and Spanish (5.71 per cent).

It is clear that the 1926 catalogue of Espasa Calpe was bent on marketing the new and appreciably expanded publishing enterprise. While it promised accessibility to great works in the Universal collection, here it places more of an emphasis on literary sensibility, which is described as part of what we could recognize as the impact of modernism. Its emphasis on modernity is one that encompasses 'problemas de orden material o moral' for which new types of expression are needed. It promises a diversity, which can be perceived in the examples of writing from different countries: 'este movimiento revolucionario tiene infinitos matices, aspectos dispares, multiples tendencias, según el país en que se produce y el clima social en que se desenvuelve'. Yet what it offers in the light of this revolutionary movement is not something to feed intellectual curiosity, but rather something for the emotions: 'La literatura de hoy, fiel reflejo de los hábitos, progresos, vicios e inquietudes de nuestra época, tiene, por lo tanto, para nosotros no sólo un poderoso atractivo artístico, sino un enorme interés emocional' (Espasa Calpe 1926: 37). The preamble further asserts that the collection has been compiled from the best produced in the whole world, adding to this assertion of breadth the curious detail that the writers selected are of 'alta solvencia intelectual'. This assurance of reliability doubtless refers to the long-term didactic promise of the collections of this house that between them they will make the reader informed. But the detail that they have included writers from Latin America suggests a view of the 'whole world' that is somewhat enlarged but not massively so.

The prime impression, however, given by this 'contemporary' collection is that much of it is ephemeral. Of the items in the 1926 collection, some of those continued, and added to, will become canonical: Proust in French, Thomas Mann and Schnitzler in German, Hardy in English, Unamuno in Spanish. But other writers who have new titles included, are less obviously so, existing more at the periphery of literary history. What is not clear, and possibly it was not at the time, of course, is the degree to which texts or authors later perceived as canonical greats were perceived as such in their

day, and the fuzziness in this area is emphasized by the relative evenness
of marketing tone adopted. The 1926 catalogue (of the new Espasa Calpe
venture) includes new titles, but the most striking feature is the way in which
they are firmly marketed and presented to the reader in enticing manner. The
marketing line is not univocal, but there is clearly an angle in the presentation. Brief paragraphs of explanation and commentary accompany the listing
of texts, and there are photographs of the majority of authors concerned
(disturbingly not well aligned with the items in question). The reader is made
promises, given reassurances that the works in question will bring him or her
up to date with the latest in artistic developments, and, if offered material
that is on the edge of the scandalous, this will always be tempered by high
artistic quality. The marketing of foreign items has little or no reference to
national specificities, but rather they tend to be offered as containing time-
less truths. The heroine of Jammes, *Rosario al sol* is 'una de esas figuras que
quedan como clásicas' (the 'que quedan como clásicas' demonstrating a faux-
reluctance to enter into aesthetic discussions of the classical). One axis of
marketing is to promote interest in the world of the psychological, frequently
coloured by *novela rosa* discourse of emotionality. It should be noted that this
is not restricted to foreign works. *The Well-Beloved* by Hardy is promoted as
an 'estudio completo de la inquietud humana', while *El funámbulo de mármol*
by d'Almeida is implicitly guaranteed as offering psychology rather than
sensationalism through its description as a 'libro de extraña intensidad, de
fuerte profundidad psicológica'. The comment on *Tres dramas* by Giacomo
makes the elite/popular combination of appeal more obvious, in that they are
termed as works that are 'fuertes de intenso dramatismo, reveladores de la
psicología popular italiana y logrados con arte supremo'.

It is here that the delicate line between elite appeal (works of prime literary interest, of 'high aesthetic' (and, it is frequently implied, moral quality)
and an implied popular appeal (works with dramatic and even melodramatic
qualities) begins to emerge. Espasa Calpe's potential readership is broad,
and certainly its range of collections is in line with this. It is clearly not
limited to the elite range reached by the Revista de Occidente press, nor
does it make the unadorned emotional appeal of the many forms of brief
novel that existed in the 1920s and 1930s (see Paris VIII 1986; Santonja
1994, 2000; Sainz de Robles 1975). At the same time, some of the classi-
fications of novels included imply norms of nationality that might be both
elite and popular. Thus with Kuprin's *Yama*, subtitled *La mala vida en Rusia*.
This is promoted as a 'libro cruel, descarnado, audaz' with the concluding
comment that it is 'Una de las mejores novelas del genial novelista ruso'. It
is thus made to relate to a Hispanic set of writings on the 'mala vida' (see
Bernaldo de Quirós and Llanos de Aguilaniedo 1901), and with popular and
elite fantasies about the nature of Russia, which is simultaneously perceived
as full of primitive cruelty (as made evident in Chapter 6). At the same time

there is an implied invitation to be a member of a group that can judge that these are of his 'best' novels. The issue of how to balance the writing-up of novels in a manner that will entice and thrill the reader, while including him in a critical group, is exemplified nicely in the write-up of Thomas Mann's *Death in Venice*. Its subject matter, of male homosexual love, is presented as a novel 'donde un tema escabroso y atrevido ha sido resuelto con enorme arte y belleza' with the reassurance that it has been 'discutidísima y admirada por la crítica mundial' (Espasa Calpe 1926: 43).

The implied canon of foreign writers in the Colección Universal and the Colección Contemporánea is therefore limited, spanning well-known figures and quite marginal ones, and ostensibly including writers for their readability and marketability (while appealing to the purchasing clientele on the basis of their desire to be thought discriminating). Other collections, smaller in scope, have a more significant foreign presence in numerical terms. 'Los poetas' has a strong French presence, bulked by Jammes, who appears in the Colección Contemporánea. But it also displays a willingness to go outside the conventional frame (as with Mann), and includes Whitman's *Leaves of Grass*. More striking still is 'Los humoristas', claiming to print selections of 'humorismo mundial', presented with a moral tone that by now will be familiar:

> En las largas horas de tedio o de melancolía; en la fatigosa aridez de los viajes; cuando un esfuerzo o un dolor haya abrumado o acongojado su espíritu, busque usted la amistad, ingrávida y amable, del libro del humorista.
>
> (Calpe 1923: 20)

Represented by Spanish, French, English, Russian, Czech and Hungarian humour, and with no items from either Italian or German, the selection is singularly uneven. More than this, it is not clear that the selection of humour is based on any sense of spread: the English list is dominated by Arnold Bennett, the French one with a set of unknowns (Benjamin, Courteline, Véber). Hungarian, with eight items (a third of the whole collection) is even more puzzling. The clue to selection here, however, is not that Hungary appears to have been perceived as a major source of humorous writing, but simply that the presence of Andrés Révesz as translator has ensured a vigorous collection. Révesz (although with no evidence of being on the books of Biblioteca Nueva, for example) was prominent as a journalist in *El Sol* through the 1920s, with over thirty articles in that paper in 1920 (taken as a randomly sampled year), and showed himself to be a resourceful and talented correspondent, dealing with Eastern Europe in general as well as his native Hungary. His strong showing in the humour section therefore is more likely to be related to his personal activity and dynamism than to any intrinsic merit.

A different style of collection is that of 'Literatura selecta', chosen to be

offered in a handsome binding. It is a subset of the Colección Universal, and
its relationship is that between 'integrity' and 'durability' (in terms of reputation). Hence the announcement:

> De la *Colección Universal* que, aunque selecta ya, aspira sin embargo a la
> integridad, hemos recogido las más fragantes flores, las más brillantes de
> color y las más bellas de aspecto, para ofrecerlas en forma algo más sólida.
> (Calpe 1923: 31)

The nicely turned justification is that they should have a more durable
binding, since 'en lo espiritual, ya tienen ganada la inmortalidad'. Within this
select band, the names of foreign writers (with retrospective wisdom about
canon) are more predictable, and the collection is dominated by major French
writers – Lamartine, Voltaire, Prévost, Gautier, Stendhal – making up 46 per
cent of the whole, with Sterne, Jane Austen and Darwin representing English.
German is absent except for Eckermann, *Conversaciones con Goethe*.

Some collections, such as poetry, or of the sciences, are highly focused.
The Colección Universal and the Colección Contemporánea take their principal remit to be a literary one, while adding in some general culture. But just
as Ortega had the concept of 'Nuevos hechos, nuevas ideas', so Calpe had
the corresponding one of 'Actualidades científicas y políticas'. Yet the two
collections, notionally with a similar objective, look quite different. Ortega's
collection, discussed above, had an overwhelming majority of German titles,
and science, sociology and metaphysics dominated. The Calpe collection
includes science, but its international science is limited to Schlik, *Teoría
de la relatividad*. The gloss on it in the catalogue is plainly reassuring: it
promises to make the theories widely accessible and affirms that 'la lectura
del libro no exige conocimientos especiales de matemáticas' (Calpe 1923:
82). The only other scientific entry in this section is Pittaluga's volume on
public hygiene, a simple *folleto*, timely and prompted by discoveries of the
First World War. Two items, by H G Wells (*The Salvation of Civilization*) and
Bertrand Russell (*Principles of Social Reconstruction*) could be classed as
sociology, but with the science volumes just mentioned, they make up less than
a quarter of the 'Actualidades' collection. This compares with a quarter of the
'Nuevos hechos' entries being on science, with a further quarter on sociology.
Two further features make the Calpe collection distinct: the proportion of
English writers, and the number of works on contemporary Russia. Indeed,
the concept of 'Actualidades científicas y políticas' could be construed in
this case as consisting of how to react to Russia after its revolution, and of
taking some lead from England on the nature of this reaction. The collection
contains a number of travel writings that give first-hand accounts of visits to
Russia, and the commentaries on these items emphasize the degree to which
the accounts have a hands-on feel to them. The 1926 version of this collec-

tion is largely based on that of 1923, with some strengthening of the Russia-related items (notably by Julio Álvarez del Vayo) and with some additions to the contemporary history section.

The Calpe 1923 catalogue has a striking collection intended for boys. Though billed as being of 'alto valor literario y educativo', this is plainly adventure literature. It has two modes of appeal: to adults who will recollect having read of the adventures in the series and for whom the authors are associated with 'la lucha primitiva y ruda con los elementos de la Naturaleza y de la Humanidad rudimentaria'; and to boys, for whom they will provide moral fibre, through the mode of reading about bravery. The books are thus 'una especie de iniciación en el valor y en el sufrimiento, en la resistencia física y en la audacia espiritual, formando valores morales que cada día se aprecian más en nuestro tiempo' (Calpe 1923: 33). It is clear that this world of heroism made available to inspire boys for the future is largely drawn from English and American writings, and in many the prominent note is that of striving not just against difficulty but against the primitive. Literature of exciting travel is then headed by Jules Verne, having in common with the adventure stories the idea of man against the primitive, or man against the elements. The 1926 Espasa Calpe catalogue markets on this basis, on entertainment that comes from 'novelas sensacionales, de audacia y lucha. Visiones de países lejanos, pugnas contra la naturaleza hostil, contra los salvajes o las fieras' (Espasa Calpe 1926: 62). The 'Biblioteca blanca' of Calpe 1923, meanwhile, not precisely aimed towards girls, had offered not excitement but taste, not adventure but select literature, travels of the mind rather than travels of the body. The lack of focus in this collection is thus that it is literally effaced in the 1926 catalogue, where it is announced in the index, but indistinguishable in the main text. The logical extension of the adventure collection is that of 'Los grandes viajes modernos', with accounts of travels to the North Pole, to Africa, to the Antarctic, to the tundra of Siberia. The emphasis of this collection contrasts with the images of fighting with primitives that dominate boys' adventure literature: adventure, in adulthood, takes place in extreme zones.

The combination within these catalogues is of what seems to be assumed as 'European culture' (German and English philosophy, sociology, with some political implications, conservative rather than otherwise), and a sense of exotic distance. The latter is exemplified in literature for boys (adventure, heroism, exploration), but is not restricted to such areas. It features widely in *Residencia*, and indeed is the surprising hallmark of a publication that might have contained more of what was specifically Spanish, and more of what was 'European culture'. But as will emerge in Chapter 5, the culture of the *Residencia* was distinctly English in tone and aspiration, with the resultant emphasis on the modern-day adventures of mountaineering and speculative archaeology.

The many and varied collections of science of Espasa Calpe allow us to get some feel for the degree to which different areas of science in Spain sought foreign sources. In some areas we can see a mainly Hispanic authorship (as with the Manuales Calpe de Ciencias Médicas). Here some of the directors (Ramón y Cajal, Goyanes, Pittaluga and Lafora would later be seen high in the list of supporters of the World League of Sexual Reform) (Sinclair 2007), only Madinaveitia having no obvious connexion with the movement. The same group of directors was in charge of 'Obras varias de biología y medicina', where the works published clearly draw on German and English sources, with the occasional French title. Between them German and English account for 74 per cent of the 1923 list for this collection, with French a mere 7.4 per cent. And if, in cultural terms, the First World War had divided Spain into 'aliadófilos' and (predominantly right-wing) 'germanófilos', the scientific collections of the postwar period demonstrate that science at least still draws on Germany for information. Hoffman's work on *Los médicos alemanes en la guerra mundial*, translated by Jiménez de Asúa and Vetter, the first of whom will be prominent in the Sexual Reform movement in Spain, recounts the advances made in medicine and surgery by Germany in the war. The prominence of German works continues in the collection of studies edited by the *Revista de Medicina y Cirugía Prácticas*, where they account for 42 per cent. They are, however, outpaced by French contributions (52.6 per cent). There is no absolute pattern, and the 'Biblioteca médico-quirúrgica: Colección de manuales prácticos' of 1923 has a predominance of 72.7 per cent French works. The significance of these figures and proportions is simply to demonstrate that there are no absolute patterns. While the information in some quarters might suggest the paradigm of Germany's cultural offering to Spain being in the sciences and philosophy, whereas that of French was in literature, this is clearly not an absolute, and French has its own prominence in translations of scientific works. The scientific culture of France, therefore, to the informed, and according to the field, is just as significant for Spain as is the culture of Germany. Lastly, as an illustration of how eclectic these collections were in terms of source, we might note that in works of practical scientific access, Spanish authors predominate. Thus in the 'Catecismos del agricultor y del ganadero' only one of the 116 items of the 1923 catalogue is indicated as being a translation. The 'Catecismos' hold the role that many of the volumes of the 'Bibliotecas populares' project will exercise: that of bringing useful and necessary enlightenment to a population not anticipated as being well educated. The catechisms are in the brief format of novelettes (32 pages), and are 'de tipo de letra muy claro y legible y profusamente ilustrados en el texto'. Their aim is to 'iniciar o ampliar la cultura del agricultor y del ganadero', and to this end, summary, simplification and education come via Spanish authors.

Biblioteca Nueva

Biblioteca Nueva is an example of a publishing house in which the persona-
lity of an individual, José Ruiz-Castillo Basala, comes through. His role as
publisher, when perceived through the rich archive of correspondence housed
in the Biblioteca Nacional in Madrid, involves a high degree of direct nego-
tiation with participants (authors, translators), and the letters communicate
warmth, urgency, and above all live interest on the side of both publisher
and those involved in what was to be published. The liveliness is also to be
perceived in the various catalogues that appeared between 1919 and 1936,
while the correspondence from after 1936 attests to the determination to keep
the business going, albeit with a somewhat altered frame of activity.

   The degree to which there was lack of agreement on what constituted
a 'contemporary' collection can be seen by putting the 1926 Espasa Calpe
list, commented upon earlier, alongside the 'Colección extranjera' of Biblioteca Nueva of 1929. The lists are comparable in length, with Espasa Calpe
listing thirty-eight works, and Biblioteca Nueva thirty-five. Only five authors
appear in both lists (and then not with identical works): d'Almeida, Kuprin,
Tharaud, Schnitzler and Hardy. The profile of the two collections is somewhat
different. That of Espasa Calpe had a majority of French titles (40 per cent),
with German and English equal second (14.28 per cent), strongly followed
by Italian (11.42 per cent), and with Portuguese taking a lead (8.57 per
cent) over both Russian and Spanish (5.71 per cent). The Biblioteca Nueva
collection contains nothing in Spanish (this is a separate list), and it concurs
with Espasa Calpe in foregrounding French authors (39.4 per cent). English
(including American) and Russian come next (18.4 and 13.1 per cent respectively), with Italian and Portuguese in a similar proportion to that they hold
in Espasa Calpe (10.5 and 7.89 per cent respectively). German is in a reduced
proportion (5.26 per cent). The balance then is changed, with a clear shift
now, in the Biblioteca Nueva 1929 catalogue, to an increased prominence of
English and Russian, and a reduction in German titles. Biblioteca Nueva also
strikes out in its inclusion of Knut Hamsun, a Nobel Prize winner in 1920.

   There is also a question of the apparent durability of these authors, and
their degree of public recognition. The Biblioteca Nueva collection manages
to include not just Hamsun as a Nobel Prize winner, but also the Polish
writer Henryk Sienkiewicz, who won the prize in 1905. In addition to this,
with what might seem like foresight (albeit with a relatively unknown work,
El difunto Matías Pascal), it also publishes Pirandello, who will win the
Nobel Prize for Literature in 1934. Winning the Nobel Prize for Literature,
of course, confers recognition, but not one that is always generally accepted.
The award of the prize to Echegaray in 1904 did not meet with universal
acclaim, and indeed he is omitted from the Biblioteca Nueva companion
list of Spanish writers that goes with the Colección Extranjera. The authors

included in the Biblioteca Nueva list, vagaries of being a Nobel Prize winner aside, have in greater degree remained in canonical circles in a way that the Espasa Calpe authors did not. Espasa Calpe wanted to market the new, but it did also refer to publishing the most 'select' of foreign literatures. Biblioteca Nueva, however, includes the following in its 1929 list: Nietzsche, Villiers de l'Isle Adam, d'Annunzio, Eça de Queiroz, Twain, Baudelaire, de Banville, Schnitzler, Nerval, Tolstoy, Lautréamont, Stevenson, Loti, Apollinaire, O Henry, Galsworthy, Chesterton, Romains, Joyce and Montherlant (in addition to the prize-winners already named). Of these, only Baudelaire, Nerval and Stevenson (who figures in the 'Libros de Aventuras of Calpe 1923), besides the Nobel Prize winner Sienkiewicz, are included in the Colección Universal.

Stretching the boundaries, and the inclusion of Russia

In Chapter 6 I consider the special place that Russia occupies in Spain's relations with Europe. The sense of northern Europe in the Spanish imaginary of the foreign is primarily limited to France, Germany and England, with an almost total absence of Scandinavia and patchy representation of Eastern Europe. Yet Russia occupies that position of being included within the imaginary of Europe almost because it is virtually outside it. It is present in very different ways: in literature and non-literary writings linked to the 1917 revolution, and an interest in the politics that ensued; in travel writings; in writings intended for a proletarian market, and produced within a left-wing environment. In the mobility of the Russian element in the Spanish publishing world, and yet in its potential ubiquity, there are all the features of tactical existence. It is much more obviously marginal, in terms of culture, than the writings of nearby France, or the writings of (on the surface) more comparable Italy. (The low profile of Italy, as a mirroring southern Mediterranean country is a feature of interest in itself, as is also the relatively low profile of neighbouring Portugal.)

The Revista de Occidente made its contribution to the knowledge of this area in the series 'La Rusia actual', a list of just five works, by Ivanov, Seifulina, Leonov and Zamiatin. More obviously literary than political in the items chosen, perhaps because the dates of publication, 1926–7, fell under Primo's dictatorship, this is a relatively cautious selection, albeit consonant with its name of 'actual' or contemporary, and it is only one item short of the list of contemporary Spanish writers to be found in the 'Nova novorum' collection. By contrast, a mixture of pre- and post-revolutionary literature is to be found in Espasa Calpe, which produces a range of Russian novelists, some fifteen in all, and including Chekhov, Dostoiewski, Gogol, Goncharov and Gorki. A significant proportion of what it contained, however, is in the form of the short story. Somewhat over 9 per cent of the total of the Colección Universal is in the form of the short story, but in the Russian items this rises to 23.6 per cent. In addition to this, there is a significant presence of Russian works (to the virtual exclusion of other works foreign to Spain) in the series La novela proletaria of Vivero in 1932, and in that of La novela chica in 1924.

Where does the Colección Universal stand in terms of strategy and canonicity? If the Revista de Occidente was cautious, and – in the context of publishing under Primo – its selections a discreet tactical movement, the larger collection might be seen as more established. But it is not obvious that this is the case. Revista de Occidente as a publishing house is alternative, and tactical – in the sense that the ILE and the Residencia were: solid in its positioning of a cultural view alternative to the official state one. Yet it has its own orthodoxy, confirmed to a degree by the orthodoxy of its German-biased cultural importation. By contrast, and bearing in mind its sheer accessibility, the Colección Universal, pocket-sized, economical and (relatively) catholic in its range, has the mobility of the tactical. Alberti confirms the significance of the Colección Universal in making Russian writers available to the Spanish reading public: 'Aquella colección Universal, de pastas amarillentas, nos inició a todos en el conocimiento de los grandes escritores rusos, muy pocos divulgados antes de que Calpe los publicara. Gógol, Goncharov, Korolenko, Dostoievski, Chéjov, Andréiev ... me turbaron los días y la noche' (Arroyo Reyes 2003: 37). Consonant with this comparison, the Peruvian Marxist José Carlos Mariátegui congratulated the Revista de Occidente for having published Leonov, Seifulina and Ivanov (thus spreading the range of Russian writing available), but commented that much more needed to be done. If the Spanish reader were to gain a full panorama of Russian literature of the revolution, it would entail acquaintance with Pilniak, Babel, Maiakovski, Esenin, Fedin, Zamiatin, Lunts, Pasternak, Tikhonov, Leonov and Ehrenberg. He also commented (and the evidence of this is painfully apparent in the catalogues of the early twentieth century) that there was much still to be done in publishing pre-revolutionary writers, although his examples, Blok, Briusov, Remosov and Bieli, might not instantly spring to mind).

The much longer list of Russian works is to be found in Cénit, which between 1929 and 1936 would print thirty-four Russian titles, and a further four Russian-related works (see Santonja 1989: 77–95 for details). The strongly left-wing nature of this enterprise contrasts obviously with the profile of the Revista de Occidente and the determinedly mainline nature of the Colección Universal, but at the same time a certain mobility and eclecticism place it, like the activities of Biblioteca Nueva, into the framework of the tactical rather than the strategic.

Here we might observe a phenomenon that is partially evident in the selections in the Colección Universal from Dickens, and to some degree from Balzac: there is an relative absence of the long novels that in a modern canon we associate with nineteenth-century Russian literature. In the case of lengthy Russian novels, the evidence of the Biblioteca Nacional is that there were some editions of major works by Tolstoy and Dostoiewski, but they did not appear in the major collections discussed so far. Of Tolstoy, the collection 'La novela ilustrada', published by A Marzo, brought out *Anna Karenina* (n.d.), *War and Peace*, *The Kreutzer Sonata* (as 'Part 3' of *War and Peace*) in 1910, and *Resurrection* (n.d.), while the influential *What is art?* (*¿Qué es el arte?*), to which Valle-Inclán and others would famously respond in an *encuesta* of 1920, was published in Barcelona by Maucci in 1902. The status of Tolstoy, for this series, was beyond dispute. The flier presents various points of reference: he is the best novelist of the world since the death of Victor Hugo, and is 'él genio más excelso de la literatura contemporánea, y un legítimo heredero de aquél, tanto en la grandeza de las concepciones como en el humanitarismo de sus ideas revolucionarias'. Its ensuing comments suggest that there is a reception for Tolstoy that is beyond dispute, and of a judgement that is not in question: the implication is that to be civilized in the world one has to recognize the worth of Tolstoy:

> ¿Quién no conoce el nombre del venerable patriarca ruso y la fama de sus novelas, que tan profunda huella han marcado en la sociedad actual, combatiendo sus vicios y su absurda organización? ¿Quién no querrá admirar las obras inmortales de uno de los más grandes genios de nuestra época ...?

But the punch-line is an economic one: who could refuse to become an admirer when the price is so reasonable, 'en tan extraordinarias condiciones de baratura' (Infantes *et al.* 2003: 590 for reproduction of flier [n.d.]). Another edition of *Anna Karenina* was brought out in Barcelona by Sopena in 1912, and a further one in Madrid, with the Prensa Popular, in 1924. *War and Peace* appeared, in a particularly interesting publishing venture, in Spanish, but published by Garnier of Paris, in 1909. Dostoiewski, meanwhile, also appeared thanks to A Marzo, with *Crime and Punishment*, and a French edition of *Les Frères Karamazov* brought out by Brossard of Paris (1923). *The Idiot* (n.d.) was produced by Atenea, the press with which Ricardo Baeza was associated. Baeza's enthusiasm for Dostoiewski is further revealed in the 1921 catalogue for Atenea included at the back of Turró, *Orígenes del conocimiento*, Madrid. It lists *The Double* as being in print, and further volumes in press: *An Adolescent*, *The House of the Dead*, *The Eternal Husband*, *The Village of Stepanchikovo and its inhabitants*.

Atenea's substantial and unusual production of Dostoiewski must be attributed to Baeza whose personal library in Montblanc contains numerous Russian texts, and commentaries on them, in both French and English. The profile of Russian literature in Baeza's library is a single but arguably indicative example of the most prominent form of Russia's presence in Spain: not in direct translation, but through the mediation of better-known languages. The major role of Baeza in the selection for Atenea is evident from other items on the 1921 list, particularly the prominence of works by Wilde, H G Wells and Kipling, who are also strikingly well represented in the library at Montblanc. We can observe here, in general terms, the influence of the individual, something that emerges in the translation activity we can observe in Biblioteca Nueva, and who arguably has something of the role of Gramsci's *entrepreneur*.

Biblioteca Nueva, by contrast, does not primarily engage with the field of Russia in terms of literature, but was clearly active in the production of political and social texts. This can be seen from its collection of 'Las nuevas doctrinas sociales'. Printed at the back of Kerensky, *El Bolchevismo y su obra*, c.1920, but also in Orage, *Socialismo gremial: El sistema de jornal y los medios de abolirlo* (s.a.), it included Kerensky, Lenin, Trotsky, Tasín and Zagorsky. Its 'Colección extranjera', of 1929, however, did include four works by Andreiev, and one by each of Kuprin, Dostoiewski and Tolstoy.

Finally, a brief indicator to what the public actually read, and specifically to give a marker of the importance of Russian in the general reading market, is the following. Entertainment was clearly a prime factor in promoting popularity, so that it is hardly surprising that Edgar Wallace and Zane Gray outstripped other writers, running respectively to eighty and thirty-three editions. But there was a serious interest in what went on in Russia, evidenced by the fact that in the years of the Second Republic, and in a range of publishing houses that included Oriente, Historia Nueva, Cénit, Ulises, Zeus and España, after Wallace, the next foreign author most published was Lenin (thirty-six editions), while Gorki reached eighteen, Andreiev sixteen and Ehrenberg nine (Garitaonandía 1989: 166–7).

Translators and Biblioteca Nueva

It will have become clear that some publishing houses were directive in their policies, producing for example a foundation in German philosophy for their readers, while others were arguably responsive, as would appear from the 1929 Biblioteca Nueva catalogue printed at the back of Nóvoa Santos, *La mujer, nuestro sexto sentido y otros esbozos*, where the section on the 'Biblioteca del más allá' answered to curiosity about the life of the spirit (outwith Catholicism). But there was also the input of translators into what appeared in print.

The correspondence in the Biblioteca Nueva archive has a significant level of two factors: the financial crises continuously affecting the translators, and the degree to which they prompted (or tried to prompt) some of the translations to be undertaken by this publisher. There is ample evidence of the economic factors present in the publishing industry, and within the Biblioteca Nueva archive of correspondence in the Biblioteca Nacional approximately a fifth of the items deal directly with translations and questions of taking on work for publication involve offers to do work. We could regard this simply as evidence of the precarious economic position of any translator. But there was also a difficulty – so it would seem – with Ruiz-Castillo. On the basis of numerous letters, it appears he was less than prompt in providing payment for work done, a characteristic that could be interpreted as reluctance, but conceivably also indicating the economic tightrope on which the industry as a whole operated. Some offers of translations are moved by penury and despe-ration. This is the case illustrated by Astrana Marín's letter of 2 November 1920 [BN MSS 22.600–85] where he says, in reference to a translation of Shakespeare's poems that they had discussed some days earlier, that it will be ready in two weeks, and that he wishes to receive 300 pesetas for it on the spot, otherwise it will not be worth the trouble. Leon Bronstein's letter of 22 August in that year [BN MSS 22.600–178], less emphatic, is nonethe-less insistent and careful in trying to secure payment for Sienkiewicz, *En vano*. By contrast, Mingarro y San Martín on 1 August 1920 is upbeat and confident in promoting work that he would translate [BN MSS 22.602–197]. Even López Ballesteros, who would become famous for his translation of the complete works of Freud, has problems in collecting payment, and is notable (as in a letter of 1924 [BN MSS 22.601–183]) for the fact that he finds it necessary to present an excuse for going to collect it.

The ongoing correspondence between translators, authors and their publisher shows a range that runs from desperate begging (or importunity) to an easy friendship. The letter from Juan Cueto (BN MSS 22.600–326), recommended by Alfonso Reyes, is unashamedly open about financial need: he is in 'una situación financiera lamentabilísima', asking Ruiz-Castillo 'que eche mano de mis servicios tan pronto como le sea posible, porque mis apuros, más que grandes, son urgentes'. But we could take his account of his translator's skills both as a disturbing indication of some of the amateurism around, and as an example of what not to write to a publisher:

> Soy un poco latinista y algo he picado en todos los idiomas y aun en los dialectos – romances, menos en el rumano. En el italiano es muy escasa mi práctica; tan escasa que solamente puedo apuntar en el haber las obras completas de Manzoni, periódicos, revistas etc. En el portúgués es algo mayor y más reciente (de tres años a esta parte). En el catalán y provençal, lecturas no muy abundantes y de fecha antigua. En el francés, sobre haber leído mucho, desde los autores primitivos hasta la literatura de la guerra, tengo la enseñanza de mis correrías por Francia, sobre todo, de una temporada de cuatro meses en París, hace catorce años, en situa-ción económica mucho más dura que la actual, que es cuanto hay que

decir. Fuera de los idiomas neolatinos, sólo conozco el inglés, que he leído bastante (Borrow, Richard Ford y otros autores de menos celebridad, que han hablado de España), Byron, casi completo, incluida su correspondencia privada; Dickens, casi completo también; Goldsmith, Walter Scott, Prescott, periódicos, revistas etc. Ahora estoy con Disraeli. Esta mañana leí unas cincuenta páginas de su *Lothair*.

Julio Gómez de la Serna, by contrast, writing in 1931 [BN MSS 22.605–1], comes over as markedly more confident, although perhaps equally pressed for money, and his offer to translate André Germain, *La révolución española en veinticinco lecciones* because it is new, topical and fresh is made in a spirit of incorrigible optimism. He believes that

> no está mal y que podría tener éxito en España, un poco como visión truculenta en cierto modo de nuestra República. Son una serie de impresiones, intervius con los más destacados etc anteriores y posteriores al 14 de abril. Yo se lo digo porque además no se ha publicado todavía nada extranjero sobre la revolución española.

There is no evidence that Ruiz-Castillo took him up on this, but what the letter does demonstrate is the way that translators felt able to deal with him, and the evidence of the archive is that in general Gómez de la Serna's approach worked. Numerous letters give his recommendations, judgements and ideas about works to translate. Wilde is much in vogue at this point, and had been so in 1919 (Fernández Cifuentes 1982: 135–7) and Gómez de la Serna comments that the French version of *Salomé* is 'absolutamente inencontrable' [BN MSS 22.601.16], and that for him *An Ideal Husband* outstrips *Lady Windermere's Fan*. His own role as translator is in the pleasure of making things known, offering 'estas <u>cosas</u> a nuestro público, aún tan ciego' [BN MSS 22.601]. Wilde's will had made the task easier for publishers and translators, and he is eager to make the most of things.

Julio Gómez de la Serna at the time of these letters is an impecunious student, but clearly feels able (and determined) to affect the direction of Biblioteca Nueva's publications. Others who are more established also intervene, such as Cansinos-Assens, writing on the headed paper of *Cosmópolis* (which he directed), a review of 200 pages a month, and a run of 10,000 (or at least, so the headed paper proclaims). What he pushes for are modern French poets, and his eye is informed: Apollinaire, Mallarmé, Barbey d'Aurevilly, and it is evident that his source, one well known to Baeza, is the *Nouvelle Revue Française* [BN MSS 22.600–207]. Cansinos-Assens is a vigorous entrepreneur, one who will be active as a one-man centre of exchange in publishing, and his position is crucial as one who both translates and publishes, illustrative of the multi-valency that will nourish some of the more adventurous publishing enterprises of the time.

Chronology is also a major factor in these interventions. It is noticeable that a lot of offers come in when Biblioteca Nueva is in its early days, and 1920 is a gathering point for numerous suggestions. It is also here when a lot of enthusiasm shows through. As León Trilla excitedly expounds:

> Yo tengo en mi poder – y no hay otro ejemplar en toda España, porque lo hemos recibido directamente de Moscú – una obra de Trotsky, titulado: *Terrorismo y comunismo* y que es una contestación a lo del mismo título de Kautsky cuya traducción ha aparecido en la Biblioteca que Ud. dirige. ¿No cree Ud que sería conveniente traducirla?
>
> Poseo, además, la última obra de Lenín, publicado hace poco más de un mes en Moscú en various idiomas – yo la tengo en francés, como lo de Trotsky – que se llama *El comunismo de izquierda* y de la cual poseo también el único ejemplar que hay en España. ¿Le convendría a Ud traducirla? [BN MSS 22.602–168]

Translators may come over appear from these letters to be dependent, even minor figures. Yet they are crucial, and we dismiss their role as agents at our peril.

In many of the examples cited in this chapter, we have evidence of there having been an editorial line that was announced and followed. Such editorial lines varied over time, and certainly between publishing houses, as one would expect. This heterogeneous nature of the publishing industry, which should hardly surprise us, allows us to see the sheer range of cultural imports to Spain from Europe, and the degree to which imports occurred vertically through the reading public, and not just in the upper reaches of an educated elite. The final examples of the input of translators to the publishing process, given as an example and indication of a force possibly at work, remind us of the degree to which editorial direction could be affected, and to which publishers could be open and responsive, albeit with a habitual eye to the economics of their business.

4 Elite and Specialized Markets

Disinterested intellectual curiosity is the life-blood of real civilization.
(Trevelyan, *English Social History*, 1942)

The aim of the *Residencia* therefore is to awaken curiosity – a faculty lacking in many Spaniards – to arouse a desire to learn and the power to form personal judgements instead of accepting what other people say. Only a real passion for truth and justice can lead to the development of those habits of toleration and social solidarity which are the only hope for the future of Spain and all other countries.
(Trend, *A Picture of Modern Spain*, 1921)

Esta curiosidad, que va lo mismo al pensamiento o la poesía que al aconte-cimiento público y al secreto rumbo de las naciones, es, bajo su aspecto de dispersión e indisciplina, la más natural, la más orgánica. Es la curiosidad ni exclusivamente estética ni especialmente científica o política. Es la vital curiosidad que el individuo de nervios alerta siente por el vasto germinar de la vida en torno y es el deseo de vivir cara a cara con la honda realidad contemporánea.
(Ortega, 'Propósitos', first number of the *Revista de Occidente*, July 1923)

As observed by Collini (1991: 56), the activity of journals, and specifically that of the journal essay, is something that constructs an imagined intellectual community in a highly specific way, in that it assumes that the reader has read what has gone before. Only subtle hints and references are needed, therefore, to allude to an accumulating body of knowledge (and, one might assume, a canon of accepted ideas and discourses). The process of ongoing creation of a group of participants is different, more intense and dynamic than the activity of publishing houses, and the way in which it is able to create a community both more subtle and more controlled.

Bourdieu has argued that the coming into being of a group, and its coming into being at the level of institution, is a matter of demarcation and classifi-cation. In *Language and Symbolic Power* he describes this process:

> The transition from the state of being a practical group to the state of being an instituted group (class, nation, etc.) presupposes the construction

of the principle of classification capable of producing the set of distinctive
properties which characterize the set of members in this group, and capable
also of annulling the set of non-pertinent properties which part or all of its
members possess in other contexts (e.g. properties of nationality, age or
sex), and which might serve as a basis for other constructions.

This demarcation brings to the fore power-relations with other groups, and
stimulates reaction among those not included within the demarcation of the
group. The reaction produced is inevitably one of defensiveness:

> Indeed, any attempt to institute a new division must reckon with the
> resistance of those who, occupying a dominant position in the space thus
> divided, have an interest in perpetuating a doxic relation to the social world
> which leads to the acceptance of the established divisions as natural or to
> their symbolic denial through the affirmation of a higher unity (national,
> familial, etc.). (Bourdieu 1991: 130)

In the case of the Residencia and its publication *Residencia*, and the
Revista de Occidente, the two journals that are the prime concern of this
chapter, we are presented with initial self-forming groups that distinguish
themselves from the outside. The two elite groups formed here result, I would
argue, from a consciously directional attitude towards the formation of an
elite that contrasts with the simple act of self-recognition of 'los mejores' that
Ortega would later, perhaps rather unrealistically, imply in his 1930 essay *La
rebelión de las masas*.

As its title suggests, this chapter is not just concerned with periodical
publication and how it acted as a multiple centre of exchange. A whole
range of factors would need to be taken into account, including the technical
advances that facilitated the production of copy (Botrel 2008: 7). A far more
extensive study would be required to cover this. In addition, a conscious
exclusion from this chapter is that of the daily press as a form of outreach
towards Europe. It should be noted, however, that this is a major omission
and there is a risk we underestimate the degree to which the daily press kept
Spanish readers informed in a manner that is arguably far more catholic than
that of journals habitually under consideration of intellectual and cultural
exchange. *El Sol*, for example, or *El Imparcial*, have notable variety and
openness in their articles, and some of the variety of the former (in terms of
pieces that reflect events and situations in Europe) derives from the nature
and nationality of their contributors. Thus Andrés Revesz and Nicolás Tasín
guaranteed a presence of central and Eastern Europe in the columns of *El Sol*
in 1920, for example. While their being retained as regular columnists can be
viewed as the policy of the paper, the degree and variation of their writings
results from the way they make the most of their position. Similarly, the 178

articles written for *El Sol* by Ricardo Baeza, ranging between the desperate situation of Ireland in 1920–1 and of Russia in 1921 (when Baeza was based in London as a foreign correspondent), demonstrate the immense range of an individual as a centre of exchange operating through the press.

The crucial distinction between the daily press and the journal is access via subscription. Articles of the former are habitually acquired on the hoof, in the street, on the way to work; journals are habitually received on the basis of subscription and delivery. This latter method already guarantees some flavour of commitment to the publication subscribed to, a readiness to read what is in that particular selection. The newspaper, by contrast, while it can be chosen for its recognized political colouring and known journalists and contributors, can be virtually guaranteed to be more diverse and random in content. The review or journal consequently will operate, in Collini's terms, like a club, the ' "imagined community" of a journal's readers' (Collini 1991: 56), although the strength of demarcations between this community and the rest of the world will vary. *La España Moderna*, as demonstrated by Davies (2000), was implied as a singularly open community; *Leviatán* in the second half of the Second Republic would be open primarily to Russia and to communism, but slanted in its political view. By contrast, the *Revista de Occidente* and *Residencia*, the main topic of this chapter, are organs of communities that play to specific cultural imaginaries, purporting to support openness and yet bearing all the marks of *habitus* that shapes development to be consonant with what is known. Their styles of cultural diversity, present yet clearly shaped, contrast with the shifting profile of the *Boletín del Instituto de Reformas Sociales*, and the specific educational focus of the *Boletín de la Institución Libre de Enseñanza* in the same years.

RO and *Residencia* are unashamedly harnessed to the creation of elite groups rather than to a project of general outreach within Spanish society. The dates of publication for both take them through the dictatorship of Primo de Rivera and the Second Republic. *RO* came into being virtually with the dictatorship while *Residencia* would not appear until some sixteen years after the Residencia had been founded. One can ascribe to both the aim of fostering curiosity, that quality highlighted by Trend in his early recollections of the Residencia, and by Ortega in his mission statement for *RO* cited in the epigraphs to this chapter. We might also note the elite and specialist nature of the publishing house of the Residencia de Estudiantes (Ribagorda 2007).

The two reviews differ in significant ways. *RO* continues as a journal today, after an interruption of some thirty years mid-stream. *Residencia*, however, dwindled noticeably through the 1930s, and was never resurrected after the Civil War. What they have in common, however, is a sense of cultural imaginary that strives for civilization, and identifies that civilization as deriving – in part at least –from beyond the frontiers of Spain. They demonstrate a conscious attempt to engage with what is perceived to be 'civilized' Europe (much in the sense as delineated by Passerini [1999]), but with differing aspirations and delimitations. Each in their way sets up an implied moral universe, some of it based on assumptions about gender, and each sits Janus-like (despite their mission statements of representing elites that are forward-looking) at the gateway points to new culture and experience.

Residencia: the definition of an elite

Residencia's start date is later than that of *RO*, but its first number, January–April 1926, on which I shall concentrate, sets out to summarize and recuperate the activities of the Residencia over the preceding sixteen years. There is a tension to be aware of from the start. The Residencia as an institution had a firm cultural mission of looking to Europe in order to enrich the cultural and intellectual base of experience and knowledge of its members. By contrast, *Residencia* was essentially an alumni publication, and as such operated in the field of cultural memory, seeking to impose a collective identity through selected features. I shall discuss at further length the specific adopted 'Englishness' of the Residencia in the next chapter, but will offer views on its conservative approach to the importation of culture here. Its creation had been preceded by a publishing enterprise headed by Alberto Jiménez Fraud, supported by Juan Ramón Jiménez and subsequently José Moreno Villa, and published some thirty-five volumes, but concerned primarily with Spanish content rather than acting as a centre of exchange (see Ribagorda 2006: 314).

Viewing the Residencia in the light of Bourdieu's *habitus* allows us to understand the dual motion of the institution, one that will become accentuated in its publication. As outlined in Chapter 1, Bourdieu observes that the *habitus* has an inbuilt tendency to conservative practices, making choices consonant with its past (Bourdieu 1992: 61). The result is self-conservation through the practice of 'homogamy'. Habitually the view of the Residencia has been of a rather different nature, of an institution outgoing rather than inward-looking, a force for change rather than for conservation. Its function as a gateway has, like the gaze of the anthropologist on the species he studies, its own influence on the new experience gained within its portals.

What happens in the journal of an institution is the creation of a micro-environment. This will interact not only with the outside (Europe, the United States, the Far East) but with the other institutions of the context within which it finds itself, and against which it will seek to define itself. Some cultural contacts within an institution (and we can take the Residencia as an example, as well as the Ateneo, clubs, casinos, *tertulias*) will be casual: chance encounters, the meeting of minds through the reading of books, in the audience of a lecture or a classroom. They will exist as a subset of encounters that may be planned by the institution's intentions (invitations to outside speakers, and the provision of the necessary funds or environment for lectures to take place). Alongside the planned culture of a programme of events, and the constitution of the place that holds them (with its limits on membership and expectations about behaviour) there will be a micro-culture of resistance. The antics of Lorca, Buñuel and Dali, for example, thus fell outside the puritanical norms of the Residencia (Pritchett 1971: 147; Gibson 1997: 88, 104–5, 136; Buñuel 1994: 63–4).

The Residencia without doubt acted as a centre of exchange, a crucial point in Madrid where outside influences were welcomed in, whether in the form of residents from abroad, or visiting speakers. This is what Enric Trillas refers to in his presentation of the 1987 reprint of *Residencia*:

> RESIDENCIA nos cuenta la aventura de aquel grupo extraordinario de inte-lectuales – científicos y artistas, profesores y estudiantes, literatos, médicos, ingenieros y arquitectos – y la incansable actividad que desplegaron hasta las vísperas del desastre de 1936; revela también datos preciosos de la vida cultural y el desarrollo científico en una de las dos capitales culturales de la España del momento. Yo diría incluso que RESIDENCIA refleja, a su modo, la vida intelectual de todo el país, pues el aire de la Colina de los Chopos nunca fue solamente madrileño; hasta allí llegarán siempre gentes de toda España, haciendo de la Residencia un mirador hacia Europa. En las páginas que siguen se percibe el afán europeo y universal de cuantos se apiñan en los sencillos pero elegantes edificios de ladrillo tostado que albergaron aquel mundo inquieto y fecundo de la Europa de entreguerras.
>
> (Trillas 1987: vii)

Trillas encapsulates the well-known vision of the Residencia, the place that hosted everything exciting in Spanish cultural artistic and intellectual life, the place where Lorca was heard by Trend, where Ravel, Milhaud and Poulenc performed, where Valéry lectured. This vision is detailed in the foundational histories of the Residencia, the most detailed summary of activities and individuals being that of Margarita Sáenz de la Calzada (1986) (see also Jiménez Fraud 1972; Crispin 1981; Trend 1921, 1934). From these accounts the Residencia emerges as a crucial centre of exchange, a location where the intelligent, artistic and innovative minds of the country were able to meet, and benefit from one another's expertise and creativity, and where – most significantly in the context of this study – it acted as the forum for the reception of distinguished foreign visitors, the means for Spain to be up-to-the-minute in European cultural, scientific and artistic affairs. Among the authors in *Residencia* we find Marie Curie, G K Chesterton, Eddington, Keynes, Starkie, Trend, and other lecturers include H G Wells. Debussy is cited almost as frequently as Darwin (and rather more than Poulenc and Milhaud); Einstein has prominence only slightly more than the explorer Charles Gran-ville Bruce; Faraday shows up slightly more than Freud (and Jung is a brief single mention); Simmel (to take a favourite of the *Revista de Occidente*) is nowhere, but Isaac Newton is as much in the picture as Kraepelin.

The actual past of an institution is, of course, elusive at best. As Bourdieu elaborates the inaccessibility of the *habitus* of another, this becomes clear:

> The habitus – embodied history, internalized as a second nature and so forgotten as history – is the active presence of the whole past of which it is the product. As such, it is what gives practices their relative auto- nomy with respect to external determinations of the immediate present. This autonomy is that of the past, enacted and acting, which, functioning as accumulated capital, produces history on the basis of history and so ensures the permanence in change that makes the individual agent a world within the world. (Bourdieu 1992: 56)

In the case of the Residencia, as with so much of pre-Civil War Spain, we are left with what has been allowed to remain there. In common with other key cultural institutions of the first decades of the twentieth century, the Resi- dencia has suffered a loss of evidence belonging to the years of the Second Republic, not to mention the years of Primo de Rivera's dictatorship.

We can take as a point of comparison here the case of the Madrid Ateneo, where we have no means of tracking the membership year by year in the decades preceding the Civil War, nor indeed, of all the intellectual activi- ties it hosted. There are the surviving lists of *socios* for 1909 and 1914, but otherwise the records are patchy. We have registers of membership for the Ateneo that give us 'positive' evidence (if a name appears in the register, it indicates that the person was a member for the period listed), but there is no guide to names that have been silently removed. Absence from the list does not signify that a person was not a member of the Ateneo, since at the outbreak of the Civil War some names were removed, and never reinstated. Furthermore, we have no evidence of what happened in the period of closure of the Ateneo during Primo's dictatorship. That the dictatorship closed the Ateneo, and yet allowed the Residencia to survive tells its own story. It indi- cates the degree to which the Ateneo either was, or was regarded as, a centre with a degree of intellectual subversiveness not believed to exist in the Resi- dencia (perhaps based on the youth of the majority of the residents, who according to the yearly 'programa' it produced as its prospectus could be as young as fifteen). Alternatively it could be argued (and this is consistent with the careful attitude of Jiménez Fraud, its director) that the Residencia managed to maintain a political neutrality in a way that the Ateneo neither wished to do, nor was able to do (see Crispin 1981: 49, 73–4; Bécarud and López Campillo 1978: 7–8). In the light of the fact that intellectual and cultural life in Spain during the years of the Residencia consisted of various intersecting and overlapping circles and groups, the self-construction of the

Residencia through its journal may have been a crucial factor in its survival. The style and level of this self-construction (a bid for strategic status) was, however, at the cost of a level of limiting self-definition that the Ateneo, and conceivably other groupings, did not engage in, thus retaining the freedom, mobility and subversiveness of the tactical.

The assumed and proclaimed ethos of the Residencia balanced on a knife-edge of a determinedly lay institution that nonetheless had features of monastic rule. The nature of the Residencia as a somewhat austere place derives from the JAE, and ultimately from the austerity of Giner himself, compounded by the unorthodox austerity of Castillejo. The inheritance of the Residencia (which stood to be confirmed and compounded by *Residencia*) was thus of austerity, with a strange emphasis on non-establishment morality, remarkably akin to the English Nonconformist tradition. This emphasis is quite insistent, and the beliefs and sobriety of attitude of the ILE from which the Residencia would spring can be seen in their statutes that appeared at the head of each number of the *Boletín de la Institución Libre de Enseñanza*:

> La INSTITUCIÓN LIBRE DE ENSEÑANZA es completamente ajena a todo espíritu e interés de comunión religiosa, escuela filosófica o partido político; proclamando tan sólo el principio de la libertad e inviolabilidad de la ciencia y de la consiguiente independencia de su indagación y exposición respecto de cualquiera otra autoridad que la de la propia conciencia del Profesor, único responsable de sus doctrinas. (Art. 15 de los *Estatutos*)

The Residencia had been set up with a framework of marginality and alternative educational structure. As Giner would comment to his public, some fifty years after the founding of the ILE, 'conviene recordar que la *Institución* no ha aceptado jamás subvención ni auxilio alguno del Estado ni de las corporaciones locales' (Giner 1926: 48). This position of tactical adoption of marginality was further confirmed by the unofficial origins of the JAE. While marginal in its beginnings, what is noticeable is the importance of Giner, who continued as a distant (and sometimes not so distant) figure of authority for the institutions that came from his example. This is particularly evident in the link between him and Castillejo, the secretary, chief mover and organizer of the JAE (D Castillejo 1997, 1998, 1999). Giner was clearly a moving force in the international intentions and aspirations of the ILE/JAE/Residencia line, so that we can see the outward reach of all three as a sign of obedience to the master. This is arguably seen in the clarity of Castillejo's reply to the official enquiry as to the purpose of his visit to England in 1922 (he had gone to get married): 'I have come to further connections between Spain and England' (Claremont de Castillejo 1967: 14). The pattern of Castillejo's actual travels (as traced in his correspondence) is rather less dramatic than this anecdote suggests. Nonetheless the idea that a foundational individual (Giner) could subsequently influence so strongly the tactical movements of those within alternative establishments raises questions about their independence and spontaneity, both qualities, one would assume, of the tactical.

This sense of moral rightness in the attitude of the ILE was continued in the traditions of the JAE, mainly through Castillejo. Thus, for example, the scholarships offered via the JAE for study abroad were deliberately set at a low level. This was attributed in part to the natural austerity of Castillejo, but also regarded as a deliberate ploy so that applicants would not see the money as an inducement. They had to want to go abroad (Zulueta 1992: 190). This casts an interesting light on the ILE and JAE as centres of exchange, of course. The commitment to outreach had to be strong on the part of the applicants, and those at the gateway vigilant to ensure that only the most motivated would be able to travel abroad to secure their contact with Europe.

The Residencia was not primarily about outreach in terms of sending students abroad, although some *becas* existed to enable this, particularly those established by the Comité Hispano-Inglés, which both funded residents who went abroad, and allowed for visitors to join in the Residencia's activities (the details of *becarios* are given in *Memorias* of the JAE, which cover the years 1912–34). What is striking, however, about this institution is the degree to which its desire for cultural outreach and exchange was set in the context of austerity already noted, and yet also in the context of an institutional desire for the integrated approach to development of mind and body. These were ideals of Giner that had been implemented in the ILE, as had the intention to awaken curiosity, the desire to learn, independent judgement and true scientific method. It is this context, the 'estilo de la casa' that will come through in *Residencia*, rather than or as much as a strong sense of the task of cultural exchange. Thus in its first number *Residencia* will speak of morality, albeit in passing. The publication was set up to meet a need, responding to those who with affection and nostalgia had written in to the Residencia, and it was therefore intended to provide a cultural instrument so that those no longer in the Residencia could have access to what was going on. It was directed to those who 'han pasado horas felices en la Residencia y guardan un grato recuerdo del esfuerzo con que ayudaron a sustentar los ideales de la casa'. The foreword also expressed regret that it would be unable to do full justice to 'los sucesos que construyen diariamente la personalidad *moral* de la Residencia, en las explicaciones, fundamentos y referencias que les prestan sus sustancia *ideológica*' (foreword, *Residencia* 1926, 1 (1): 1, emphasis mine). The mention of the ideological contribution of the Residencia is apposite for the Primo years, suggesting what might be an ideology of internal opposition. It is possible also that the high moral tone could be read as an elite cornering of the market in morality in a national context where the leader was not renowned for his moral qualities. But a perusal of the pages of *Resi-*

dencia confirms that the concept of the moral significance of the Residencia continued beyond the Primo era into the years of the Republic. This in the *Anuario* of the University of Madrid for the academic year 1932–3, in the information provided about the Residencia, we read how its educational activities are complementary to those of other centres of higher education. This is not all: the moral emphasis comes first: 'Así a los *influjos morales* añade estos y otros estímulos de orden intelectual, con los que procura intensificar el trabajo de los residentes' (Universidad de Madrid: *Anuario 1932–33* 1933: 79, emphasis mine).

Residencia is a large-format publication, with the emblematic Roman head that now appears on the Residencia website. A photograph of the head was reproduced in *Residencia* 2 (3) (December 1931), 167, with a note on its associations. These include the assessment that many find it to be 'entre lo más bello y más importante que nos ha legado el arte griego' and that it is known as 'Efebo o atleta rubio', a title that says much about the institution's concept of beauty and masculinity, and its model of cultural supremacy. Its photograph appeared again in *Residencia* 4 (2) (April 1933), 55, with the same explanatory note.

In its early numbers at least *Residencia* runs to some hundred pages of text per number, liberally illustrated with photographs and sketches. This pattern is set in the first number. The balance of material in this first number is curious: well over a third of the publication is given to reports of lectures, as we might expect of the journal of an institution of cultural and intellectual exchange; about a fifth contributes a sort of local balance with what I shall term 'internal tourism', conjuring up vistas and atmospheres of Madrid; a slightly smaller proportion than this is devoted to everyday news of the Residencia. In terms of its intended function and audience, Ribagorda (2006: 314) has commented that it sits between the *Boletín de la Institución Libre de Enseñanza and the Revista de Occidente*. That is, it sits balanced between information for the alumni of the Residencia and the function of acting as a centre of exchange.

The first published number of *Residencia* necessarily fulfils a number of functions. As an alumni magazine it aims to give a sense of what is happening at the moment, while consolidating and presenting a constructed self of the Residencia, and then items from outside are offered to that constructed self. To do so it draws partly on the history, or rather on the memory of the Residencia, and in part on historical statements of mission. These statements of mission are reiterated in the final and 'official' section of the journal, as a rounding-off of the construction that has been carried out.

We can see retrospectively how the different elements of this first number reflect the variety of aims. On the one hand, some items present a direct appeal to former (and present) residents in the shape of the invitation to shared or remembered experience. This displays an awareness of the pleasures of solitude, and encourages and develops sensibility, even preciosity, and a degree of self-culture. This is a type of pedagogy which, to quote the programme of 1920, pursues 'la cultura desinteresada del espíritu', and which

> no sólo busca en ella la utilidad, sino el mejor medio de que el hombre aprenda a seguir sus propios pensamientos y a juzgar las pruebas que deben llevarle al conocimiento de la verdad; la que para alcanzar ésta piensa que el empuje intelectual debe ir guiado por el arte supremo de la vida: el arte de hacer el bien; y la que, por último, cree que hay que buscar la fuente de este difícil arte en el impulso de los sentimientos más puros que dan elevación moral al carácter humano, son un factor decisivo en su formación, le hacen justo y bueno y encienden en el alma el amor a la verdad y a la belleza.

On the other hand, a number of items in this first number could be considered to respond to the statement from the 1914 programme of the Residencia, in which the ideals of the '98 generation are readily perceived. But one can also see in it elements of an English public school education that had as its aim the formation of the leaders of the future:

> La Residencia es una asociación de estudiantes españoles que cree como se cree en la vida misma, en una futura y alta misión espiritual de España, y que pretende contribuir a formar en su seno, por mutua exaltación, el estudiante rico en virtudes públicas y ciudadanas, capaz de cumplir dignamente, cuando sea llamado a ello, lo que de él exijan los destinos históricos de la raza.

Both of these programmes, part of the Residencia's history, identity and self-construction, are brought to the reader's attention by being included in the final section of current news (*Residencia* 1926, 1 (1): 85). Although this official and final section is subtitled 'laboratorios, deportes, Sociedad de becas', there is more to it than mere reportage. It is not a total account of all the contents, but represents the major strands. There are no book reviews, beyond notices of three works published by residents. Of these, one is Ortega's *Meditaciones del Quijote* (1914), and another is Antonio G Solalinde's edition of *El sacrificio de la misa* by Berceo (1913). The third is Eduardo Torner's *Cuarenta canciones españolas*, a work advertised with some regularity in this publication.

The two programmes of the Residencia that appear in the pages of this first number are not absolutely distinct from one another, and it may or may not be significant that the 1914 programme is a more direct and directive mission statement, whereas the emphasis on solitude and self-culture comes from the later programme of 1920. What I think is striking is the way they relate (or perhaps fail to relate) to the 'solitude pieces' that are clearly addressed to the readers of the journal, although by contrast there is an implied relation to the stronger sense of 'leader-formation' material that will come in the reports of the lectures.

The 'solitude pieces' are a cluster of short articles in this first number of *Residencia*, and act as a meditative guide to identity in their echoes of *modernista* preciosity and the phraseology of the Generation of '98. There is a strong setting in history and in cultural tradition in these writings by Azorín, Cossío, Ramón Gómez de la Serna, Juan Ramón Jiménez and Tenreiro that could easily be found in a Hispanic culture of some twenty years earlier, at the date when the Residencia was originally founded. Jiménez contributed two pieces on the 'chopos', one noting the arrival of 3,000 of the trees to be planted on the new site of the Residencia (where it currently stands), and gushing with enthusiasm, and a 'Visita nocturna a "La colina"', even more self-indulgent (*Residencia* 1 (1): 26, 76). Jiménez was himself a sort of set-piece of the institution, residing in one of the pavilions from 1913 until his marriage in 1919 (Crispin 1981: 27).

These pieces of nostalgia, solitude and poetic reverie focus on the individual experience of the resident and offer it up to the readership as a historical form of self-construction in which members will be steeped in memory and affect. But there is also the public face of the institution, seen most clearly in its lectures. It is for the lectures that the Residencia has – with some justification – been remembered as a centre of exchange. But they need to be read in the context of the adopted moral tone of the Residencia. Firstly, they were not part of the direct educational structure of the Residencia, or of the intellectual *formación* of the residents. They were organized and funded by two separate groups: an inner, subscription-paying circle, the Sociedad de Cursos y Conferencias, and the Comité Hispano-Inglés (see Chapter 5 and Sinclair 2004a). Secondly, there is selection and editing (inevitably) in the reporting of them, so that what is offered to the readership of *Residencia* is a version that is consistent with the official ethos of the institution.

The lecturers invited by the Sociedad de Cursos y Conferencias in 1924, for example, demonstrate how the Residencia operated, offering a mix of local and exotic personalities and experts: Froebenius, Marañón, Zulueta, D'Ors, Cossío, Valéry, Ortega, Aragon, Cendrars, Duhamel, Max Jacob, Hernández Pacheco and Keyserling.

The lectures of these speakers receive some account in *Residencia*. There were yet others, Maeztu, Blas Cabrera and Manuel García Morente, who were merely listed. Between them they represent an excellent cultural education. One can note curious emphases in the accounts given. For Froebenius, a brief, factual résumé is given, as also for Marañón and Zulueta (in short, bullet-like sentences). Aragon, likewise, is treated with brevity. In his case the society is said to have been eager to 'conocer los temas que logran fuera de España resonancia y actualidad', and thus had thought of 'la conveniencia de ofrecer a sus socios alguna disertación sobre el gran suceso literario del día: el *surréalisme*', a striking piece of phrasing. The account goes on to say (presumably as Aragon spoke in French and a substantial section of the audience thus would not have understood him fully), that 'Más que el contenido de su trabajo, captó al público por su aire, por su voz, por su dicción y la suprema elegancia de su prosa, de cuño legítimo y radicalmente francés. Como se ha dicho por alguien, "este anarquista resulta un príncipe"' (*Residencia* 1926, 1 (1): 68). There had, however, been a careful process of de-sanitization in producing this account of Aragon, to make him acceptable in the polite society of the readers of *Residencia*. Key sections of the lecture were printed in *La Révolution Surréaliste* in June 1925, and in that version we find that the text is aggressive and uncompromising. Buñuel cites the story of how Aragon shocked the director Jiménez Fraud by asking him if there were any interesting urinals in town. This may or may not have been invention, but it fits more credibly with the outrageous behaviour of surrealists than does the image of the urbane lecture (Buñuel 1994: 62).

The initial base of the lectures provided in 1924 is of breadth and interest. What is singled out for comment in *Residencia*, however, borders on the bizarre, not least in its emphasis on energetic physical activity and exploration. Consistent with this are the two substantial articles produced by the activities of the Comité Hispano-Inglés, and which connect with another leitmotif of the '98, an adventurous and heroic spirit: a lengthy article on Howard Carter's discovery of the tomb of Tutankhamen (*Residencia* 1926, 1 (1): 3–15), lavishly illustrated, and a series of pieces (*Residencia* 1926, 1 (1): 56–62) relating to the attempt on Everest (1922), and the lecture on it by one of its participants, General Bruce. Both lectures were obvious crowd-pullers. The treasures of Tutankhamen had come to light in excavations of late 1922 that significantly combined the patronage (and financial support) of Lord Caernarvon, and the industry (and entrepreneurial spirit) of Howard Carter, a man of relatively little formal education, quick temper, but meticulous habits when it came to archaeology. Meanwhile Bruce, the stocky general who had spent years in India in the army, and who provided the organization for the attempt on Everest undertaken by Irving and Mallory, was a practical and essential part of that expedition. In the cases of both the Tutankhamen and Everest lectures, the men concerned were individualists, good at enterprise, good at organization and self-contained. Both were outgoing. Neither exemplified, however, the English public school tradition: indeed, one could observe that they were the exceptions that proved that education of that style did not provide all that was worthy in life. Rather, their presence suggested that personal commitment and direction were what counted. When the Duque de Alba presented Bruce, he singled out his qualities of the sportsman (something the Residencia was trying to encourage).

But he also made a link with quixotic activity, saying, as it were, that what Spaniards might want to emulate in him was in their tradition already:

> Estas empresas ideales son siempre gloriosas y ricas en imponderables consecuencias. Así por lo menos lo pensamos todos los que habitamos esta tierra, donde emprendió sus hazañas, siempre ideales, aunque casi siempre infructuosas, aquel noble caballero Don Alonso de [sic] Quijano el Bueno.
> *(Residencia* 1926, 1 (1): 62)

Similarly, when Sánchez Rivero speaks of Carter's work in Egypt, he makes a link that his Hispanic audience would have recognized as their own:

> El rasgo más saliente de la civilización egipcia es la fuerza que ella tuvo, la preocupación de la muerte y el espíritu grandioso que manifestó en la construcción de los sepulcros. *(Residencia* 1926 1 (1): 5)

The text that summarizes the two lectures of Walter Starkie reads as a strange, even eccentric catalogue of dramatists writing in English. Part of the eccentricity derives from a moral agenda which – like the two lectures of adventure and discovery (Bruce and Carter) – comes from a sense of knowing what was what. In the case of Starkie, however, there is a desire to actually tell his audience what was what. Unlike contemporaries in France and Argentina, Starkie is not keen to lionize Oscar Wilde, who is classified by him for his dandy performance of anti-masculinity. Attitude and style, whether in literature or life, are not enough for Starkie. Here he merges a desire that there should be values that can be understood with the 'moral' programme of the Residencia:

> Los artistas caen harto frecuentemente en el vicio de juzgar las obras de arte por la factura, figurándose que la factura es todo el arte, cuando no es sino un elemento supeditado al contenido, pues por sí nada vale. Ocurre que se encomia de artística una obra a causa de su factura. Pero si carece de contenido, que es por donde el arte se inserta en la naturaleza humana, o su contenido repugna a la naturaleza humana, esta obra, aun cuando algunos profesionales la tengan en estima, a causa de la habilidad o novedad de su factura, no es una obra de arte. Y así, la inmoralidad deliberada se erige como impedimento de la excelencia artística. (Starkie 1926: 45)

These articles on the English lectures are highly conspicuous in this first number of the journal. They present a curious spin on what the life of the Residencia was about. What were the interests, and what were the values? We can conclude something more of the meaning of the lectures by considering their audience, and contrasting it with the population of the Residencia. We find two ranges of elite, socially not identical, but with some range of overlap, and in this there is a demonstration of the potential diversity of audience for a number of cultural importations.

The lectures did not represent freely available culture. The charges of the Residencia, while deliberately set so as not to suggest a regime of luxury, were such as to exclude poorer scholars (and the *becas* initially available were later converted into *becas* for travel abroad). The lectures were open to residents, but otherwise were available to outsiders, to those who were paid-up members of the Sociedad de Cursos y Conferencias. The statutes of the Comité Hispano-Inglés, approved 6 May 1926, fixed the subscription for 'meros suscriptores' between 50 pesetas and the minimum of 250 pesetas given by the 'protectores' (who also had to have made a donation of 1,000 pesetas). The statutes of the Sociedad de Cursos y Conferencias, as they stood at 31 December 1931, had the slightly lower rate of 40 pesetas for ordinary members, and 200 for the 'protectores' (with a similar requirement of a donation of 1,000 pesetas).

An analysis of those signed up reveals an interesting profile. A list of 164 members signed up in June 1925 has risen by 1926 to 225, with an organizing committee of eleven. Of the 225 members, no fewer than fifty (22 per cent) had an aristocratic title, and within this aristocratic group (nearly a third of those listed), women clearly outnumber men (62 per cent). This aristocratic emphasis is reflected in the group of 'Socios protectores' (two countesses, and one marquis, out of a total of eleven members), and in the members in general (seventeen men and twenty-seven women with a title). Very few of these members, incidentally, appear as matrimonial pairs. The gender break-down of the organising group is that three out of the eleven are women, and ninety-eight of the group of *socios* are women, some 44 per cent of the total. It is not possible to identify exactly the nature of family groupings from the list, but it looks as though there could be some nineteen matrimonial pairs, so that of the sixty-six men who were *socios*, about a third had brought along their wives, and there would appear to be some daughters. Indeed, the gender profile of the list as a whole leads one to wonder whether in some degree what might have happened was not that husbands brought their wives to the event but that wives brought along their husbands. The figures for the academic year 1928–9 continue to show a similar profile, though somewhat attenuated, with women representing some 43 per cent of a total of 512 members, and titled members accounting for 15 per cent of the membership (see Sáenz de la Calzada 1986: 179–80).

Furthermore, some of the lectures included royalty in the audience. The public lecture by Bruce, for example, was also the occasion of one of the visits of the royal family to the Residencia ('Visitas regias', *Residencia* 1926, 1 (1): 77). The commentary on a photograph of Alfonso XIII on an earlier visit to the Residencia, one of three on the same page, could have come out of the most fawning society journal: 'tuvo Su Majestad la bondad de animar los primeros débiles pasos de la Residencia, prestándola el apoyo moral de su afectuoso interés'. It should be noted that this attitude to the king is found elsewhere in accounts of educational institutions in this period, and that the assumption made of the king's interest overstates what elsewhere was the sign of royal patronage, although the king did hand over his summer residence at Santander for the use of the University Summer School in 1931, an act that can be seen as a piece of astute social politics on the part of the king, or at least some social face-saving (Madariaga de la Campa and Valbuena Morán 1999: 45–58).

It was clear that the Residencia needed to survive in the regime of Primo, and what mattered here was not the attitude of Giner, but rather that of Jiménez Fraud, adjudged by Crispin at least, to be of diplomatic *convivencia* ('de ecuanimidad senequista') with the regime of Primo (and consequently with the monarchy) (Crispin 1981: 36). A detail that Bécarud and López Campillo note, however, is that Alfonso XIII, king during Primo's dictatorship, was not known for his intellectual sparkle. They recount an anecdote told by Ortega who was introduced to the king at a high-society social occasion. When the king asked Ortega what he taught in the Faculty, Ortega replied 'Metafísica', at which the king commented, 'Debe de ser muy complicado' (Bécarud and López Campillo 1978: 12, their source being José Pla, *Madrid* [Barcelona 1932: 61–2]). The presence of the king at the Residencia is not linked to his intellectual curiosity. Rather, we might see it as part of the social scene within which the lecture by Bruce took place.

What is striking about the picture of the Sociedad de Cursos y Conferencias is that its profile might be said to reflect various other audiences, whether the congregation of a church, or what is sometimes termed the 'blue-rinse brigade' of lecture-goers still found at events in some large public institutions in capital cities of Europe. The nature of this audience is also striking in the face of the publication of the Residencia (as opposed to its activity of lectures), which is coloured by an atmosphere that combines Spanish austerity (though one which takes a self-indulgent form) and English masculinity. It is of course a record of the potential audience as it would have been after the visits of lecturers such as Einstein (1923), since the society was formed after his visit (Crispin 1981: 48). It is the audience that would have been there for Valéry and Claudel, and for the ethnographer Froebenius. Despite the attendance of residents the atmosphere of genteel high society is difficult to avoid. The mischievous reader might believe that there is potentially more than a little prefiguration, if history can prefigure literature. That scathing portrayal of a literary *tertulia* that Luis Martín-Santos will include in *Tiempo de silencio* in 1961 has, perhaps, more than one antecedent.

It is not absolutely clear that the audience of the lectures was, in sociological terms, distinct from the readership (or intended readership) of the journal. But we can infer something further from the material substructure of the journal, in which there is a combination of marketing and subtle self-marketing. On the one hand, the numbers of the journal contain exactly the sort of information that we might expect to find there: advertisements for other journals of an intellectual nature, including *Arquitectura Española* (bilingual in English and Spanish), the collection *Biblioteca de Ideas del Siglo XX*, directed by Ortega (full of good mainline titles in current thought, science, law and aesthetics), the *Revista de Filología*, the *Revista de Pedagogía*. An indication of cultural exchange (besides the bilingual *Arquitectura Española*) is *Universitario*, the publication of the *Asociación Intelectual Americana*, published in Paris. But there is other advertising. Here we are, in the 1920s, and suddenly the advertising suggests that slick world of avant-garde existence, with Pirelli tyres, photographic equipment, typewriters, *artículos de sport*, and items of medical treatments ('Biol', sold at the Farmacia Gayoso, for pregnancy, lactation and fatigue). The reader appealed to here is not obviously the bookish and austere student following in the steps of Giner or Castillejo. The implied reader is rather the stereotype of sportsman later satirized by Lorca in *Así que pasen cinco años* (1931), the man about town wanting to get the right equipment for his car and fashion-statement accessories for the rest of his life, or to get the latest medical compound for the mature woman in his life. As the advert for Heno de Pravia soap puts it, the item sends out a message to others: 'en el lavabo, es indicio de buen gusto y de esmerado culto a la higiene', while that proclaiming the products sold at Julio González y Compañía in the Gran Vía (with a delectable Oriental *art nouveau* woman holding the advert) tells how the shop stocks 'las últimas y más selectas creaciones en Perfumería Nacional y Extranjera...' (*Residencia* 1926, 1 (3): xix, xxiii). The Hotel Gran Vía proclaims that it has 220 rooms with bath 'en el mejor sitio de Madrid', and the cry '¡¡EUREKA!!' announces the solution to one's problems in footwear is to be found at three Madrid addresses (*Residencia* 1926, 1 (3): xxv).

Revista de Occidente: visions of consolation

The case of *Residencia* shows how careful shaping of material resulted from the objective of creating, and speaking to, a specific audience. The elite nature of this audience was implied in the ideals (and the published aims) of the institution of the Residencia. *RO* and its associated publishing house (discussed in Chapter 3) was specifically engaged in the education of the intellectual, and the formation of a readership, and was deliberately and explicitly non-political. Distributed primarily through subscription, as were many other journals of the time, its intended readership was a well-educated and cultured elite.

As an academic by profession, Ortega had a fierce belief in the need to disseminate culture (acting on this at times by lecturing to large audiences in cinemas), while also believing that elites were an essential element in bringing about such dissemination. Other ventures besides *RO*, such as *El Espectador* (1916–34), would run on subscription only (and with Ortega as the sole contributor); *España* (1915–23), which again included in its agenda that of opening Spain to foreign culture, was political, unlike *RO*, and Ortega left it in 1915 as it moved politically further to the left (Dobson 1989: 28). He published in the daily paper *El Imparcial* (in publication until 1933), and in 1917 joined with Nicolás María de Urgoiti in setting up another daily, *El Sol* (in publication until 1939). Through his participation in both of these papers it is arguable that Ortega's impact on the public was more far-reaching than through *RO*. In addition, the medium of the daily press provided a more obvious forum for reader reaction: within the pages of *RO*, response to articles published occurred occasionally in the form of other articles, but there was no letters page for immediate feedback on ideas.

The received view on *RO* is that it constitutes one of the prime channels through which Spain had its cultural contacts with the outside world. In broad terms this cannot be contested, but what does bear examination is the degree to which it was not an entirely open centre of exchange, but one that operated to try to place Spain in line with certain currents of thought in Europe. One striking feature of the way in which it slanted and selected its material concerns gender, and specifically gender used in social and political analyses. By tracing the outlines of these contributions, and the eventual response made to them in 1931 by Rosa Chacel, I shall argue that *RO* looks both forwards and back. It thus joins with certain elements in European thought to respond to perceived areas of crisis through a strongly gendered vision that is aimed at consolation. In presenting these images of consolation, and opting for an idealization of relationships between the sexes that could be read individually, and as national metaphor, *RO*, without being overtly political (a direction consciously avoided by Ortega) was able to engage in the projection of structures of society that in a broader sense could be construed as political.

The view of gender promoted through a series of articles – first in the years of Primo de Rivera's dictatorship, and then through the years of the Second Republic – is essentialist and tidy. In so doing it runs tactically against the context of public life of the time, offering a consolation of neatness against the current of contemporary liberal social developments, most notably concerning the emancipation of women, both in Spain and Europe. Thus while *RO* has a reputation for looking forward and outward, this particular, and by far from negligible aspect of its activity and the specificity of its imports suggests a type of retrenchment of social attitudes that inevitably carries an implied political message.

The articles on gender show two things: they demonstrate Spain's awareness (or perhaps Ortega's awareness) of currents of thought in Europe that he wishes to become part of the fabric of the intellectual *habitus* of his country; and secondly, they show a view of relations between the sexes that is set in a structure of stability. This is a significant structure to present within Spain in this period, given that a purely surface political and social stability during the dictatorship gave way to overt and disruptive instability during the Republic, resulting from extremes of social and political progressiveness on the one hand, and a conservative championing of traditional values on the other. Spain was, of course, not the only European country to experience social and political disruption in this period, and arguably the proffering of an imaginary of consolation would have been as relevant in England, France or Germany. But where Spain stood to be 'different' from elsewhere in Europe was in the concept of where stability of society (and relations of gender and love) might lie. Outlining gender relations that echoed patriarchal structures, and that, because of those structures, offered a sense of social stability, responded to a conservative tradition. At the same time, however, it was also one that was far from absent from more liberal standpoints. These included the articulation of 'proper' gender positions that would be found in the work of Spanish sexual reformers in the 1920s and 1930s, particularly among champions of eugenics such as Marañón and Pittaluga. Their articles, for example, looked towards a utopian future in which the disorders caused by disease (and thought to be linked to degeneration) might be removed. Love, or at least relations between the sexes, was presumed to occur within a structure in which there might be 'proper' gender roles, a 'proper' functioning within society, and these relations would thus contribute to a civilized future.

Implicitly, and occasionally explicitly, the imaginary of consolation stands in counterpoint to the instability of political and social life in the West in this period and maps out gender relations in which – one deduces – 'love' and civilization might occur. The emphasis is on social relations, rather than on individual affection, and love is rarely if ever discussed explicitly. Apparent exceptions such as Bertrand Russell's essay of January 1930 on the place of love in human life, or that of Rosa Chacel on the 'Esquema de los problemas prácticos y actuales del amor' are in fact largely philosophical or sociological.

The selection of authors who would have their work published in *RO* was patently in line with Ortega's strong editorial policy. We can take as an example of this those publications with a bearing on psychoanalytic thought. In this area Ortega was cautious and selective, and while six articles by Jung appeared between 1925 and 1936, there is a striking sparseness of reference in *RO* to the work of Freud. Three of his works are reviewed, *Wit and its Relation to the Unconscious* (Manuel García Morente, in September 1923), *The Ego and the Id* (by the psychiatrist José Sacristán, in November 1923), and *The Interpretation of Dreams* (by the psychiatrist Gonzalo Rodríguez Lafora, in October 1924). In the number of April/June 1925, Sacristán reported on an article by Freud published in *La Revue Juive*, in which he responded to his detractors. After this, Freud's presence in *RO* is in the form of brief references only, and at no point are excerpts from his work published. This 'retreat' from Freud would appear to relate to Ortega's own shift of enthusiasm for the works of Freud. He had promoted the translation of Freud's *Complete Works* by Biblioteca Nueva in 1922, but later moved to a position of increasing distance from Freud and reservations about his theories.

In terms of the imaginary of consolation that *RO* pursues in relation to matters of gender, it is as though Freud might disturb a vision of the Imaginary, or simply a cultural imaginary, in which a social structure guaranteed some stability and meaning. Curiously, it is this vision that is presented to the elite readership, almost assumed to be unable or uninterested in engaging with the challenges posed by the writings of Freud. This might be read in terms of what could be imagined as – if not Freud's usefulness – then his timeliness and appropriateness to the Spanish context. His *Civilization and its Discontents* (1930), for example, did nothing to produce a reassuring vision of society but, on the contrary, emphasized the aggressive nature of man. Through its selection of articles *RO* appears to assert that – whatever the conflicts and difficulties of the Western world in the interwar years – structure and meaning still obtain. It is curious in the light of his attitude to Freud that Ortega would later voice his own concerns about the role of the masses in modern society in no uncertain terms in *La rebelión de las masas*.

Ortega's intention in setting up his review was to bring into being a set of others with whom he could discuss things of the day. For Evelyne López Campillo, the chosen non-political nature of *RO*, to which I have referred, constitutes a reduction in Ortega's ambition (López Campillo 1972: 55–6). Yet Ortega's aims ('Propósitos'), published in the first number of *RO*, suggest something other. He speaks of wanting to appeal to the 'curiosity' of a readership envisaged as 'calmly' interested in culture and the arts. This curiosity is free-floating, detached from hierarchies and divisions of social and cultural structure, a type of curiosity that is neither exclusively aesthetic nor particularly scientific or political. It is what the alert individual feels in his desire to confront and know the depths of contemporary reality (Ortega 1923a: 1). These aims can thus be seen as the expression of a different ambition. In part they contain the general ideal of producing an educated and cultured population by exposure to the 'best' ideas from Europe and elsewhere. But something more complex is suggested in Ortega's explanation of the reference to the West ('occidentalidad') in the title of his review. Rooted in the belief that there is a Europe that is cosmopolitan and cultured, history had changed things. The cosmopolitan spirit of before the First World War, he says, could be seen as a surface style of internationalism, in which national differences and peculiarities were 'annulled', whereas the postwar cosmopolitan spirit of the West was one that now existed in a more realistic way.

War had brought closeness through conflict, but this did not prevent those
involved from having to rely on one another more and to have co-existence.
Ortega conjures up therefore an idea not of tough love, but of a tough togeth-
erness between countries, born of the difficulties of their recent contact/
conflict. This is coupled to the idea that many feel the current world to be
one they experience as chaos. He hopes that *RO* will bring some light to the
situation, and more significantly, that it will put its readers in touch with the
'new architecture' currently being reconstructed in the West (Ortega 1923:
2). Simultaneously, then, the experience offered by this review is of difficulty
and encounter, of order for the chaos of experience, and hope that Spain will
be brought into the development of the countries of the West. The articles on
gender in *RO* might be considered as an element not wholly consonant with
the forward-thinking nature of Ortega's aims for the journal given that they
offer strikingly calm and reconciled views on how to understand gendered
difference. Yet they are outward looking. In publishing articles on gender that
form an imaginary of consolation, and specifically in choosing articles that
in their majority are authored outside Spain, Ortega subscribes to an ideal
of love and gender relations that is European rather than Spanish, cultivated
and civilized rather than passionate and individualistic (the contemporary
stereotype norms for Spain). In short, he sketches out an ideal that will be
soothing and consoling in troubled times. That it has an embedded imbalance, insofar as woman is frequently figured in the articles as 'superior', and
yet excluded from the world of action, maps well on to the model of courtly
love, in which woman appears as a superior, and at times unapproachable
being. Within this emphasis what is striking is how the redemptive figure of
the Virgin from Catholicism is transformed into, or supplanted by a mythical
view of woman as redemptrix. An implied message from the metaphors of
the articles is arguably that there could be an orderly and 'civilized' world
not just in the sphere of gender relations, but elsewhere. *RO* thus presents an
alternative form of public life, in intellectual exploration and debate, in the
exchange of ideas without acrimony or political agenda.

The articles on gender (some two dozen appeared between 1923 and 1936)
are thus tinged with a desire to analyze and interpret the present with a view
to a future that is intuited as uncertain. They appear at the average rate of
two a year in the period up to the Second Republic, after which they are
much more sparse. A chronological view of the articles demonstrates how
Ortega created over time a collection of others with whom he could converse,
simultaneously creating a corpus of ideas. The review as a whole had a strong
pedagogical intent. There are numerous introductory footnotes or epigraphs
that place the authors of articles in modern society, that offer an evaluation
of their importance to the cultured reader. A discussion that would take in all
the authors of articles dealing with gender is not possible here: they include
Kretschmer, Spranger, Frank, Russell, Giménez Caballero, Pittaluga, Dantín

Cereceda, Kierkegaard, Chacel, Simmel, Marañón, Keyserling and Jung. I shall concentrate on a small selection that represents Ortega's desire to give his readers the ideas of those he considers to be foremost European thinkers, underpinning their work with local writers whose work might be considered 'scientifically respectable'.

One line that can be followed runs through Georg Simmel, Marañón and Pittaluga, and then Keyserling and Jung. The initial introduction of writers such as Simmel is readily able to be interpreted as *RO* acting as a centre of exchange, making its readers aware of Europe. The inclusion of Marañón and Pittaluga (and others from the circle of the Residencia and the JAE) has, however, a different impact on both the imported work and the work that comes to be its local Hispanic context. The result can be understood as the creation of a new sphere, that of the institution that is the centre of exchange. Not only do things pass through here, but in so doing they form their own ethos and context, and a place for the elite that is familiar with them to move and think.

Ortega makes a special point of introducing Simmel to the readership of the *RO*. Simmel had died in 1918, some five years before his articles started to appear in Spain, and it is evident that Ortega's aim in bringing Simmel to the attention of the Spanish public was strongly didactic. He had become acquainted with Simmel's work when he went to Berlin in August of 1906, where he attended his lectures, Simmel becoming a major influence on his work (Orringer 1979: 30). Ortega's note accompanying Simmel's article on 'Lo masculino y lo femenino. Para una psicología de los sexos' (November and December 1923) declares:

> No creo que se haya hecho hasta ahora análisis más agudo y penetrante de las diferencias entre la psicología del hombre y de la mujer que el presente ensayo del filósofo Jorge Simmel. Me permito recomendar a los lectores de esta Revista una lectura atenta de estas páginas excepcionales que tanto aclaran el conflicto perdurable entre lo masculino y lo femenino.
>
> (editorial note by Ortega to Simmel 1923c)

The essays reproduced in *RO* are, incidentally, straightforward translations of the originals, not adapted specially for the Spanish reading public.

But what Ortega was doing here was championing one who had been marginal in German academic culture when he first made his acquaintance. His experience of Simmel in Berlin was that he valued in particular the work of this sociologist who, albeit with six books published, was nonetheless not far up the academic ladder (Orringer 1979: 20). So in a sense what Ortega does is to try to make the marginal central, or the tactical strategic, using the fresh force of the tactical, the oblique and innovative thought of Simmel to give edge to the offerings of *RO*. Ortega was happy to publish other areas of Simmel's work elsewhere: between 1926 and 1927, seven volumes of Simmel's sociological works appeared in the Revista de Occidente press, largely centring on the sociology of groups. Yet although Simmel came to be highly regarded as a pioneer of social analysis, the fact that his writings on gender are acknowledged as a problem area in his output by current scholarship was either not perceived as such by Ortega, or was skirted around. It is conceivable that by publishing the essays on fashion first (1923a; 1923b) Ortega was establishing him as an authority, in order to strengthen the effect of the essays that deal with gender. The status of Simmel's writings on gender has been much debated, and an excellent evaluation of the debate is offered by Witz (2001). She notes that many current evaluations rely on a curate's egg motif to explain the unevenness of the writing. Her own reading, by which Simmel's ontology of gender consigns woman to the periphery, while his sociological imagination releases man into a more fertile working area, is a discrimination singularly helpful in situating him in the corpus being established by *RO*.

The elite readership of *RO* was presented with a less than liberal view of gender relations, albeit presented (at least by Simmel) in innovative fashion. In 'Lo masculino y lo femenino' (*RO*, November and December 1923) Simmel argues for a traditional (Platonic and Aristotelian) split between the worlds of the masculine and the feminine. The crux of his contribution lies in his attempt to define and place woman outside the familiar binaries, so as to secure her a sense of 'authentic femininity', and in so doing he follows the tradition of Herder, Goethe and Nietzsche, rather than that of Kant and Hegel (Witz 2001: 358). He is not simplistic, yet there is a patriarchal traditionalism underlying what are presented as contemporary and challenging analyses. While he appears to retain the sharp critical edge of historicity that had raised the level of his discussion of fashion, he slips between this and a disturbing essentialism. Thus man's position of social superiority, his 'posición de fuerza', recognized historically, means that he considers his position less than woman does hers with the result that man is more objective. This 'objectivity' becomes a type of 'objective truth', valid for both men and women (Simmel 1923c: 220–2). Yet the fact that Simmel perceives the supposed 'objectivity' of the world as one associated with the masculine (as a social and historical fact) is one of his major insights, albeit one not entirely comfortable for those excluded from that field of objectivity.

Simmel argues biological difference to be the foundation of social difference (225), a schema within which woman was more bound up with her sexual being than man. Viewed retrospectively, we can see how the style of this argument on gender will be consistent with that presented (from the Hispanic side) by Marañón, and what emerges is Ortega's strategy in the sequencing of the articles in *RO*. More generally, Simmel's view on gender was consistent with the organicist strand of thinking on gender and sexuality in Spain in the period (Richards 2004). Simmel does something quite curious in this paper. He argues that woman was more conscious of her subordinate place in society, but maintains that the difference with man, based on biology, matters less to her, precisely because of the nature of that sexual difference. Appealingly (and this is where we can see the beginning of the narrative of consolation), he views her as removed to a place out of history and strife by virtue of her sexuality, and sees her reposing in her femininity as if in an absolute substance (Simmel 1923c: 225). He thus invites approbation for his acuity in perceiving that gender difference is a matter of construction and social norms as well as any biological foundation, and then affirms that the difference in fact lies in sexuality. His very emphasis at this point nonetheless suggests some need to overcompensate the weakness of the essentialist argument, and proceeds to assert that for her, being and sexuality are profoundly identified (226). The idea that this identification should be 'profound' invites the reader to acquiesce to some spiritual appeal. At the same time the observation that woman relates to her own sexuality independent of her relationship to man simultaneously sets her free from her observed subservience and appears to make her the positive and self-determined possessor of the essential nature ascribed to her.

Why did Ortega so support Simmel? One simple answer is to be found in Ortega's own disarmingly patriarchal judgement made of the poetry of Ana de Nouailles in July 1923, his liberalism of earlier years no longer evident (López Campillo 1972: 31). Here he balanced on a knife-edge in relation to the feminine similar to the one evident in Simmel: woman is 'superior', and as such she is unsuited to the making public of feelings that are associated with lyric poetry, revealing as she does the monotony associated with the 'eternal feminine' (Ortega 1923b: 37–8). By this Ortega cunningly relegates woman to a position of superiority, abstracting her from the field of existential struggle that is the world of the masculine. Thus Ortega articulates the way that the liberal mind can operate in two directions in order to preserve the terrain of power and interest ascribed to the masculine by traditional gender structures. Woman is apparently praised for her devotion, her total absorption of herself in her role of the feminine (by which, among other things, she will never be in a position to challenge man in his ambitions). But in a move that betokens sour grapes in the face of this conceded moral superiority of woman, she (with the products of her intellect) is dismissed as of little interest. The logic of the dismissal lies within the characterization of woman as genre rather than individual. Only man is engaged in existential struggle, and thus only the contents of *his* soul will be of real interest.

Specialized markets: education and labour law

A clear sense of the intended public can be gleaned, as shown in the preceding pages, from *Residencia* and the *Revista de Occidente*. No less clear is that of professional journals that clearly perceived their brief not just to be that of outreach, but that of networking with Europe. Here I will comment briefly on two major publications, the *Boletín de la Institución Libre de Enseñanza* and the *Boletín del Instituto de Reformas Sociales*. Sampling of their pages at roughly ten-year intervals provides a profile of their window on Europe and their activity as gate-keepers for intellectual imports.

The *Boletín de la Institución Libre de Enseñanza* (*BILE*) came into being months after the founding of the Institución Libre in 1877. It took as its *lema* article 15 of the founding of the ILE:

> La Institución Libre de Enseñanza es completamente ajena a todo espíritu e interés de comunión religiosa, escuela filosófica o partido político; proclamando tan solo el principio de la libertad e inviolabilidad de la ciencia, y de la consiguiente independencia de su indagación y exposición respecto de cualquiera otra autoridad que la de la propia conciencia del Profesor, único responsable de sus doctrinas.

With this brief taken from the ILE the *BILE* proclaimed its non-confessional nature and independence from parti-pris, whether in the area of belief, education or politics. Declaring itself neutral in its intellectual orientation, by this limitation it set out to be broad and open in coverage, an openness that was explicitly oriented towards the world beyond Spain.

When we look at the *BILE* in the early decades of the twentieth century, its activity is nothing if not serious, and we can track some of the intellectual orientation of the ILE, and some of its assumptions about its readership. In 1904, for example, it is clear not only that its educational antennae are directed firmly towards Germany, but that it has expectations that some at least of its readers will be able to access German material directly. Thus in the summary of 'Revistas pedagógicas' for June 1904 (*BILE* 28: 531) three out of the four reviews covered are German. The summary translates the titles of the reviews, which are *Die Deutsche Schule* (German Schools) of Berlin, *Die Kinderfehler* of Langensalza and the *Monatschrift fur das Turnwesen* (Gymnastics Monthly) of Berlin, and gives a summary of their contents in Spanish. The implication is that some readers will feel encouraged by the titles to go ahead and work their way through the German originals. The other detail signalled by these journals (the fourth of which is the *Educational Review* of New York) is the degree to which ideas on education at this date were imbricated with concerns about hygiene, child development, normality (or the lack of it), psychology and the body. By contrast with this section, however, the 'Revista de revistas' of this number of the *BILE* includes five from France (*Revue Bleue*, *La Renaissance Latine*, *La Revue*, *La Grande Revue*), one from Italy, the *Nuova Antologia*, and the English reviews *Strand* and *The Critic*. Although the titles of these publications might suggest concerns that were predominantly of a literary or artistic nature, there is a clear sociological interest that drives the selection, one that encompasses both hygiene and sociology.

Ten years later, in the number of 30 June 1914 (two days after the assassination of the Archduke Ferdinand that would set the events of the First World War in train), the summary of pedagogical journals has disappeared. Meanwhile the Francophile tendency of the 'Revista de revistas' is still in evidence, and Domingo Barnés's summary of the *Revue Internationale de l'Enseignement* not only taps French sources, but uses a French gateway to further sources.

England is not absent from the horizons of the *BILE*, but it is far from prominent (with the exception of the awareness of Herbert Spencer, whose death in 1903 was no doubt responsible for some focus upon him in 1904). Emphases unsurprisingly reflect the background of contributors. Thus, for example, Manuel García Morente, who despite his initial immersion in the French educational system was frequently a channel for importations from Germany through his activity as a translator, has a focus that is primarily German in his article on 'La universidad' on 30 June 1914. The list of educational systems he refers to includes Germany, France, Italy and Belgium, but not England. His article, the transcription of a lecture he had given in the Ateneo in Madrid (yet one more sign of subsidiary channels of dissemination of material interacting with one another) demonstrates with clarity his careful, even conservative approach. As he launches into initial detail on the faculties in a German university (theology, jurisprudence, medicine and philosophy) his emphasis is on conditions that encourage an attentive attitude to learning.

Another decade further on, and the 'Libros recibidos' section in June 1924 continues to demonstrate the educationalist's interest in the psychological and the psychiatric that was evident in 1904. This evidences continuation of interest through Primo de Rivera's dictatorship, despite the type of censorship that would be embodied in the clumsy and tardy closure of the *Primeras jornadas eugénicas españolas* (Sinclair 2007: 54–5). But beyond this, the impression of the *BILE* in this snapshot of the Primo years is one of a reduction in its outgoing nature.

The profile of the *Boletín del Instituto de Reformas Sociales* (*BIRS*) is sharp in focus, arguably more so than that of the *BILE*. Linked to the Institute named in the title that was set up by royal decree on 23 April 1903, *BIRS*, a younger, less established review, when compared with the *BILE*, is still in the flush of its first enthusiasm in 1904. Its priority is the condition of the working man, and its mission described in its first number (in 'Al lector' 1904 1:1, 1–2) is to

> *preparar la legislación del trabajo* en su más amplio sentido, *responder a las consultas de los Ministerios* con que se halla inmediatamente relacionado, y a *todas las demandas atendibles,* y *cuidar de la ejecución de las leyes del trabajo.* (emphasis as in original)

A fundamental role in this is to gain and propagate knowledge about labour laws in other countries. Appearing monthly, *BIRS* would supply a stunning level of information about labour law, labour conditions, with work on sociology, economics, education, and it communicates a strong sense of information emanating from the immediate 'central' (France, Germany, Italy) countries of Europe, and of Spain's active interrelationship with these countries in this area.

Given what would be the strife-laden profile of labour relations in Spain in the early decades of the twentieth century, it is striking that the Instituto de Reformas Sociales was created by the Ministerio de la Gobernación. This opened the way for Spain to be in contact with labour law and practice elsewhere, strengthening its understanding and appreciation of advances made abroad. It was planned that there would be two sections for the journal, national and international, and that they would cover the activities of the Institute itself, aspects of the labour market, production and economics, strikes and unemployment and the means of dealing with them through arbitration, an overview of social conditions affecting workers, legislation and an extensive coverage of conditions and procedures from other countries. In its organization there was a decided intent to combine workers and bosses, with Largo Caballero representing the former (and being part of the section on socio-economic relations) and Eduardo Dato the latter (along with José Zulueta). Largo Caballero and the criminologist Rafael Salillas were members of the organizing committee (Consejo Dirección) (see further details in *Foro de Seguridad Social*, March 2004, http://www.foross.org/revista11/a08.php).

Using the same ten-year sampling as with the *BILE*, what is striking is the shift in balance of the sources of information. In 1904 there is a distinct, even an overwhelming preference for French sources (habitually about 50 per cent), including a notable number of German and other sources that are made available through translation into French. The conclusion to be drawn here seems obvious: what has driven the selection is a strong pragmatic feel for accessibility through the French language. In July 1904, furthermore, the three works selected for review (rather than simply for listing) are in French: Paul Louis, *L'ouvrier devant l'Etat. Histoire comparée des lois du Travail* (Paris: Alcan, 1904), Daniel Massé, *Législation sur Travail et Lois ouvrières, Classification, Commentaire, Jurisprudence, Legislation comparée, Projets et propositions e lois* (Paris: Berger-Levrault, 1904) and Charles Gide, *Les Sociétés coopératives de consommation* (Paris: Colin, 1904). 'Europe' as experienced in these pages is mainline: France, England, Italy and Germany, with occasional references to countries further east.

The profile of the bibliography in *BIRS* changes radically by and during 1914. The system of the journal has also changed, now supplying not only titles that are recommended, but information about books available through the library of the Instituto de Reformas Sociales, listing book requests and loans. This information is logged according to the subject matter of the books, so that it is possible to track through the period the shifts in the perceived importance of different disciplines. The level of detail in this section is such that it provides the base for in-depth and detailed study of Spain's understanding of social and industrial issues in the period, and an appreciation of the social accessibility of ideas in this field.

The period sampled includes the weeks in the run up to the First World War, so that, as with the *BILE*, we can see a shift of views after war has been declared, specifically through the foreign journals that have been consulted. In July 1914 nine German reviews are cited (comparing with seventeen from Spain and Latin America, eight from France, five from England and two from Italy), and each of these has a varying number of articles listed as of interest. By September 1914, however, German reviews have disappeared entirely and the number of Spanish and Latin American references has ballooned. Interestingly, in October 1914 German references are back, and of ten items cited, eight are on the war. These are the exception rather than the rule, the only other articles commenting on the way coming from English publications. It is also clear from the data of September 1914 that if German reviews have been momentarily side-lined in that number, there are still five German books that have been acquired by the library (with implications that there were readers using the Institute who could read German).

What is also noticeable about *BIRS* by 1914 is a distinctly international flavour, despite the effect of the war on some of the items, so that as the months go by there is some emphasis on Spanish-language sources, but not to the exclusion of others. Information by this date in the section 'Crónica del extranjero' is arranged according to topic (such as strikes or reports from international conferences) rather than according to country: Spain has, despite its otherwise clear isolation and/or neutrality in relation to the war, become European.

The details available from 1914 relating to the activity of the library suggest a steady application (by the populace at large, or at least the populace that frequented the Instituto) in the process of self-education. Here the regular section of 'Servicio bibliográfico' allows us to track trends and visualize enthusiasms (or needs). It is also possible to compare the profile of books served in the reading room and books loaned (that is the culture of public consumption, or perhaps consultation, as opposed to the culture of private reading which, arguably, might have been on a more systematic basis, compared with the *ad hoc* likely character of consultation in the reading room). Top of the list of books consulted in July 1914 were social science (58) and law (102), proportions altered in the books loaned to social science (62) and law (43). A local observation that one could make (or perhaps it should be considered as a speculation) is that reading increases in the winter months, a phenomenon that would link to the greater prevalence of reading in the countries of northern Europe when compared with those of the south. Thus by November 1914, social science consultations were steady at 58, while those of law rose to 145, and loans in law rose to 71, with social science steady at 64. Overall consultations in this month were 372; a month later they stood at 601, with social science reaching 115 and law 219, a rise reflected but not replicated in the loans. That this might have been a seasonal (winter) trend is, however, disconfirmed by the data of April 1915 which list consultations at 721 and loans at 267.

In April 1924 the number of books served in the library has increased by more than double (1,371) with law at 657 clearly outstripping social science (79). But in May 1924, in a move that mirrors the drawing-in of the *BILE*, the number of foreign reviews referred to has gone down. A further indication of the influence of Primo's regime is the reference in May 1924 to a 'Sección de anormalidades en la vida del trabajo: estadística de las huelgas Marzo de 1924' by which strikes have been deemed to be 'abnormalities'. June 1924 sees the last number of this journal, which we can assume to have been under pressure by the regime. Its mission to provide international information to its readers has not been challenged to the point of extinction, but its burgeoning activity evident in 1914 has by this date been noticeably curtailed.

The examples of the *BILE* and *BIRS* provide a significant corrective to the elitist impressions that we glean from *RO* and *Residencia*. Here are two clearly professional journals, directed towards specific audiences, contrasting with the catholic (but elitist and intellectual) outreach of the other two discussed. What they indicate is that there is a much broader field of intellectual exchange that needs to be taken on board if we are to look at the extent of Spain's contacts with Europe. We neglect at our peril a real and effective area of exchange that exists at the level of both the professional and the ordinary. The existence of professionally oriented journals in Spain has been a significant feature of its periodic publications from the early nineteenth century, and the degree to which these publications facilitated a real experience of European contact is one to which – in the interests not only of simple cover, but an understanding of a real depth and vitality of outreach and contact – we need to pay attention. The international networks that such journals facilitated (here exemplified in the key fields of education and social legislation) provide us with a view of 'ordinary' trading of knowledge and establishment of contacts.

To cite a minor but telling example, taken not from the field of periodic publications but from conference activity, we can turn to official international contacts between Spain and elsewhere. The papers held at the Archivos de Administración General (AGA) in Alcalá de Henares include documentation relating to international conferences to which Spain was entitled to send delegates. The records for the years 1928–30 (the final years of the dictatorship) make generally dispiriting reading. The international conference of Orientalists held in Oxford in 1928, is a case in point. Here we can track the long sequence of enquiries, couched in careful diplomatic terms of politeness, about whether the authorities in Spain are able to inform the conference organizers about a potential delegate (none was forthcoming, after seven months of exchanges). Similar problems were presented by an international horticultural conference in London in 1930. But by contrast, the fourth conference of poultry-breeders held in London in July 1930, was a lively affair, well organized, and apparently a success (see AGA 54/14077 for all of these). Contact between one country and another does not always have to be at the level of elites and power-wielders. For a country to feel really involved in the international flow of information and networking, participation at the level of the ordinary and everyday, by specialists meeting with their fellow specialists, is fundamental as a process not simply of dissemination of knowledge, but for an experience of interests in common that unite despite national boundaries. In a number of ways it could be regarded as distinct from the activities built largely on national imaginaries that concern us in the next two chapters.

CULTURAL IMAGINARIES AND SPECIAL ATTACHMENTS

5   Spain's Love-affair with England

What does it signify to be an anglophile? More specifically, what did it signify to be an anglophile in Spain in the early twentieth century? Some pointers to the significance of England for Spain in this period have been given. What Collini has to say on the nature and functioning of the intellectual, as discussed in Chapter 1, is relevant here, given that he envisages the intellectual as having a 'qualifying performance' that subsequently endows him with authority to pronounce on topics outside his field (Collini 2006: 52–6). This apparent championing of amateurism, in contradistinction to the concept of authority, which might be conveyed in academic systems where a more acute sense of hierarchy obtains than in the English one, suggests a number of key skills that might be valued. Simplifying Spain's love-affair with England, we could posit it as consisting in an identification with individuality. Of the key skills valued one is the prioritization of mind or judgement over simple knowledge (in terms of the possession of facts, or of a corpus of knowledge). Another is the implied belief in the need to go beyond the capacity of the intellectual to pronounce on that which is not, strictly speaking, always within his original narrow academic or professional field. That is, it entails a sense that there could be a similar capacity in those who receive such pronouncements and to judge them accordingly, a capacity to understand, to make their own and thence to move on their own intellectual track.

It will have come to the reader's notice that, contrary to current usage, my reference in this book is to England and not to the United Kingdom, or Britain. This is simply because in the early twentieth century 'England' is the point of reference for Spain, not some more subtle political understanding of the unit of the UK. This is despite the fact that the events that would lead to the Irish independence in 1922 (and to which the sixty-four articles published in *El Sol* by Ricardo Baeza between 1920 and 1922 bore eloquent witness) did not pass unnoticed in Spain. Notwithstanding this the term 'England' is what habitually stands in discussions of cross-Europe comparison, most specifically in contrast to France and Germany, such as those of Maeztu (1916), Madariaga (1928 [reprint 1980]; 1931) and Ortega (1930). References of those who write on Spain in relation to other countries in Europe are without exception to what is English rather than British.

As indicated in the title to this chapter, the dominant strain in Spain's vision of England is to do with the individual, and with templates of belief (or more predominantly of behaviour) that are based on a sense of the individual. Having a vision of a type of individual provides at the national level (but consistently expressed in terms of the individual) a model for identification. Thus a recurrent emphasis in the writings of Spaniards who draw on and promote the English experience as useful for Spain is on the idea of personhood, habitually associated with wholeness. This is perceived with regularity in the writings on educational topics (which encompass the bulk, if not the whole, of the material to be considered in this chapter). The question therefore is habitually that of how one is to form the man (and less explicitly, but not excluded entirely, the woman). In the wake of a Nietzschean search for the superman, as articulated in *Thus Spake Zarathustra* (1883), the model of the English all-rounder is frequently to be seen as what must have seemed an attractive and more manageable aspiration. But, consonant with the idea of choice and judgement implied in Collini's concept of the intellectual (based largely but not exclusively on the evidence of the intellectual in England), there is also the idea of being one's own person. This person, it is implied, is formed through choice, rather than by some submission to authority, and would be the result of natural decisions. Recognition of some given elements of history might be necessary, but in the anglophile model there is usually implied a high level of confidence in the ability to develop, and to be nurtured in personhood by means that might be indirect rather than direct.

This search for the 'person' was sketched out by Costa in 1898, and although he did so without specific reference to England, the terms of reference he used recur in multiple depictions of England via the Spanish imaginary of these years. Costa declared, as part of his campaign for a Spain that would be better (and better connected) that certain things were needed from education:

> Lo que España necesita y debe pedir a la escuela no es precisamente hombres 'que sepan leer y escribir': lo que necesita son 'hombres'; y el formarlos requiere educar el cuerpo tanto como el espíritu, y tanto o más que el entendimiento, la voluntad. La conciencia del deber, el espíritu de iniciativa, la confianza en sí mismo, la individualidad, el carácter; y, juntamente con esto, la restauración del organismo corporal, tan decaído por causa del desaseo, del exceso de trabajo y la insuficiencia de alimentación; tal debe ser, en aquello que corresponde a sus medios, el objetivo de la escuela nueva. (Costa 1981: 25)

This chapter takes as its focus some of the range and some of the curious limitations of Spain's contact with England, and most specifically on what concerned the view of the individual. But the title, 'Spain's (selective) Love-affair with England', is intended to signal the important element of the imagination, or indeed, the imaginary in that relationship. There are real events and sites of cultural contact: visits, letters, translations of books, real reporting from foreign correspondents such as Ramiro de Maeztu and Ricardo Baeza. But many of these events and sites of contact, I would argue, are coloured from or before the start, by concepts of the other nation, ideals and projections. Furthermore, the process of reception is one that involves self-definition, and the definition of the other, with subtle re-adjustments to both. As noted in Chapter 3, Benedict Anderson (1983) has accustomed us to think of 'imagined communities', constructed thanks to the print culture. These 'imagined communities' include the community of the receiving nation, and the community of the 'exporting' nation, as well as the community of the Other that is produced by individual groups and institutions. In addition, the imagined communities of the Other are significant in the creation of the self-image of the receiving nation, and hence the peculiar and indeed charismatic quality of the 'exporting' nation. The export is characteristically not promoted by the nature of the exporter, but rather represents a desired import from a set of specifications in the mind of the importer.

The English in Spain

Most of the emphasis in this chapter will be on the field of education, where there was serious and intentional importation. But some preliminary consideration of other contacts between Spain and England would be in order to set the scene of factors contributing to Spain's view of England (which might or might not be considered to be identical with Spain's view of the English).

The experience that some Spaniards at least of the twenty-first century have of the English will come from specific sources such as football crowds, charter-flight golfers taking refuge in English enclaves on the coast, stag and hen party trips to the capital. They may be considered typical within certain parameters, but perhaps not to be entirely typical of the country at large, and certainly not of its culture understood in broad terms. We could speculate that in similar manner there was variation resulting from the partial nature of contacts that derived from earlier English visitors to Spain.

Almost perversely, the experience Spaniards had of the English through those who came to visit could be expected to be atypical of the norm. Visitors who came to observe and proselytize (or sometimes to take refuge from that very Englishness that was felt to be the national characteristic) would necessarily come to populate Spain's idealistic imaginary of the country, yet might not be considered to be characteristic of those who resided in the nation producing the visitors. Of these travellers, among the most famous were

Richard Ford, whose *Handbook for Travellers in Spain* appeared in 1845, and George Borrow, whose *Bible in Spain* had come out two years earlier in 1843. Both of these writers documented what they saw, with an emphasis on the colourful, the marginal and the picaresque. Given that the full title of Borrow's work was *The Bible in Spain, or, the Journeys, Adventures and Imprisonments of an Englishman, in an Attempt to Circulate the Scriptures in the Peninsula*, it seems likely that his experience, and that of those who came into contact with him, might not have been entirely run of the mill. One of their lesser-known predecessors was Joseph Townsend, who travelled to Spain in the late eighteenth century and produced in 1791 a three-volume work describing his findings, *A Journey through Spain in the Years 1786 and 1787; with Particular Attention to the Agriculture, Manufactures, Commerce, Population, Taxes, and Revenue of that Country*. For Spaniards in the early twentieth century the fact that Borrow and Ford were still emblematic of a particular type of Englishman is confirmed by the date of the first translations of their works into English. Manuel Azaña translated *The Bible in Spain* into Spanish in 1921, and Enrique de Mesa in the following year translated Ford's *Handbook* (having translated Gautier's *Voyage en Espagne* in 1920, first published in French in 1883).

We can only speculate about the impression of England conveyed to the local population by these early travellers. The predominant impression given of Spain in these writings (as they would be in Gautier's *Voyage en Espagne* of 1883) is of a country that is primitive, being a land of gypsies and tricksters. The result is that Spain in such writings becomes a primitive Other for the civilized European (English) visitors. But, reversing the lens of observation, we might surmise that those who came to inspect Spain or to look at its anthropological and other curiosities were in all likeliness themselves viewed as oddities. If they were to provide the basis for the Spanish imaginary of England, their contribution was going to be an eccentric one.

But there was of course an English presence in Spain consisting not just of visitors. Pockets of industrial settlers were to be found through the nineteenth century in Bilbao, Barcelona, and in Cádiz and Jerez in the South. Such settlements had their influence on local social arrangements, so that in Bilbao there was the club of the Sociedad Bilbaína, which had a room, the Gibraltar Room, used as the meeting place for British industrialists and expatriates in Bilbao. In addition, in order to give emphasis to the English nature of the settlement, the football team was named the Athletic Club, rather than the Atlético (Grayson 2001: 32). The details of the settlements associated with the Rio Tinto mines in Huelva in 1873 are striking. Here we find in the late nineteenth century and the early years of the twentieth century 'La Colonia Inglesa', a separate settlement for the British community, which operated much as the Indian Raj. Cultural markers for this group present a virtual caricature of English life abroad, including the cult of Santa Claus, the non-operation of the British-built railway line to Huelva on Queen Victoria's birthday (an occasion that was also commemorated by an egg-and-spoon race), croquet, amateur dramatics and a Ladies Only afternoon tea party in the clubhouse on Wednesdays (Grayson 2001: 47).

Among other notable visitors to Spain in the early twentieth century we find members of the Bloomsbury group. The visits of Virginia Woolf, first in 1905, then on her honeymoon in 1912, and then on an extraordinary visit to Gerald Brenan at Yegen, with Lytton Strachey and Carrington in 1923, occasioned writing from her that was remarkably in the mould of Ford and Borrow. Her account of the difficulties in finding an inn, recounted in an article of 1905, suggests quite sadly the degree to which she appeared to participate in an English inability to cope with foreign languages (Morris 1993: 192–6). An even less probable visit would be that of Lytton Strachey. As Michael Holroyd summarizes, all ills befell him:

> The ruthless Spanish cuisine, with its emphasis on potato omelets, dried cod, and unrefined olive oil, played havoc with his delicate digestive system; he caught Spanish influenza; he nearly trod on a Spanish snake; he mislaid his pyjamas; he injured his knee and announced that he was liable to faint at any moment, though requiring no assistance to recover; and at all times he refused absolutely to exchange a word with any of the natives. (Holroyd 1971: 793)

Brenan, by contrast, had gone to Spain in 1919, in a manner akin to that of Laurie Lee: sleeping rough, making out as best he could (Brenan 1957, 1974; Gathorne-Hardy 1992: 141). Brenan clearly found Spain extraordinary, wondering in relation to the villages he saw about what 'strange mode of life went on there' (Brenan 1950). Nonetheless he clearly acclimatized in a way that others of his generation failed to, becoming part of the community in Churriana where he and his wife Gamel eventually settled.

If these visitors were considered to be 'English' then a fair degree of eccentricity must have been part of the qualifying features. Woolf is in general remembered not for her presence as a visitor, but rather – and perhaps predictably – for her position in modernist experimental writing, as celebrated and noted (as was Strachey also) by Marichalar (1928, 1929) in the *Revista de Occidente*. In addition Strachey would be the vehicle for a further promotion of Englishness in his three-part account of the life of General Gordon in 1928, also published in the *Revista de Occidente*.

But central Bloomsbury visitors were not the only ones. An early visitor who fared and evidently acclimatized rather better than Virginia Woolf was Havelock Ellis. The essays that constituted Ellis's volume *The Soul of Spain* (1908) appeared in serialized form in the review *La España Moderna* between April 1908 and December 1909, an arrangement put in motion by Unamuno as soon as the book came out. Unamuno also arranged at this point for the book to be translated (Davies 2000: 85). This vision of Spain presented by an outsider has its counterpart in Brenan's two authoritative works, *The Literature of the Spanish People* (1951) and *The Spanish Labyrinth* (1943).

Finally, if some of these rather eccentric English visitors conveyed special features of Englishness to Spain, their effect was arguably compounded rather than tempered by the activities of the Comité Hispano-Inglés, active in the Residencia as discussed in Chapter 4. Here Trend and other hispano-phile academic visitors might have been observed to present some contrast with those who were involved in the CHI. In the latter the particular nature of what was 'English' was defined by the nature of representatives who moved in diplomatic or high-level international circles. By contrast Trend and his companions would support more experimental contacts. The archive of the correspondence between Trend and E J Dent (Archives of King's College, Dent papers, and University Library MSS Add 7973/T), currently studied by Karen Arrandale, illustrates this at various points. Enthusiastic about Falla and full of reserve about Salazar (who would be a regular contributor to the *Revista de Occidente* between 1924 and 1929, and who was music critic of *El Sol*), Trend would distinguish on 11 October 1922 between music that would 'frighten' Fox Strangways but which Einstein would love. Salazar he was critical of for his judgements on English music, and he told Dent on 27 October 1919 that Salazar had met all the wrong people in London, convinced that Goossens was the 'only modern British composer of any importance' and that Vaughan Williams was 'quite out of the "main line" of English music'. Salazar had – to counteract this – the good sense, in Trend's view, to support Falla (see also Knighton 2009 forthcoming). Arguably, and taking the members of the Comité Hispano-Inglés as a case in point, there are heightened oddities of national character that may be perceived in those who live abroad and who, on a regular basis, need to communicate their national character and ethos to the receiving country. Specifically, when we look at this in the context of the discussion of the Spanish imaginary relating to the English, the CHI provides ample evidence for some of the wilder generalizations about the English, eccentricity and the value of the strong and active physical being.

The CHI can be understood most simply a way of the English helping the Residencia, and the archive at the Palacio de Liria in Madrid of the Duques de Alba shows its aims and intentions. The CHI's activity strengthened the cultural provision already made by the Sociedad de Cursos y Conferencias (SCC) whose aim was to bring the best of European culture to Spain. The SCC's speakers for 1928–9, for example, included Ferenczi and Mme Jean Victor Hugo (to speak on film and show *Joan of Arc*). It intended to bring, for that year, Princesa Bibesco, Paul Morand, Jean Cocteau, Jean Giraudoux, Abbé Brémond, the Duc de Broglie, Fabry and Scherrer, and considered that they were almost bound to accept the invitations. In addition it hoped to bring the Copeau theatre to Madrid, or to put on an exhibition of contemporary Spanish painters living abroad, and to have show of modern dance, and to put on a concert of original works by Falla. What is noticeable, even surprising, in all this, is an absence of English names: the SCC was presenting a Europe not as seen by Giner and his disciples and contacts, but by a body that, as shown in Chapter 4, was largely aristocratic.

The English contribution meanwhile, coming from the CHI, and as documented in the Liria archive, planned the following for 1923–4: Howard Carter on Egyptology, Bernard Shaw on literature, Reginald McKenna on finance, Robert Cecil and Lord Balfour on politics, and Rudyard Kipling on literature. In June 1925, the committee speaks of inviting speakers liable to be best known in Spain, and who would attract the attention of the public, naming Wells, Kipling and Bernard Shaw. The fallback position was 'perhaps' to invite John Galsworthy or Lytton Strachey. After this last name there is an 'etc', the reach of which provides fuel for the imagination.

The emphasis of the CHI, however, was not on literature. It had a clear practical aspect (contrasting in this with the SCC), shown in its intention to invite the chief engineer of the Ghezira dam (because of the interest for Spain in hydraulic engineering), and politicians such as Churchill (who wrote in December 1934 that he was unable to come because of the weight of work concerning the India bill). Keynes and Eddington were successfully invited for 1929. The views of the committee were summarized in a letter from the Duque de Alba dated 21 June 1935 to Colonel Bridges (from whom Alba was clearly hoping to gain financial support for the CHI). He tells Bridges how the committee has organized lectures by 'British men of letters, scientists or explorers of international repute'. Yet an examination of the letters of invitation and the penned notes and thoughts about invitations show there was a strong feeling that what was appropriate was entertainment and spectacle, and that some large proportion should relate to English colonial activity. Lord Zetland was approached. What he offered in 1929 was a slide-show of Sikhim, the Chumbi Valley and Bhutan, although he thought he could alternatively produce something that would be useful background on India (something that might have been of more interest to the British than, one would have thought, the Spanish audience of the Residencia). In similar vein is the note about the idea of inviting a Dr Christy, former governor of Uganda and Somaliland, and author of a book on *Big Game and Pygmies*, to speak on pygmies and the gorillas of Kivu. Arnold Lunn, who could have been expected to report on his 1932 famous exchange of letters with Haldane on *Science and the Supernatural*, in fact offered something rather more tame to the CHI. He wrote on 13 April 1936, saying he was enclosing the substance of his lecture and that he was still trying to get slides of the Olympic Games. 'One way or another about a third of the slides will be of racing events, and about two-thirds of scenery and ski-mountaineering. I think this is about the right proportion, don't you?' In this manner, virtually verging on parody, the CHI did much to confirm the image, or indeed the imaginary the Spanish had of the English, or the British, as a race of explorers and sportsmen. Presumably all other values were meant to follow.

Spaniards in England

Bohemian and modernist writers visiting Spain were not, however, the only or the main source for concepts of Englishness. To a large degree they were formulated and fostered through investigations into educational developments, as will be shown in the latter part of this chapter. In this area of activity we find thoughts that resonate with more general writings by Spaniards on Europe, and its constituent countries. Such writings indicate how – according to the Hispanic imaginary – there were grounds for believing that there was a basis for a special relationship between Spain and England that was founded on fundamental areas of likeness in national character.

A prime source of ideas about what constituted Englishness was bound to come from those Spaniards who went and took up residence in England, and reported back on their experience. They contributed not necessarily so much to an imaginary about the English as to the belief that this was a country with which ordinary lived relations were possible. We might remember in connexion with this that the whole period 1900 to 1931 is marked by the voluntary presence elsewhere in Europe of Spaniards who were frustrated by the development (or lack of it) in Spanish intellectual, academic and political life. They can be viewed as seeking a voluntary personal exile, one reflected in numerous novels by Pío Baroja, notably *Ciudad de la niebla* (1909), which celebrated London as a centre of fog, free-thinking and anarchy (see Murphy 2002; Alberich 1966). Significant clusters of Spaniards would form in London, as well as in key locations in Germany (Leipzig, Marburg, Berlin, Dresden), and in Paris. They included those who translated for major publishing houses, and hence became a source for reporting back on local culture. During the Republic there was a significant increase in Spaniards abroad, not prompted by exile but deriving from the participation of notable numbers of intellectuals in politics in the Republic that they were called to serve through their appointment to a number of international posts. Their links with other countries, via the ambassadorial network, would prove invaluable during and after the Civil War when many sought refuge in other countries and would need local support.

Of the early settlers in London one of the most significant was Ramiro de Maeztu, whose younger sister María would head the Residencia de Señoritas, founded in 1915 (see Zulueta and Moreno 1993). Maeztu was the first

Spaniard to become an English correspondent for a Madrid-based paper, and, according to Madariaga (another famous interpreter of English culture to Spain and vice-versa) was the interpreter to Spain of English reaction to Spain's disaster of 1898 (the loss of Cuba).

Maeztu set a trend for other Spanish correspondents to be based in London. The point that Madariaga makes is that this was preferable to the alternative form of correspondent, who previously would have been based in Paris. The complication, as Madariaga saw it, was that if the Paris-based correspondents were to give Spaniards a vision of the rest of the world, as perceived from Paris, the disadvantage was that it had passed through a sort of 'proceso de simplificación al que todas las cosas complejas e irracionales han de some-terse en la mente de Francia para transformarse en ideas claras, sencillas, racionales y universales a la francesa' (Madariaga 1931: 60). Madariaga himself would be an interpreter of Spain to the English, a fact evidenced by his book *España* of 1931 being commissioned by an English publisher, and published first in English. The consequences of having a world view communicated through Parisian eyes was, according to Maeztu, the basis for a feeling of inferiority among Spaniards, a feeling that Spain was a sort of France that had not quite turned out as God intended. The significance, then, of Maeztu becoming a correspondent in London was that – according to Madariaga – he was reporting from a different base, and that whereas according to Madariaga France had the tendency to see Paris as the centre of the world, London had interests that were too vast and complex for this to happen. In addition, he added, the 'English spirit' was not 'geometric and abstract, but empirical and organic' (Madariaga 1931: 61).

While he was in London Maeztu did more than report back to Spain. He wrote on a fortnightly basis for *New Age*, the review edited by Orage during 1908–22 (see Passerini 1999: 107–11). Maeztu published in *New Age* from January 1915, beginning significantly, with an article on 'England and Germany: Two Types of Culture'. He went on to publish some sixty-nine articles, being a key contributor in the years 1915–16, and continuing partially through 1917–20. In his first article of 1915, Maeztu is curiously fixated on the concept of the English gentleman, something that – in divers ways – also nuances the view of the English held by other Spaniards of the period. The idea of the gentleman in this article centres on behaviour, style, and a sense of disengagement from the material world (an area of interest and activity that Maeztu, conveniently and simplistically, associates with the Germans). The keynotes of the English gentleman, according to this article, are to do with restraint, willpower, self-awareness and awareness of others. The image Maeztu conveys is one of containment, in which there is mastery over the body and mastery over the actions. If Maeztu writes with some evident approval here, it is because of the self-control that he sees as central. His understanding therefore of the aim of the person who teaches boys in a public school is not that he should impart knowledge, but educate the person. This model was frequently taken by Spaniards at this time to indicate what was English, and assumed to be capable of being extended to all classes. Speaking of the master in a public school, Maeztu asserts:

> What concerns him in the first place is that his pupils shall be clean, healthy, energetic, truthful, incapable of betraying their comrades or of lying, respectful towards others and self-respecting. Everything else – whether these boys are to be good mathematicians or good linguists or good technicians – is an entirely secondary matter. (Maeztu 1915: 303)

At the same time we might note that in 1902 in 'Cómo muere un super-hombre' Maeztu had valued the potential for feeling within the English as a key factor: he asks (rhetorically?)

> ¿No es posible que la superioridad anglosajona dependa únicamente de la mayor ternura de sus poetas, de la mayor filantropía de sus clases ricas y de la mayor religiosidad de su población? (Maeztu 1902; see Fox 1977: 33)

It is of course unclear what his source was for believing in the greater religious attitude of the English, but this was a judgement that preceded his residence there, and is an example of the sort of projection that could be engaged in. It is also in this pre-residence period that he wrote his four articles on anarchism in *El Imparcial* (November-December 1901), in which he attributed the success of anarchism in some countries, and the lack of it in others, to relate specifically to the level of culture in that country, so that England, Germany and Scandinavia, with their higher rates of literacy, were less prone to it (Maeztu 1901; see Fox 1977: 190). This takes no account of the phenomenon that Baroja was to observe – and replicate in his novels – namely that England, because of its relatively stable nature, would become the home to numerous exiled anarchists.

Maeztu's intentions at this period are progressive, and repeatedly take the form of a simple belief that things could be made better. *Hacia otra España* (1899), with its diatribes against a superfluity of lawyers in Spain (their presence only serving to make litigation more likely, especially in rural areas), also strongly recommended the virtues of agricultural colleges. Such places would supply an education that would be more *useful* in Spain than academic and abstract programmes of learning. Maeztu was listed on 29 January 1915 as one of the contributors to the progressive review *España* (at a date exactly coincident with his article on England and Germany in *New Age*, noted above). He thus forms part of a front line of intellectual reaction against a Spain perceived to be old and 'podrida': his name sits alongside Ortega, Baroja, Pérez de Ayala, Eugenio d'Ors and Gregorio Martínez

Sierra. The specific nature of his activity in this publication is not obvious, but through 1915 *España* brought out a series of 'Figuras contemporáneas'. Although they are all published anonymously, it would be unsurprising to find Maeztu had penned many, if not all. The names of the English (and Irish) singled out here come in the category of being the usual suspects: they are part of what would be the circuit of the Residencia and *El Sol*, and include H G Wells, Chesterton, and – in the arena of politics – Lloyd George, Keir Hardie, Winston Churchill and Lord Kitchener. The choice of Churchill at this date is interesting, both for the early recognition of his significance, but also for the qualities noted as positive:

> Ha sido el niño mimado del moderno liberalismo inglés. Representa espléndidamente a una raza de hombres que un día supieron conquistar el mundo; un día ya lejano. Es intrépido, esforzado, aventurero, caballeroso, deportista y noble por nacimiento.

All of these features fit with the qualities of the English that are embodied in the choices of travellers and adventurers (as well as military men) to speak at the Residencia de Estudiantes. But the reservation made is a striking one. Churchill is noted as being an excellent orator (a quality for which he would be celebrated and valued in the Second World War), but it is also commented that because of this he has sometimes been considered in England to be light-weight. Showiness does not fit in with those attributes of the English to be valued when viewed from abroad.

This example of the real presence of Maeztu in London, and Madariaga's commentary upon the significance of his residence there, encapsulate essential elements in the Spanish relationship with England. There was indeed a grounded basis for their perceptions of Englishness. At the same time, as Madariaga's comments reveal, perceptions of other nations, and indeed of one's own, were the subject of much interest and speculation: the writing of national identities was a major pastime in this pre-Civil War period, and Spain and England are no exception (at least in Spanish writing).

Madariaga produced schematic and reductive comparisons between the English, the French and the Spanish (Germany for some reason being completely out of the discussion). In three essays published originally in 1928, 'Carácter y destino en Europa' (repr. 1980), what he associates with the English is the idea of 'fairplay', and consequently of action (contrasting with the French concern for 'le droit' and the Spanish concern for honour) (Madariaga 1980: 19–20). As with Maeztu, Madariaga's imaginary about the English turns upon a relationship with the body and control through exercise of the will. It is an individually centred relationship with the self and its consequences, and one that contrasts with what he sees as a French adherence to a sense of system and of the law. The Englishman is also perceived as one who is above all empirical, practical, only given to thinking if there is an immediate use for it. His sense of hierarchy derives from who happens to be useful; his sense of structure from what makes sense at the time: thus his 'organización espontánea es libre, instintiva, vital, omnipotente, natural simultánea con la acción, no escrita' (Madariaga 1980: 35, 42).

Madariaga's set of contrasts is highly schematized and is worryingly reminiscent of the philosophical method of Entrambosmares in Unamuno's *Amor y pedagogía* of 1902. But under the contrasts we can see how there is a basis being sketched for the possibilities of identification between Spaniards and the English. The former are characterized by passion and the latter by action, but insofar as both of them are integrally formed by these attributes (rather than by adherence to a code of law or behaviour), Madariaga is presumably positing a fundamental level of affinity between them. Thus the individualistic and passionate character of the Spaniard (as celebrated by the generation of 1898) is here transformed into a new version in which individual will and judgement, valued in the English, are glimpsed as what might be core principles for the Spaniard also. In a disarming generalization made in his *Bosquejo de Europa* (1951, repr. 1980: 307), Madariaga concludes that the three most intelligent nations of Europe are France, Germany and Italy, and that the most mad are England, Russia and Spain (a feeling of affinity to be borne out further in Chapter 6).

A different angle on the English is offered by Julio Álvarez del Vayo, a man who would eventually be one of Spain's prime foreign correspondents, reporting from London, Paris and Moscow. In his autobiography, *The Last Optimist*, he is acute in his depiction of the attractions that foreign places held for him. In the case of Russia, this would be via his reading of *Anna Karenina*. When Álvarez del Vayo thought about London, it was as a place of mystery and excitement, its allure intensified by the veil of fog. In many ways, it is a figuring of England, and specifically London, that has continued to be projected by Spanish television, in the much favoured re-runs of Victorian mysteries, and tales of terror. Álvarez del Vayo saw London thus:

> I saw it from afar, wrapped in a mysterious fog that covered outbursts of passion, artificially repressed by the cult of good form; or protecting, as they walked along the banks of the Thames, men with pinched faces and fiery looks born of all earth's injustices, who were plotting to avenge their comrades and preparing for the greatest social upheaval of all times.
>
> (Álvarez del Vayo 1950: 37)

This anticipation of London (echoed in Baroja's *Ciudad de la Niebla*) was, however, also balanced by Álvarez del Vayo's real experience. Funded by the JAE for study in London, he went to the London School of Economics, where he encountered Beatrice Webb who, with her husband Sidney, was central to

the activities of the Fabian Society (originally founded 1884). Álvarez del
Vayo produced two reports, one on the National Insurance Act (1912), and a
summary of his study of economics in England (1913) (see the *Archivo de la
Secretaría de la Junta para Ampliación de Estudios (1907–1939): Cuadro de
Clasificación*, held in the library of the Residencia de Estudiantes).

Álvarez del Vayo was clearly much impressed by the Webbs, and a chance
remark demonstrates the gaps in the English culture that would reach Spain.
Beatrice Webb, he says, objected to the plays of Bernard Shaw, and to Gran-
ville Barker, saying of the latter that he 'brought to the stage not a true
presentation of a solid English middle class, but the artificial creations of his
own erotic unease' (Álvarez del Vayo 1950: 42). Granville Barker would form
a part of the strange selection of English literature brought to the Residencia
de Estudiantes by Walter Starkie in his lectures given on 22 and 23 December
1924, and published in *Residencia* – a demonstration of the eccentricities of
cultural export that can occur (Starkie 1926).

A point made by Álvarez del Vayo about the Spaniards in London in those
early years is that they were not like those intellectuals who would flee from
fascism in the Civil War. Rather they were

> voluntary refugees who fled from the mediocrity of the Spanish universities
> and were trying to advance their education by foreign study. Most had gone
> to Germany and France; only a few had come to England. They were jour-
> nalists, writers, and artists who desired to renew our old Spanish culture,
> which had been disconnected from the world by the reactionary isolation
> of the monarchy and still more isolationist attitude of the Catholic Church.
> (Álvarez del Vayo 1950: 47–8)

In retrospect his observations can be applied to others commented on in this
chapter.

As a final note in this section, we can return briefly to the exceptional
example of Baeza, product of Spain but example of a fully Europeanized
Spaniard, and whose view of England both complements and contrasts with
that of others mentioned in this chapter. Although little recorded in canonical accounts of Spain in these years, Ricardo Baeza (1890–1956) can be
regarded as a one-man centre of exchange. An energetic translator, dealing
with several languages, he was a major channel for works by Wilde, Shaw,
Shakespeare, Somerset Maugham, Galsworthy, Eugene O'Neill, Graham
Greene, Conrad, Thornton Wilder, H G Wells and Malinowski, while also
being the vehicle for Gabriele d'Annunzio and Pirandello, and for the work
by Ibsen (translated from English), Dostoiewski and Merezhkowski (translated from Russian) and from German, the work of Hebbel and numerous
biographies by Emil Ludwig. Between 1920 and 1928 he would produce over
280 articles for *El Sol*, of which some sixty dealt with Ireland, and sixteen of

which were the fruits of his stay in Dublin that enabled him to write first hand about the political troubles there. Many of the *El Sol* articles confirm Baeza not just as a cultural bridge, but as one concerned to understand and interpret politics. His writings on Ireland form a part of this, as do his impassioned articles about famine in Russia based on his visit to Russia in 1922 (some seventy-five of his articles deal with Russia, and include perceptive writing on canonical Russian literature).

Baeza's wide translation experience, and his mastery of prime European languages, make him a reference point that is both exceptional and yet symptomatic of the range of cultural contact and exchange that was possible in this period. In addition to this, his personal library in Montblanc further testifies to his catholic and energetic cultural activity and curiosity. The library is clearly that of a modern humanist, in which one could read widely on history, philosophy, literature. The divers languages we can associate with Baeza through his translations are well represented, both in the original and in translation. It also illustrates, through the reviews taken (*Nouvelle Revue Française*, *Sur*, *Revue de deux mondes*, *The English Review*, *The London Mercury*, *The Gramophone*) and encyclopaedias (of Buddhism, music, Islam), the sheer breadth of Baeza's interests.

Within this rich context, it would be misleading to say that England and the English were central to Baeza's imaginary. But some profile of his interests can be inferred from the authors he chose to translate. These include specifically Wilde and Wells, but also show his interest in mythology (the library contains – not surprisingly in the light of the exchange of letters with Ortega noted in Chapter 3 – a complete set of Frazer's *Golden Bough*). His library also has no fewer than twelve works by Havelock Ellis, contrasting with a mere two by Freud, including the *Introduction to Psychoanalysis*, a French edition of 1922, two by Jung and a Spanish translation by Azaña of 1930 of Bertrand Russell's *Vieja y nueva moral sexual*. The presence of Ellis and Russell exemplify an interest that is further displayed in Baeza's possession of contemporary Spanish psychology, psychiatry and work specifically having a bearing on sexuality. Thus for Baeza, England arguably represented (as it would for Hildegart Rodríguez) that place where explorations of the variations of sexual life and practice might be found (see Sinclair 2007: 8–13). But Baeza is also remarkable for the fact that in his journalism written from London, he is keen to report back and inform on current affairs in England (the miners' strike in May 1921, on Churchill's foreign policy in April 1921, on the new Parliament in Ulster in June 1921, on the English reception of Dante in September 1921). Baeza operates as an international and as a European, rather than a Spaniard out to make contact with pre-selected aspects of Englishness.

Education and the quest for Englishness

There were, however, other ways in which Spaniards ventured abroad, and this goes hand in hand with developments in education. There was the sustained and dramatic programme of liberal educational reform stemming from the setting up of the ILE in 1876, followed by other educational institutions, including the Residencia de Estudiantes in 1910 (with the Residencia de Señoritas in 1915) and the Instituto-Escuela in 1918 (Zulueta 1988, 1992; Zulueta and Moreno 1993). Central to the project of reform were two ideas: one, that education needed to be released from a deadening strait-jacket of curriculum, and a framework of examination that did little, if anything, to develop the mind and interests of the student; the other, that if Spain was to advance in this area, it needed to learn from abroad. It was believed by some that Spain had specific things to learn from England, less tangible than practical, although there was an interest in the structures and mechanics of English educational systems, not just in aspirations and implicit or explicit values. And while education can be considered to be a singularly practical field in which to traffic knowledge it also provides us with an example of how educated imaginaries and cultural desires came to operate.

Giner de los Ríos is the lynch-pin in fostering Spain's cultural love-affair with England in the early twentieth century. Whereas Sanz del Río had led the way in encouraging study abroad for Spaniards in the second half of the nineteenth century, Giner, as the *abuelo* (grandfather) of the reformers of the 1920s and 1930s, had been decisive in his early years. When he and Cossío attended an international conference on education in London in 1884 they were proud to be able to present it as an example of progressive education.

It was through Giner that José Castillejo became the mainstay of the JAE, building on what was already a strong mentoring relationship. Castillejo's wife is the source of an apocryphal story about Giner and Castillejo. According to her biography of her husband, *I Married a Stranger*, Giner was directive and imperious, and Castillejo compliant. But the story reveals some of Giner's beliefs. She recounts that Giner reproached Castillejo for having come top in his university law examinations, saying, 'I daresay you will get over it, but you will never lose the scar,' and then 'If you had not bothered to study so thoroughly the set books for the examinations you might have been quite well read and known something by now.' He then asked him if he knew French, and being told that Castillejo only had school French told him to go and learn it and then see him again. After six months, when Castillejo returned, saying that he could read and speak French fluently, he was then told to do the same with German, and complied (Claremont de Castillejo 1967: 72–3).

The version of Castillejo's travels that can be gleaned from his correspondence (D Castillejo 1997, 1998, 1999) is not quite so rapid. But there was clearly direction being given by Giner. In particular Giner believed in the necessary complementarity of education in Germany and education in England. You had to go to Germany to train as a scientist, but then go to England, which was 'para el hombre' (letter to Castillejo, 21 October 1903; D Castillejo 1997: 192). When Castillejo writes to his father from Berlin on 13 March 1904, this is what he lays before him: clearly for his studies he needs to remain in Germany, but

> En cambio para mi *educación* como hombre y para mi aptitud social y mi conocimiento del estado moderno de los problemas me conviene visitar Inglaterra. Además D. Francisco considera éste indispensable y espero sus instrucciones. (D Castillejo 1997: 206)

Giner reiterates this advice, adding a gloss about being a gentleman: England was for making a man, but, he added, it could be for making a gentleman, a term that resonates with Maeztu's concern noted earlier. For Giner being a gentleman is fundamental in England, and his additional comment on Germany recalls the generalizations of Maeztu in his 1915 article cited above: 'allí hasta el zapatero quiere ser *gentleman*, y así el hombre y el *gentleman* casi vienen a ser lo mismo. Inglaterra es un gran contrapeso a Alemania' (D Castillejo 1997: 208).

The mention of the *gentleman* is a recurrent pivot of interest within the Spanish imaginary of England. Much of what Giner has to say in matters of education can be couched in terms of humanist development, and certainly his admiration was for an educational framework that allowed for a holistic emergence of the individual. But of course where he was to find this idea in England at least was not in education at large, but in the elite education offered by the public schools and by Oxbridge. It comes as no surprise that Giner goes on to advise Castillejo to visit schools of all varieties, then Eton, and then the universities of Oxford and Cambridge. We should, however, note Giner's grasp of the breadth of educational practice in England, which comes with his recommendation to look also at Manchester as an example of the 'other sort' (letter of 30 April 1904; D Castillejo 1997: 215). Later, in a swings and roundabouts pattern of influence, we find a mention in a letter from Trend to Dent on 3 December 1919 of his attempts to persuade Spaniards 'who think Leeds the only English university which is really up to date', that there were other options.

Castillejo took Giner seriously. Although he had spent long periods in France and Germany (mainline Europe), from the start he took Giner's direction as a personal and paternal mandate, almost a mission. In the background to this, one might mention also Castillejo's relation to his own father. In his early correspondence, his father is the main receptor of Castillejo's observations. From 1896 on, when he is in Madrid studying, he sends a detailed account of his doings, both within the university and without. The letters convey a number of things. One, that Castillejo is being given a privileged education, and it is one not extended to his three sisters. Second, that he does not write to them, or if he does so, the letters are framed to take into account their anticipated field of reception. As his son David points out, he will also send pedagogical details to Giner and domestic news to his family (D Castillejo 1997: 229). This will be particularly marked after the death of his father in 1905. The early letters also reveal Giner's influence. From a letter to his father on 22 January 1901, we learn of what happened when he went to see Giner about his thesis. The advice he received from Giner in relation to the activity he should pursue outside his work is revealing about Giner's ideas and values. If Castillejo did not spend Sundays in the country and an hour and a half walking each day, said Giner, they would cease to be friends (D Castillejo 1997: 61). The emphasis is on physical activity, regulation or regularity of habits, and the force of patronage; friendly, firm, and outside the strict bounds of the educational, Giner is an all-round mentor to the manner born. But it could also be construed, from what Castillejo will later say about English education, as syntonic with Giner's approval of English educational practice, mirrored by what he offers at the ILE.

In his first journey to Europe (a form of tour being even for a Spaniard a part of a young man's education), Castillejo is clearly carrying out some sort of instruction to look into education. It is striking that, although his formal studies were in law, all his foreign visits include the study of educational establishments, and this becomes intensified over the years so that they come to form his main motivation in life. His later holding of a university post in law seems to be the least of his concerns: a slight irony here. Thus in Zurich, in August 1902, he visited a considerable number of educational institutions, including the *Pestalozzianum* (D Castillejo 1997: 107).

The publication where Castillejo presents a résumé of his views on the English is an extraordinarily detailed volume on English education, *La educación en Inglaterra* (1919). It is the fruit of many contacts and – by this date – numerous visits. What he has to say reveals a mixture of considerable practical experience and observation. But at the same time, it is possible to view it as guided by a *vision*, even an *imaginary vision*. Thus England may have been perceived for what it was, but it was also, arguably, perceived as or for what it represented.

The introduction to Castillejo's volume sets its context by commenting on England in relation to the First World War. In terms of specialist technical and professional training, the country had not been well prepared, and the education Castillejo describes is one that is recognizably, even bordering on the form of a caricature, that of the public schools:

> Sus mejores escuelas seguían siendo las de preparación general; sus bachi-
> lleres aprendían poco y jugaban mucho; sus más famosas universidades
> conservaban el Griego y el Latín en el dintel de todas las carreras y dedi-
> caban su principal esfuerzo a producir mozos robustos, alegres, elegantes,
> tibiamente oreados al calor de las literaturas clásicas y de lecturas bíblicas.
> (J Castillejo 1919: xii–xiii)

But the point he goes on to make is crucial, namely that what England offered
Spain at this point was a success story. Having faced Germany, a technologi-
cally advanced and superior nation, it had nonetheless won. The background
to this is Spain's feeling of inferiority, something on which Madariaga had
commented in relation to Maeztu, as noted earlier. In the period before the
war, comments Castillejo,

> No se creía a Inglaterra solamente pueblo de ignorantes, sino nación
> corrompida, inclinada al snobismo y la molicie, dominadora de pueblos
> salvajes, explotadora de regiones vírgenes cultivadas con brazos esclavos
> o mercenarios, país de traficantes y banqueros sin conciencia, amantes de
> la paz en que medran, débiles, asustadizos e inexpertos ante una situación
> de fuerza. (J Castillejo 1919: xviii)

The usefulness of England as an example for a Spain that had lost its
remnants of empire in 1898, and felt backward in cultural and professional
stakes, was clearly appealing. We might also notice how far Castillejo is
building on traditional views about the Spanish nature, views that Giner and
others were keen to combat. But the point is that the mention of snobbery
and 'molicie' (being soft or pampered) sets up a model for identification, in
that they have Hispanic counterparts in the sense of honour, and the tradition
that the noble do not work. This is embodied most famously in *La vida de
Lazarillo de Tormes* of the sixteenth century, in the figure of the starving
nobleman. It will be re-cycled ten years later by Madariaga in his characterization of the Spaniards as a race of passion, but also – curiously – possessed
of a type of passivity. What Madariaga argues is that the passive character
of the Spaniard, one that makes him open to the flow of life, is complementary to that of the Englishman, who is always ready to put his personal
activity into life. In fact, he concludes, the attraction of the Englishman for
the Spaniard is based on a capacity for anarchism. Because of his sense of
discipline, he regards the Englishman as one who has been successful in a
sort of embodiment of anarchism:

> El español admira en el inglés la disciplina personal, libremente impuesta;
> precisamente por libre y espontánea, cosa que agrada sobremanera al
> español, siempre anarquista, pues se da cuenta de que el inglés, precisa-
> mente por su disciplina, es el anarquista perfecto. (Madariaga 1929: 288)

Presumably it was thought that there were lessons to be learned here.

Similarly one could make a link between what Castillejo observes about the English downplaying of emotions, and the way in which the generation of 1898 had proclaimed 'stoicism' to be a fundamental feature, even a virtue, of the Spaniard.

> La serenidad con que el inglés se despide de sus hijos, que van a la guerra o envía a luchar con las enfermedades y los peligros en las colonias; la tranquilidad con que ve venir la muerte, tienen quizá equivalente único en las imágenes que nos han transmitido las estelas griegas.
>
> (J Castillejo 1919: 10)

Indeed, Castillejo could be virtually quoting from Unamuno when he talks of the effect of climate on character. That of England influences its inhabitants, offering little scope for the imagination, so that he is thrown back on himself:

> de modo que el espíritu se reconcentra, se hace fuerte dentro de sí mismo y se nutre de su propia substancia; es más subjetivo y personal; suple lo que le falta de sensaciones exteriores con el ejercicio de la facultad más íntima: la voluntad, que desata sus fuerzas hacia la acción y goza dominando y moldeando el mundo. (J Castillejo 1919: 11)

England came out of the war successfully, says Castillejo, and while it realized that it had a backlog to make up in terms of technical preparation of its citizens, its 'human' education still showed its values. Indeed, the English had been vindicated in this experience of war, and their example demonstrated how far one could be influenced by their upbringing. Here Castillejo reverts again to the concept of the *formación* of the gentleman, a formation of the *person* rather than an accumulation of different aspects of factual knowledge:

> una formación ampliamente humana, donde es factor esencial el cultivo, afinamiento, ejercicio, flexibilidad y sensibilidad de todas las potencias, espirituales y corporales, mucho más que el contenido concreto y tabulable de los conocimientos, los procesos y las artes. (J Castillejo 1919: xx)

And in relation to knowledge, Castillejo's belief was that what should be at stake was still the person, and their senses. His comments here reflect the philosophy and practice of the ILE, would be central to the ideas of Steiner and Montessori, and still act as a keynote for progressive education. What matters in education is the act of giving 'a la percepción de los objetos más importancia que al recuerdo de los nombres' so that the aim of the educator was to promote 'el interés del educando hacia las cosas que estudia' (J Castillejo 1919: 66).

Clearly in these comments there was a primacy given not just to the idea of the individual, but to the values of the healthy body. The ideal of *mens sana in corpore sano*, associated with the English in the examples given above, was one that struck the imagination of progressive Spanish educationalists. Exemplified in Giner's advice about exercise, it would be taken up in the excursions of the ILE and those of the Residencia de Estudiantes, an institution that by the 1920s was clearly into sporting activities as can be seen from the significant space they occupied in their publication *Residencia*. The English were thus praised (by Castillejo, and Madariaga) for being robust, and for making their bodies intentionally so by rude exercise and privation. Clearly the example here was more that of Brenan with his heroic marches across the wilds of Spain rather than that of the delicacy and fussiness of a Virginia Woolf or a Lytton Strachey. But it also needs to be seen in the more general context of a European concern with degeneration. Spain fully shared in this concern, which found its way into a promotion of eugenics, public hygiene and concern with race (see Pick 1989; Cleminson 2000, 2003; Álvarez Peláez 1988; Nash 1992; Nordau 1892; Bernaldo de Quirós and Llanas de Aguilaniedo 1901). A central issue would be how to hold on to masculinity (not doing so, according to Nordau, would be a sign of degeneration). This gives local point to Castillejo's generalizations on the positive elements of the English and their principles on education: 'ante el horror de bordear un afeminamiento de la raza, prefiere cultivar una cierta rudeza' (J Castillejo 1919: 6).

Two further features of what Castillejo sees as the basis for English education are significant. He values what he (or conceivably Giner) would like Spain to possess: the capacity to abstain from rules and regulation, and the cultivation of an elite. This coupling (J Castillejo 1919: Chapter 2) is one that relates as much to the Spanish situation as to the English one. Castillejo comments on the degree of internal freedom in English education, and notes that many schools have a room where the pupils can do what they like, something that he sees as related to the project of self-realization (D Castillejo 1997: 54). But also, with implications for comparing Spanish education with that of England, he observes that there is remarkable freedom from government control. The result is that the syllabus and structure of universities and schools differ not only from region to region, and town to town, but institution to institution (D Castillejo 1997: 263).

A comment that Castillejo makes about the nature of family life also has a bearing on his ideals in relation to institutions. There is the value given to the world of the child (for this one should also read, perhaps, the world of the independent institution): kept away from adult society, the child gains freedom from conflict that might be experienced prematurely. But yet more apposite is Castillejo's comment (1919: 29) on the element of respect between parents and children. It is this that enables the child to realize that he receives the respect he deserves, and also to know how much respect he owes to others. When we read this in the context of evidence throughout Castillejo's correspondence of the gross and unpredictable interference of government with education, his idea of mutual respect can be construed as one that is as vital to him at an institutional level as it is at a personal one.

One of the noticeable features of this selective love-affair that Spain has with English life and culture is its concept of education as led by Eton and Oxbridge, that is, education for a small number and with an extraordinary level of both intensity and personal freedom. In a sense this concentration is obvious, in that the leading progressive movement in Spanish education is a private one, both at the level of school, where the ILE leads the field, and in university education, where we have the brainchild of the ILE, the Residencia de Estudiantes. But we might feel that there is an odd mismatch between this cultivation of elites in restricted locations and a concept of education that is liberal in virtually all possible meanings of the word. It would be clear for Madariaga (1929: 117) that this restricted range of English institutions produces the leaders of the nation. Later, Ortega y Gasset, one of the younger members of this generation, would outline in *Rebelión de las masas* and *La misión de la universidad* a concept of elite that was individual, in his concept of the minority man as 'el que se exige mucho a sí mismo' (Ortega 1930: 181). Clearly the meaning that those of the ILE had in their creation of elites, one echoed by Ortega, was that only if you have able leaders could you lead the rest of the population to prosperity and safety. An example of the degree to which the Residencia would act on this was the Misiones Pedagógicas, an endeavour of cultural outreach that had roots back in the journeys of philological research by Menéndez Pidal (D Castillejo 1998: 191–2). In addition there was Castillejo's ingenious plan of July 1912 in response to the uncertain success of taking parties of Spanish primary-school teachers to France. The participants on these visits did not seem to derive clear cultural benefit from them, and Castillejo suggested that perhaps they could be sent inland. As David Castillejo glosses the conversation between Castillejo and Luis Santullano, who had taken the previous trips, and on which Castillejo reported to Giner in a letter of 24 July 1912:

> Las excursiones de maestros y obreros por países extranjeros se podían convertir en lo contrario: equipos itinerantes que viajarían por España educando a la gente de los pueblos. Aunque no tuvieran nada que ver, conscientemente, una cosa con otra, es una curiosa casualidad que inmediatamente después de organizar tres grupos – de obreros, maestros y extranjeros – se les ocurriera algo parecido para España.
>
> (D Castillejo 1998: 734)

A detail so obvious in the discussion thus far that it might be overlooked is that in the consideration of education all the references have been to the education of men. This is scarcely surprising, and yet this generation of Spanish educational reformers was acutely sensitive to the different condition and education of women in other countries. The number of men produced by the ILE and its offshoots and who then went on to marry women who were not Spanish is truly remarkable (see Labanyi 2010 forthcoming), and the phenomenon is suggestive of their sense of the limitations in a rapidly changing world of the education offered to women in Spain.

Castillejo, who would eventually marry Irene Claremont, serves as an interesting example here. Writing to his father from Berlin on 23 March 1903, he revealed some of his preferences in relation to women. The German woman, unlike the French (who he perceives as full of artifice), is 'naturalmente buena madre, es naturalmente chica honesta y es también con la mayor naturalidad y frescura, sin rodeos ni disfraces' (D Castillejo 1997: 143). A Spanish girl, by contrast, was characterized by her ignorance: he commented that one could speak of nothing sensible to her. The following year he mentioned, writing from his summer visit to England, his pleasure at seeing English youth at sport, and significantly mentions the girls, who appear to be able to go about the activity without fear of flirtatious approaches from boys (D Castillejo 1997: 269). The implied reservations about Spanish education (whether social or formal) and its effects would appear to be about pretension, possibly *lo cursi*, and a cultivated ignorance coupled with social hyper-awareness that could not fail to complicate and distort social relationships.

In 1910 Castillejo appears to have decided to act upon his beliefs about what might be educationally desirable for women by taking his younger sister Mariana to England. His intention, evident from his letters to Giner, was somehow – against all the odds – to convert her into a feminine counterpart of himself, as the student he had been, who had travelled and been fascinated by other countries and their educational institutions. But the letters relating to Mariana, while they bear testimony to Castillejo's *beliefs* about what England could offer to women, make devastating reading. This is not so much for the failure of the experiment as for Castillejo's blindness to his sister's nature and her difficulties. In relation to Mariana he shows himself to be an able and committed administrator, but one who cannot enter into her skin. He looks over her shoulder, and (literally) corrects the letters she writes to her sisters (D Castillejo 1998: 228). He is frustrated by her social shyness, and her concentration on the immediate (and often, for her, difficult) relations with those about her.

There is something verging on the autistic in Castillejo's dealings with Mariana. Conceivably this could be because she typifies for him the uneducated and culturally hopeless style of woman he had commented on when writing from Berlin in 1903. Typically, after she had spent some unhappy months in Cambridge, and transferred to a much more congenial family in

Windermere he wrote to her on 9 December 1910: 'Creo que irás tomando ya confianza y libertad con esa familia y charlando con ellas, si has curado un poco tu mutismo habitual. – Dependerá de cómo estés de salud. ¿Sigues mejor?' (D Castillejo 1998: 405). His comment on her 'mutismo habitual' blunders into her private world: no sense of family respect here.

Castillejo hoped to transform Mariana into something else. What was his model? In Spanish terms, clearly someone like María de Maeztu was the sort of woman he hoped for. María de Maeztu, for instance, would write from Marburg, on 15 March 1913, full of enthusiasm about voluntary attendance at class in Germany. She wants to be a co-worker in the educational enterprise.

> Tenemos que empujar entre todos, con todas las fuerzas de nuestro espíritu esa obra de enviar gente a Europa, para humanizarla. Es increíble lo que se gana y se aprende. Y después hay que laborar, ahí, ahí, para que este trabajo no se pierda. Hacer labor de Seminario fuera de la Universidad, y sin que los jóvenes – hombres y mujeres – que allí acudan vayan *por* y *sólo por* el título, sino por el placer de los placeres de aprender a pensar.
>
> (D Castillejo 1999: 28)

But there is also Castillejo's vision of the Englishwoman. It appears to consist of two elements, equally interesting, and equally belonging to a specific type of imaginary. One is of a delicate, floating creature (shades of Virginia Woolf?), and the other is of a natural, quite physical and hearty being. The latter was exemplified by his wife-to-be. In 1917 he would write to his family on 17 August of the delights of plunging at 8 am into a pool of water at 16°, in the middle of rain and wind, with three girls of the Claremont family, one of whom was Irene (D Castillejo 1999: 363).

By 1921 he had formed an attachment to Irene, and now conceivably, when writing of Englishwomen, was guided in his writing by his love, but seeming to opt for the ethereal rather than the hearty model. He writes to his sisters on 19 December 1921, and the 'tipo de mujer' he describes is a delicate visual image of the new woman of modernity:

> Este nuevo tipo de mujer es un ser etéreo. Come unos granos de semilla, unas galletas o una manzana y, en una vuelta al estado primitivo, ha reducido el traje a un símbolo: cuatro cintas que se adivinan cruzando el cuerpo en el interior y un par de cintas y una écharpe al exterior, quedando el cuerpo tenuemente velado como tras un vapor coloreado de marrón o de verde claro. Cientos de estos seres flotan por calles y praderas sobre un fondo terso, limpio, pulimentado, de asfalto o de yerba, se encaraman en ómnibus y tranvías, invaden teatros y museos, y cuando se cansan de bailar y correr van a posarse en el rincón de un hogar y encienden una conver-

> sación humorística que chispea de vez en cuando bajo la capa grisácea de
> los tópicos indiferentes. (D Castillejo 1999: 497)

Clearly Irene presented the right combination of culture, wit, physicality and
yet a certain delicacy. Their marriage in 1922 would last until his death in
exile in 1945.

6 Spain's Love-affair with Russia

In this chapter I shall examine a second case of identification and desire. In a cultural love-affair located largely in the imaginary, Russia constituted a masculine Other, a desired and exotic brother for Spain, while its revolution provided the possibility of a realistic engagement with a different culture. But there was a further gendered dimension. The imaginary that concerned England and Englishness had had its primary focus on the concept of the gentleman, the amateur or the eccentric (with only brief excursions into feminine aspects of the cultural imaginary). The imaginary that concerns Russia is one that also involves the feminine, and specifically we find the figuring of Russia as the exotic woman. In addition to this, in travel writings on Russia, despite periodic attempts to figure women as individuals, non-essentialized and newly formulated in their post-revolutionary situation, we find that there is also a myth of woman as flesh and groundedness, a creature that is the repository of positive experience.

The relationship of Spain to Russia in this context can be considered as the attraction of exotic br/Others. There are two facets to the discussion: there is a desire on the part of Spain desire for identification (with Russia) that involves becoming a particular type of subject, and there is desire which is for an object. There are a further two areas of interest, in that Russia is variously regarded by Spain as an object of political interest or as one of artistic significance. In both cases, a structure of desire, in the two forms of identification and possession, can be perceived. This chapter will not concentrate on Spanish political visitors to Russia, discussed by the excellent article of Gómez (2002), since my emphasis is on cultural imaginaries, but the political dimension was clearly a major factor in Spain's broad perception of Russia.

The period that is most relevant to the functioning of this double cultural imaginary runs from before the Russian Revolution until the middle years of the Second Republic in Spain. That it went beyond is evidenced by the phenomenon of the children of Republicans being sent to Russia to escape the Civil War, an act of desperate idealism that was eloquent about the sense of a brotherhood with the other margin of Europe.

Inevitably political event has a bearing on the materials produced in relation to Spain's cultural imaginary of Russia. As elsewhere in Europe the 1917 revolution in Russia prompted live interest in Spain (Fernández Cifuentes 1982: 149–55). Consequent upon it, for those who were observers committed to socialism or communism, was a vision of the new State as one that would be capable of embodying a whole series of political ideals. This political focus on Russia from within Spain continued through the 1920s, and Spaniards (along with other travellers, like H G Wells) visited Russia to examine the new state for themselves. Then in the 1930s, with the advent of the Second Republic, political interest in Russia flourished anew, with a marked increase in the popularization of literature relating to it. Some of the travel books of the 1920s had already been directed at a wide reading public rather than an elite one. This popularizing trend continued through the 1930s, most noticeably in small pocket publications, novelettes for the proletariat, while journals such as *Leviatán* (1934–6) took up from the travel writers the cause of making Russia known to a more educated reading public.

But there was also a different strand of interest in Russia that ran alongside the wave of writing that took it as a political and social reality to be conveyed to the public at large. At around the time of its revolution Russia was adopted as an icon of high art in Spain, and, as this was gradually elaborated, Russia came to be (paradoxically) conceptualized as primitive and consequently close to Spain. From this point, and then through the 1920s, a significant number of writers took up and promoted the vision of Russia as a primitive Other of Spain. Doing so allowed for an interest in Russia to be based on fantasy, and for notions of Spanishness to rest on concepts of the primitive. Where the two political and artistic/imaginary strands come together is in the degree to which they both presented a vision of Russia that was exotic and eroticized.

In order to discuss this complex double relationship, based largely on national imaginaries, I shall begin with the interest shown in Spain for Russia as a new political state, and will track that interest through the travel writings of the 1920s. I shall then retrace my steps to the dawn of interest in Russia as an artistic icon, and emblem of the primitive, and the elaboration on this primitive identity through the 1920s at the same time as the travel writings were being produced. I shall then look at the way in which a number of writings, even in the liberalized political climate of the Second Republic, continued to propagate the vision of Russia as the primitive, exotic and erotic (br)other of Spain.

As will have become evident by this stage of the book, there is a central ambivalence in Spain in the early twentieth century in relation to other countries. On the one hand there is its urge to become a part of a mainstream Europe consisting of France, Germany, England and Italy, a desire both developed and promoted by progressive educational leaders and supported by the activity of publishing houses and the press. In this desire the concept of mainstream Europe is shared with others. It is curious and significant, however, that England is included, because as Luisa Passerini has observed, England at the period saw itself somewhat on the margins, so that its view in the 1930s was that Europe was 'elsewhere' (Passerini 1999: 10). But while, as she goes on to note, England considered that it 'had a special mission to save Europe from its folly', such equanimity in the face of difference (an equanimity that expressed itself as superiority) was not found in Spain. Indeed, the evidence through all the chapters of this book is of clear desire to join in European activity.

But there was something else, more elusive, more intuitive than intellectual, which consisted in the conviction that life, and certainly inspiration, was elsewhere, an 'elsewhere' that was felt with more passion and less detachment than that British feeling of Europe being elsewhere. Part of this conviction about life being elsewhere is what inspires and underpins the philosophy and activity of the Misiones Pedagógicas through which desolate *pueblos* peopled by underprivileged inhabitants were simultaneously seen as an obvious target of cultural outreach and as the ultimate repository of traditional culture (see Chapter 8). It is within the concept of 'elsewhere' that the relationship with Russia figures. Central to Spain's imagined relations with Russia was the belief that both countries were palpably at the margins of Europe, and that they had much to gain from their commonality.

Ambivalence about Spain's relationship with other countries was not spread evenly throughout the national body. Rather it was the product of the layers and fragmentation of Spanish society, and the degree to which affiliations were bound to investments in class, politics and an urge towards either continuity or discontinuity. What is striking in the case of Russia is that various favoured connotations of the country are to be found in both elite and popular or populist literature. Furthermore, in the early decades of the twentieth century Spain was undeniably involved in a project of nation formation, in which its sense of itself and other nations was in part, but not exclusively, the result of the print culture. The 'imagined community' of self and other thus operated, not least, via the concept of a community of readers who could thus engage in this print culture. This would relate in some degree to the activity of spreading culture and knowledge that is discussed in Chapters 7 and 8.

Spain's cultural love-affair with England is one that I have described as selective, and one that focuses, as it were, on the person of the lover. With its interest in the creation and cultivation of a model of personhood, to a striking degree identified with the character of the English gentleman, its concentration is upon the one that will be the subject, a moving and desiring agent. It is thus a case of one country idealizing and projecting a series of desires upon the culture and identity of another nation, with a view to a state of nationhood that could be achieved.

The love-affair with Russia is characterized by different features, and the model that most suggests itself is that of model of courtly love, a central concept of which is a sense of distance between the lover and the beloved. This is a cultural enthusiasm that borders on an infatuation. The beloved (Russia) moves between being an object of desire and (as in the case of the love-affair with England) a model of a strong subject offering the possibility of identification. The degree of geographical distance involved enhances the possibility of idealization, and simultaneously of the idealizing of the self that is in love with such an ideal. The more distant the country, the more and the greater the projections that can be entertained in relation to it, as shown so compellingly by Said in *Orientalism* (1978). A remarkable combination of resonances would be picked up by Ernesto Giménez Caballero in *Genio de España* associating Russia in general with barbarian Asian hordes ('Rusia si era pueblo un poco *bárbaro*, no era *pequeño*') and singling out Lenin as 'el marxista, Genio de Oriente' (Giménez Caballero 1932: 237, 261).

The memoirs of Álvarez del Vayo provide not only insight into imaginaries concerning England but also an example of the many dimensions of the meaning of Russia for Spain in this period. He writes of a significant interest in his boyhood days, spent in El Escorial. Like many schoolboys, perhaps, he was not most interested in what he was expected to read, but he did have an interest in reading. He recounts:

> If I felt a constant aversion for textbooks, other books soon began to attract me and were, in fact one of the causes of my poor work as a student. One day a copy of Anna Karenina accidentally fell into my hands. It was a Spanish version and, like all the pirated editions of foreign works then published in Spain, undoubtedly translated from the French and badly mutilated; but it had a grand drawing in colour as the frontispiece, showing an alluring woman with large green eyes and body wrapped in pine-marten skins. I went off to enjoy the book in solitude on one of the little hills near El Escorial from which Madrid could be seen in the distance. As I read, I became greatly attracted to Count Vronski, the hero, and I felt as never before the seduction of Madrid, which I had never visited in spite of its nearness; there, I felt sure, must certainly be women like Anna Karenina.
>   (Álvarez del Vayo 1950: 16–17)

Álvarez del Vayo was born in 1891. Although at this point in his autobiography he does not specify his age, he is still at school, so presumably in his teens, and we can thus assume him to be writing in the first decade of the twentieth century. Written in relation to the desires of an impressionable age, but recounted of course in maturity, what does this vignette convey to us? It tells of a clandestine literature of high quality (Tolstoy, no less) that existed alongside official textbooks. It tells of how this foreign novel had entered Spain: a pirated edition translated from the French, a far from unusual practice at the time. The fact that texts did not enter Spain unscathed is indicated in the phrase that it was 'badly mutilated', a mutilation perhaps as much at the hands of the translator as at those of the censor. Anna Karenina is obviously the exotic and alluring woman in the novel of that name. But the illustration Álvarez del Vayo refers to suggests a mixture of the fairy-tale (green eyes for witches, or mermaids), and – in the indication that she is 'wrapped in pine-marten skins' – something between the exotic and decadent (in the style of Sacher-Masoch's *Venus in Furs*), and the primitive. He refers also to his feeling of identification with Vronski, the aristocratic hero, and, curiously, an immediate feeling of being drawn to Madrid. Russia is thus associated with attractiveness, excitement and urban modernity, even though Anna is clothed in pine-marten skins. This primary experience of Russia, effected via its literature, is full of feeling, escape, romanticism. It is the alternative to the humdrum, to required tasks of education, to the boring. It is not yet associated with another range of attractions, those pertaining to the political and, most specifically, to the event of the 1917 revolution that would be exciting for many in Spain (and elsewhere).

Russia, the political icon

If Álvarez del Vayo and others went, funded by the JAE, to Germany, England and France to study, their travels were given a new direction by the Russian revolution of 1917. From the 1920s onwards, a spate of travel literature appeared, and would continue, in varying guises, until the Civil War. It was a reporting back that was fuelled by the desire of the travellers who wanted to see a Russia that had had a revolution. There was clearly an agenda to their visits, based on the supposed relevance of what Russia had done for what might happen in Spain in the future. That is, the visits were undertaken not just for information but because the revolution was thought of as providing an object lesson (at least), or encouragement (at most). Here, as elsewhere, there is the significance of the 'imagined community'. Travellers were going to see whether what they imagined tallied with the social and political reality (Gómez 2002).

Some of the reporting back took place in the daily press. Through 1920, for example, there was extensive writing on Russia by Nicolás Tasín, one of the prime translators for the publishing house Biblioteca Nueva. His pieces appeared in *El Sol*, frequently on page one, and at times twice a week. Five articles by H G Wells on 'Rusia en las tinieblas' appeared in *El Sol* in October and November of 1920, in positions of prominence, two of them occupying a whole page. Newspaper coverage did not end here. Between 1920 and 1929 no fewer than seventy-seven articles by Ricardo Baeza appeared in *El Sol* that touched on Russia in some manner. Particularly noteworthy are the articles of 1922 where he reported on the famine in Russia. Even in these pieces of strong and compassionate writing, where Baeza urged that some official action should be taken by Spain, we find him articulating what would be a leitmotiv in the Spanish view of Russia. Thus he claimed that Spain had a particular reason to offer aid, that of its 'brotherhood' with Russia:

> de todos los pueblos de Europa, el más afín a Rusia, el de una subscons-ciencia más pareja, el más capacitado para entenderla y compartir sus ideales, es, sin duda, España. Insertada entre Europa y Africa, como Rusia entre Europa y Asia, ni España ni Rusia son naciones enteramente occi-dentales. Esta semejanza radical nos lleva con frecuencia a soñar una cierta hermandad de destinos ... (Baeza 1922: 5)

One of the first travel books published was that of Fernando de los Ríos, *Mi viaje a la Rusia soviética* (1921), a volume that ran into a second edition in 1922, with numerous subsequent reprints. Also well known was the work of Ángel Pestaña, who had visited Russia for the creation of the third inter-national (presided over by Zinoviev), and who wrote *70 días en Rusia*, of 1924 (a work that is more critique than travelogue) and his more formal-sounding *Informe sobre mi estancia en la URSS: documento para la historia obrera* (1968; and see Ruiz-Castillo 1979: 12). A fairly steady drip-feed of works continued through the 1920s, some of the most significant titles being Soriano, *San Lenín. (Viaje a Rusia)*, Paris [1927], Álvarez del Vayo, *La nueva Rusia* (1926), Hidalgo, *Un notario español en Rusia* (1929), Chaves Nogales, *La vuelta a Europa en avión. Un pequeño burgués en la Rusia Roja* (1929), and R Llopis, *Cómo se forja un pueblo. (La Rusia que yo he visto)* (1929). Two things are noteworthy about these titles. First is their emphasis on direct witnessing: they talk about the Russia they have seen: Fernando de los Ríos speaks of 'mi viaje', Pestaña of 'mi estancia', Llopis of the Russia 'que yo he visto'. Secondly, there is their social position. There is some emphasis, at least in the work of Diego Hidalgo and Chaves Nogales, on the fact that they are middle-class visitors. The implication is that they are respectable persons, curious to see how Soviet Russia is faring. On the other hand, not all of the writers are bourgeois in class or affiliation, the example of Pestaña being a case in point, as illustrated in *Lo que aprendí en la vida* (1933), and Llopis, as educationalist, was firmly committed to spreading educational access.

When Spain entered the Republic, the style of publications on Russia did not change in an obvious manner, at least in the area of travel writings. Chaves Nogales, for example, brought out *Lo que ha quedado del imperio de los zares* (1931), written in light and lowbrow style. Somewhat more hope-fully, Díaz-Retg published *En Rusia, la revolución empieza ahora* (1931), as though his hope was that the revolution was beginning not just in Russia, but in Spain also. Personal testimony continued, as with Hoyos Cascón, *El meri-*

diano de Moscú o la Rusia que yo vi (1933), and Zugazagoitia, with *Rusia al día* (1932). And names that have remained as part of the canon – unlike most of those I have cited so far – began to appear. The Peruvian surrealist poet César Vallejo brought out *Rusia en 1931: reflexiones al pie del Kremlin*, and Ramón Sender, known now for his novels, published *Madrid-Moscú. Carta de Moscú sobre el amor (a una muchacha española)* (1934). All of this was without reckoning on the number of publications pertaining to Russia translated into Spanish. Here the works of Henri Barbusse figured with particular prominence.

The other notable feature of Spanish publications about Russia in the Second Republic (with the exception of the cover in reviews such as *Leviatán*) is the wave of works that appeared in popular novelettes, for example in the series of La novela proletaria in 1932 (see Santonja 2000: 201–38). These novelettes did not, however, concentrate on a representation of the Russia of the 1930s. The revolution had taken place in 1917, but the Russia portrayed by these publications of the 1930s bore a strong resemblance to the Russia whose plight and fate had caused engagement and enthusiasm among workers and intellectuals some fifteen years earlier. That is, while there was a reality of Russia that had captured the imagination (albeit not one directly experienced by many of the writers concerned), it was a reality that had become part of an imagined or imaginary community, fixed in a time-warp. But although there was this strong element of the imaginary in their portrayal of Russia, the nature of these novelettes as medium was avowedly that of committed art. Undistinguished in their form as literary creations, they were of the most basic, with simple plot lines and stereotypical characterization. There was little chance of the political point being missed, let alone of being conveyed with any subtlety.

In a sense these novelettes were responding to a concept of committed art that had been aired in the wake of the 1917 revolution, when social unrest was particularly rife in Spain. In 1920, a number of artists and writers were questioned as to the proper role of art in relation to society. This was formulated in the guise of Tolstoy's two questions from an essay of 1896: 'What is Art?', and 'What should we do?' Famously, Valle-Inclán had answered (in a way that anticipated Ortega's views of 1925) that as soon as art began to have utilitarian or practical intentions, it lost its value: art was a game, and that was what was special. But in answer to the question 'What should we do?' he was clear: 'No debemos hacer arte ahora, porque jugar en los tiempos que corren es inmoral, es una canallada. Hay que logar primero una justicia social' (quoted in Dougherty 1982: 102). With the advent of the Second Republic these questions would be revived, and the example of Russia served as both theme and mediator.

Among the examples of this simple and committed literature is Nazarli's novel, *El traidor* (1932), billed as authentic, a 'novela revolucionaria caucasiana', and which tells a cautionary tale about industrial life in the Caucasus in sentences so short and simple that it could easily serve as a reading primer. Here was art at the service of the people, both edifying and instructing. It is evident that other novelettes were clearly intended simply to communicate excitement and manly ideals. Such is the case of *Nuestra odisea en Villa Cisneros* by Tomás Cano (1932), the advert for which appears at the back of Vivero's novel *A tiro limpio*, and which declares that it will be a 'Colosal folleto, que deben leer todos los proletarios. ¡Viril relato! ¡Prosa vibrante! ¡Descripciones inolvidables!' (but did not appear). In like manner, Pestaña's novel *La caída del dictador* (1932) was referred to as a booklet that would enable the proletariat to be educated about Russia.

Yet not all of these novels were completely naive in their placing of art at the service of politics or people, nor were they all populist alone in their literary references. In another novel in the series La novela proletaria, by José Antonio Balbontín, *Una pedrada a la Virgen* (1932), based on a real event (Santonja 2000: 206), a number of things make the novel not an obvious propaganda tool for an uneducated readership. In this re-telling of the life of the Virgin Mary, Balbontín makes a reference to Gorki. This is of little note, since Gorki was one of the Russians widely translated in Spain and whose work was published at economical prices. His accessible and engaging prose must have made him a natural for this type of publication, so the reference is not one of high culture. The mention of 'una pobre madre – parecida al prototipo de la novela de Gorki' (Balbontín 1932: 13) is one that the intended readership would have understood, although the reference to a prototype suggests a reader with a sufficient level of sophistication to read this on a higher level than that of simply reading for the plot. But in the last pages of the novel a more explicit appeal is made to an implied reader whose level of reading includes aesthetics and not just a political or social message. Balbontín makes an elite reference to Ortega's theory of distance and aesthetics in *La deshumanización del arte* (1925a): referring to Ortega's depiction of a painter looking at a dying man, and his subsequent comments on the relation between distance and detachment of artistic perspective, Balbontín protests, and Tolstoy's views on art re-appear:

> Sentí, una vez más, la repulsa de Tolstoy, la aversión de toda conciencia honrada, frente al arte deshumanizado. Si el arte no sirve para reflejar y embellecer la gran pasión humana, si el arte no siente humanamente los dolores del pueblo, ¿para qué sirve el arte? (Balbontín 1932: 28)

In the context of this novel, within the world of art, Balbontín re-appropriates Russia as a signifier for non-dehumanized art. Art has a commitment to society. The implied context for discussion, however, is one that rises above the level of simple communication with an implied social target. If Russia had the function for Spain of a signifier to denote an art of commitment, a non-dehumanized art, this function was by no means simple.

There were however other novelettes of this type that expected sophistication from their readers. Another contribution to La novela proletaria, *Un periodista* (1932) by Ramón Magre, presupposed a reader sophisticated enough to be familiar with Russian cinema, since his protagonist, who is a journalist, gets into trouble for his review of Eisenstein's *Battleship Potemkin*, and for his reporting of *Ivan the Terrible*, both of them too revolutionary for his editor. This was fresh news, given that Soviet film had been banned under Primo de Rivera, only reaching Spain in 1930 (Gubern 1999: 327), contrasting with a much wider dissemination of other European avant-garde film through Giménez Caballero's Cine-Club and screenings at the Residencia de Estudiantes through the Sociedad de Cursos y Conferencias (Gubern 1999: 260–389 for full information). Meanwhile the Hungarian writer Emil Madarasz, in *La lucha del soldado rojo* (1932), presented a satirical account of men in the Russian navy having difficulty in engaging with the Marxist idea of commodity fetishism, illustrating how the opacity of the language of this theory passes right over the heads of the sailors.

Furthermore, if a level of brotherhood between Spain and Russia was asserted, it was not necessarily put in terms of a proletarian brotherhood. In Rodrigo Soriano's *La bomba* (1932) the concept is of a brotherhood of literary exchange. He is excited at the thought of a combination between the two nations, and alleges that there is a mysterious intuitive link between them. What is striking here is that although *La bomba* appears in the series of La novela proletaria, the literary references for both Spain and Russia are to their respective literary canons. In a flash of Orientalism Soriano configures Spain as the nation that gives (in terms of literary inspiration) to Russia, thereby boosting Spain's sense of its national value:

> No era nueva para mí esta telegrafía misteriosa del español y el ruso porque nuestra historia y la suya son iguales: Norte brumoso, normando o céltico y Mediodía, radiante, morisco y voluptuoso. Galicia y Riga, Córdoba y Odessa, cruz y turbante, media luna y cruz ... Los escritores rusos, tan helados y cirujanos en su parco estilo, tan solo parecen entusiasmarse cuando evocan a España. Pouchkine evoca a Don Juan con la gracia de un sevillano. Gogol, imita a Cervantes en sus 'Almas muertas' y al 'Gran Tacano'. Lope de Vega y su 'Fuente Ovejuna' son más populares en Rusia que en España. Y Dostoyewski, el estilista frigorífico y austero, ante el crimen y el suplicio impasible, pues fue descolgado del patíbulo cuando ya el dogal le ahogaba, interrumpe, algunas veces, sus tristonas y enigmáticas novelas para derramar haces de luz, y diamantes refulgentes, sobre la soñada Alhambra; o entona aquel canto a un Don Juan fantástico, aun más sugestivo que el de Tirso y Zorrilla, en 'Los Hermanos Karamazov'.
>
> (Soriano 1932: 10–11)

As this quotation begins to highlight for us, Russia functioned as far more than a political icon (however complex) for Spain. Distinct from its role as a potential flagship for issues of art and commitment, as outlined above, was Russia's place in elite discussions where art was far from being viewed as an instrument of social and political change. From a time just pre-dating the 1917 Revolution until the Civil War, Russia functioned as both an artistic icon and a container for Spanish imaginary fantasies about primitive national essence.

For a measure of the degree to which Russia was present in Spanish literary culture in this period, we can consult its presence in publications of the time. Espasa Calpe's Colección Universal had some 377 titles, published between 1919 and 1943, of which thirty-eight were translations of Russian texts, representing close to 10 per cent of the total. This compares with 137 titles for French, forty-two for German, fifty-six for English and eighteen for Italian. Because of its size, availability and a price within the reach of all, this collection was arguably more influential in Spain than the various series of foreign works published by the Revista de Occidente. While some names, such as Chekhov, Gogol, Gorki, Goncharov and Dostoiewski, would form part of the traditional Russian canon, the majority of the authors translated are less well-known: Andreiev, Sibiriak, Averchenko, Chemelev, Garin, Sologub, Afanasiev, Bunin and Kuprin. Publishing houses such as Cénit (see Santonja 1989: 39–99) and Biblioteca Nueva were likewise prominent in the publication of Russian texts, taking their lead at times from their translators, particularly Tasín, who combined translation with journalism and networking for publishers (Ruiz-Castillo 1979: 14–16). The archive of the Ruiz-Castillo correspondence in the Biblioteca Nacional attests to the degree to which Tasín was pro-active with Biblioteca Nueva about which texts to translate. In 1916 Luis de Zulueta, a prime mover in the Residencia de Estudiantes, and prominent in educational reform, listed in Ortega's journal *España* his twelve chosen books to provide an introduction to literature. First on his list was the *Odyssey*, and the last was Tolstoy's *Resurrection*. He equated them and differentiated them, saying of the last that it matched the first: 'Éste es clásico, visión luminosa de mares y de verdes costas: aquel es romántico, cristiano, bañado en la claridad de la vida interior' (Zulueta 1916: 4–5).

Despite Zulueta's enthusiasm for Tolstoy, in Spain, as in many other European countries, enthusiasm within the field of the novel shifted from Tolstoy to Dostoiewski. This would take the form, not least, but not solely, of Ortega's championing of Dostoiewski in his 1925 essay *Ideas sobre la novella* (1925b). Here Dostoiewski is praised, as it were, not for giving but for withholding, for requiring the reader to supply the imaginative links, and thus requiring the reader to participate in the activity of reading in a manner that exacts more of him. For Ortega, the Russian novelist is the height of modernity, and thus the nodal point for the regeneration of a genre of writing that is dying on its feet. Or, to exploit further the image of the lover and the beloved, Dostoiewski played the showing and hiding game associated with the elusive beloved (Ortega 1925a: 387–419; 1925b: 353–86; see also Fernández Cifuentes 1982: 299–301).

But Russian art came to Spain in another, more flamboyant way, one that gave rise to some of the more fanciful theorization about the fraternal relationship between the two countries. When the Ballets Russes visited Spain with Diaghilev in 1916–17 the enthusiasm aroused was not simply aesthetic but was related to concepts of national identity. Essentially, Russian music, with its style, presentation and its presumed import in terms of cultural messages, was appropriated into an ongoing debate in Spain about national identity. When what was Russian was praised, it was virtually for not being itself. Thus Calvo Sotelo commented on Russian music put on by Diaghilev, and reclaimed it for Spain: 'La música que ha compuesto Balakirev ... es de escasa consistencia. Legítimamente rusa sí lo es, pero no por su opulencia o aparato, sino por su melodía clara e impecablemente meriodional ... a ratos casi española' (Calvo Sotelo 1916; Hess 2001: 96–100).

Clearly political views entered into the aesthetic judgements offered, and part of the pro-Russian enthusiasm needs to be understood in terms of the First World War, and the issue of which side was to be supported. Spain was not a participant in that war, and although its reaction to the First World War was not absent, it was lower-key than one might expect. What was significant was the dissent between those who supported Germany and those who supported the Allies, and the way in which aesthetic judgements were attached to other generalizations about those involved. Thus if *germanófilos* tended to be on the side of law and order, upper-class industrialists, Carlists, the military, defenders of 'authority' and 'decency', with *aliadófilos* supporting workers, Republicans, regionalist bourgeois (from Catalonia and the Basque country), and liberal intellectuals, aesthetic consequences followed on directly. Hence French composers during and after the war referred to German music as 'bloated and decadent', and there were, by contrast, values deemed to be French, and which encompassed what was 'Latin' or 'Mediterranean', or 'Latin/Slav' (Hess 2001: 43–4). The contrast with what was presumed 'decadent' implied a possession, if not of virility, at least of a clearly defined sexuality. Russia's position in the war, as the country suffering military defeat by Germany early on, would move it towards the position of being favoured by *aliadófilos*, as implied by the Latin/Slav connexion.

The Ballets Russes were only part of Spanish elite enthusiasms in music. In a long-lasting debate about modernity in art (never quite separate from politics), Stravinsky was also – somewhat surprisingly – appropriated to Spanishness via the 'Latin/Slav' concept. During his 1916 visit to Spain (the first of many: he continued to visit through to 1936), Stravinsky's prime supporter was Manuel de Falla, the composer, who had commented on the strong links between Spanish and Russian music (Hess 2001: 161). This concept of a Russian/Hispanic bonding continued: Stravinsky in interviews in 1921 and 1924 in Spain commented on it and suggested that its basis was in common 'Eastern' roots (Hess 2001: 10). It was thought that 'Spaniards, like Russians, created unspoiled, innocent music rich with the essential ingredients of melody and rhythm; as such they shared an enduring wisdom' (Hess 2001: 172).

Independently of this, Falla also promoted the idea of the Eastern roots of Spanish music, and in his collaboration with Lorca in a competition for Cante Jondo this was given full expression. For both Falla and Lorca, the Orient was ancient, and full of values. Lorca's two lectures on the Cante Jondo (1922 and 1931) expressed the belief that Spain shared in such Oriental cultural treasures. He moves almost seamlessly from asserting that in this tradition of Spanish song there are gypsy roots (which come from the Far East, from India), and at the same time something 'ancient' in the Andalusian core of the music. In the case of Falla and Lorca Russia was barely brought into the equation, but their fantasies about Spain's links to the Orient provide evidence that this was a widespread feature of Spain's imaginary concerning its national identity. Thus this area of Spanish culture is one which 'nos une con el Oriente impenetrable' (García Lorca 1922: 1003). Its songs are linked with the 'primitivos sistemas musicales de la India' (which he implies are the 'most primitive' forms of song that exist). The proof of the 'rightness' of the music of the Cante Jondo, an import via the gypsies, who had left India in c.1400, was that it had served as the inspiration for Debussy, Glinka and Rimsky-Korsakov. It had thus inspired the adduced Latin/Slav artistic alliance, or – perhaps more in line with the cultural approach of the music critics – this artistic brotherhood (García Lorca 1922: 1010).

One of the most influential elite organs to promote the idea of Russia as Spain's primitive other or brother was *RO*. Early in the life of the journal, Ortega proposed the idea of an Asiatic Russia, the characteristics of which were recognizable as those attributed to Spain:

> Es curioso que en Rusia ha traslucido siempre una sensibilidad parecida. La religión de Tolstoy no es sino eso. Lo mejor del hombre es lo ínfimo; por esto, entre las clases sociales lo más perfecto, lo más 'evangélico' es el muyik. Sólo es digno de saberse lo que el muyik es capaz de saber. En una novela de Andreiev, el mozo virtuoso se siente avergonzado de serlo ante una prostituta y cree obligado descender hasta su nivel, precisamente para elevarse verdaderamente.
>
> Sin embargo, a esta inversión de la perspectiva en la apreciación de los valores no llega el alma rusa por soberbia, sino merced a una peculiar sensibilidad cósmica y religiosa que revela la filiación asiática del mundo slavo. (Ortega 1923c: 277)

Russian literature revealed an estimation of the humble, and this was arrived at because of a sensibility that – even in Ortega – can be intuited as one as resonant with contemporary myths about the nature of Spain.

In 1926, and again in *RO*, Keyserling, whose work was taken up with some enthusiasm in Spain in this period, observed that both Spain and Russia had specific, if different, contributions to make to Europe. For both countries the contribution was related to their 'primitive' nature: he qualified Spanish primitivism as the representation for Europe of its distant past and Russian primitivism as subhuman and superhuman at the same time:

> España penetra, pues, en la síntesis 'Europa' como representante de lo cósmico primitivo, como representante de lo que era antes de toda historia y seguirá siendo. Y lo hace, digámoslo una vez más, en un sentido fundamentalmente opuesto a Rusia. El primitivismo ruso tiene un carácter francamente *no* humano; es subhumano y superhumano al mismo tiempo.
>
> (Keyserling 1926: 140)

Insofar as Spain conceived of itself and its relations as 'primitive', this was undoubtedly related in part to the nature of the *RO*. Espina articulated the nature of Russia in a way that would necessarily have been understood as having a close relationship to Spain, at least in terms of the Spanish national imaginary. Russia was a country of extremes and mysticism:

> Las reacciones sentimentales del ruso, mezcladas nebulosamente a sus ideas y sus impulsos, las alternativas frecuentes en la acción, desde la energía sobrehumana y rectilínea hasta el repentino desmayo, vagamente fatalista y místico, que anotan sus novelistas y psicólogos, el aislamiento en que ha vivido Rusia, durante largo tiempo, de la cultura occidental y la impermeabilidad de sus grandes masas campesinas a las sugestiones ilustradoras de la ciudad. (Espina 1926: 372)

For Espina there was no doubt about the underlying brotherhood of the two countries, based on Oriental associations:

> Si con algún país europeo tiene relativas semejanzas, es con España, y por la misma causa. Por el contacto oriental que Rusia mantiene con Asia, y España también, a través de Africa. Ambas vetas orientales, de distinto signo, pero de fondo común, originan ese parecido que en muchos aspectos físicos y morales se advierten entre el ruso y el español. (Espina 1926: 373)

An erotic imaginary

It has become a cultural commonplace in Western Europe to associate the Orient with sensuality, with exotic Others whose allures attract because they lie outside Western norms. So too with the Oriental connotations of Russia for Spain. But in this case desire undergoes a bifurcation. The response to Russian art and ballet contained claims for an underlying brotherhood between Russia and Spain. Later, this would become more specific in relation to gender, and in the 1930s the virile example of Russian workers would be brought to the attention of the proletariat in La novela proletaria as an object for masculine identification.

In both of these areas, therefore, the style of desire was of identification. What happened in travel literature, however, was that there was an ongoing imaginary relating to masculine desire, in which Russian women were observed and interpreted as emblems of the sensual. Thus encounters with Russians on their own territory tended to be reported back in terms of an attraction that was earthy. At one level the formulation of this attraction in terms of icons of the feminine was conventional: masculine desire was for the feminine. This, however, could come in diverse formulations. The mode of representation of Russia, and its inhabitants, is less formulaic in the travel writings than in the aesthetic or nationalist theories in which Russia was conjured up as Spain's mystic and primitive Asiatic other. Yet recognizable patterns to the way women are represented suggest that there is a mixture between observation and the imposition of the frames of the imaginary.

García Morente commented on how the reporting back from Russia was inevitably framed. It was tinged with memories of how Russia had seemed in books. His insightful comment on the travellers' writings was that they seemed to be like Russian novels, while the Russians portrayed in them seemed all to be characters out of Dostoiewski. Rightly, he pointed out that art and literature have their effect on the way we see things, and that this was precisely what had occurred with Russia:

> Con la novela, la música, el teatro y la escultura hemos aderezado cierta imagen romántica de Rusia: un Rusia lejana, entre asiática y europea, con planicies frenéticamente melancólicas, con lentas melodías angustiosas, con seres extraños e incomprensibles, capaces de cometer los crímenes más sombríos como de realizar las mayores heriocidades y las más delicadas renuncias; y todo ello bañado en un ambiente inmenso de hondo fatalismo, de milenaria, cósmica resignación, un menosprecio absoluto de la vida individual, un anhelo de fundir todos los vivientes en la única gigantesca ondulación de la estepa inabarcable. (García Morente 1925: 126–7)

While it was possible, he added, that the journalists writing about Russia might have contradicted the romantic vision of Russia, they seem in fact to have confirmed it.

One possible reason why Russia was approached with preconceptions about a romantic land was its contrast with Spain. Arguably this was related to the difference between the experience of the travellers in relation to Spanish women, and what they expected to be the experience of Russian women. With regard to conceptions of the latter, literature had had its effect. As Álvarez del Vayo had commented, 'Anna Karenina cut loose a fibre of my sensibility hitherto intact and sowed the seed of an interest in everything Russian, which I have never lost' (Álvarez del Vayo 1950: 17). Here his comment was on a novel that was a gateway to future experience. Yet only a few pages later he wrote on another possible factor in his desire to explore: what he felt to be the repressed nature of Spanish women. When writing of courtship of the Spanish woman, it is clear that he viewed it as a disappointing and frustrating affair: 'The Spanish woman refutes the legend spread abroad which presents her as irresistibly sensual and warm. … Rarely was she a flirt, and she exercised an impressive control over her emotions; in a word, she was the antithesis of Carmen' (Álvarez del Vayo 1950: 20). What added, therefore, to the travellers' agenda of finding exotic Russian women who would fit their imaginary concept of them was a sense of disappointment in relation to local domestic realities.

One of the travel books produced in this period, Diego Hidalgo's *Un notario español en Rusia*, presents an interesting resistance to the idea that Russia would contain alluring and sensual women. Published in 1929, his account is strikingly more sober than most of the other texts cited earlier. Moreover it is presented in the guise of letters addressed to a friend, a correspondence that recounts Hidalgo's visit to Russia in September 1928. This format, a literary device rather than a reality, lends a mixture of intimacy and documentary accuracy to the writing, and also sets it apart from other travel writings.

The note Hidalgo strikes is that of the masculine explorer. He comments on his age and disposition:

> Ya estoy cansado de esta vida aburguesada que llevo. En vez de ir a San Sebastián o a Biarritz a admirar las horizontales de moda, y en vez de ir al Raposo a gozar de la paz del campo y de la familia, venciendo la resistencia de mis cuarenta años corridos, y sabiendo que, según me dicen, me expongo a pasar las mayores calamidades y a encontrar quizá la muerte, quiero ir a Rusia, y sea lo que Dios quiera. (D Hidalgo 1929: 29)

His desire, in this light, to rush off into the blue, and find something fresh and dangerous, has the appearance of a sort of male menopause. Making references to Robinson Crusoe, he packs razor-blades, cologne, quinine, aspirin, boot-laces. His preparations imply that instead of viewing himself as the member of a nation linked by brotherly solidarity to another nation in a state of primitive development, he is a being of a civilized world, visiting a less civilized one.

The distinct note struck by Hidalgo is of reluctance to indulge in sensationalism. It is true that in the waiting room of the Soviet consulate in Paris he records his impression of a motley array of people, with their 'exotic' bodily exhalations: 'Hasta los olores son también una rara mezcla de humanidades heterogéneas y exóticos afeites' (Hidalgo 1929: 42). But he records in detail encounters with Russians and foreigners alike in Russia, always with the note of the one who observes and questions in sober manner. There is some idealism, some desire to believe that the revolution has gone well, and instead of associating the Oriental or the Asiatic with exoticism, he comments simply on the degree to which they suffer a better (political) fate than in other European countries.

As far as the women of Russia are concerned, Hidalgo's interest appears to be bounded by considering questions such as eugenics and abortion (now become social realities, and much under discussion in Spain at the time of writing). He thus keeps his fantasy about exotic Oriental Others under wraps. Indeed, he reverses it, keeping it for his return from Russia. Where others had gone with idealism, but had found themselves engaged with the myth of liberated women who might be simultaneously sensual and available, Hidalgo simply reported an implied absence of such finds at the end of his book on his arrival in Warsaw:

> No he salido aún de los pórticos de la estación, cuando ya una mujer joven, vestida a la última moda, sombreados sus ojos por el humo de sándalo, rizadas sus pestañas y coloreadas artificialmente las mejillas, se me aproxima y me lanza la mirada discreta de la cortesana.
> Estamos en Europa. (D Hidalgo 1929: 242)

Russia is preserved as intriguing, but not as the home of alluring sexuality.

Another text suggests initially that it will follow this distinction, and will keep the image of Russian women firmly within an idealized imaginary. Thus in the account of Russia given by Eugenia Lefèvre and Pedro de la Cerda (the former possibly the pseudonym of the latter), *El sol de los Soviets* (1931), the Russian women of the Red Cross are divine carers, idealized by their menfolk. In Chapter 2, the memoirs of a male writer, Slav woman is spiritual, an Other from whom he is wrenched away. Woman elevates man:

> Misiurof me arranca de la visión divina; hermosa poesía de la mujer ideal radiando felicidad, discurren en terrenos paraísos perdidos sin el torpe deseo; ávida de dichas naturales eleva nuestro ser espiritual, conduciéndolo

su alma generosa, por todos los cielos, prometiendo un vivir sublime, jamás sentido y siempre inolvidable. (Lefèvre 1931: 28)

Yet in this text the idealized woman of this text is not just divine. The illustration of Anna Karenina quoted earlier provoked a *Venus in Furs* image, decadent and seductive. Lefèvre is more subtle. Fur coats are essential and normal clothing for women in Russia. But then Lefèvre elaborates on something more intimate: close-fitting silk underwear, still retaining suggestive possibilities as the fabric of the skin is put in contact with the fine fabric of the undergarment:

> es un artículo de primera necesidad, nunca de lujo; las mujeres ponen sobre su blanca piel de raso, una combinación ajustada de pura seda que conserva la belleza de la piel, abriga mucho sin perder la tradicional esbeltez y agilidad eslava, tan precisa para los bailes y ejercicios fantásticos que agigantan sus encantos. (Lefèvre 1931: 38)

Lefèvre's presentation of the exotic Oriental Other with its mixture of idealism and a certain level of decorum is as titillating as is the brief image of the non-Russian woman portrayed by Hidalgo.

A sharp contrast is to be found in Rodrigo Soriano's work of the years of Primo de Rivera's dictatorship, *San Lenín* (1927). The motif of fur is here again, but Soriano moves his descriptions into the arena of the decadent by making a play on the fact that the same word 'piel' in Spanish is used for the fur of an animal and the skin of a human. He describes how he arrives in Moscow with expectations of seeing one sort of 'piel', and – with a titillating throwaway line – sees the other. The abruptness of his phrasing suggests a simplicity of attitude, even a crudity, to what he wants to see, and what he does see:

> A ver pieles. Sólo veo la piel humana en el mes clásico de los desnudos. Pechos descubiertos, brazos al aire, lindas nucas, rosadas como resones que tuvieran por rabillo el más ligero y lindo de los bucles rubios.
> (Soriano 1927: 35)

Soriano sees human skin not furs because he has arrived in summer not winter. But he continues to play with the unclear boundary between hot and cold, just as he also plays with the vision of the unclothed women that slides between the sculptured and classical (and therefore acceptable), and an incongruous and primitive image of the women as animal inhabitants of the seashore, as polar bears:

> Las bellas letonas del ensueño, a la lívida luz del Norte que las amortaja en blancuras, entran en el mar cual marmóreas estatuas o marfilinas esculturas

de museo antiguo. Venus del hielo, besan las aguas temblorosas, como
Venus al surgir de las azules, estas aguas del Norte, de un blancor tan bello
que parecería a un poeta gárrulo zumo de azucenas, reguero de nenúfares.
¡Oh, divina playa, divina evocación de los invernales hielos, que luego la
convertirán en aburrida reunión de focas, tertulia de ballenatos, 'peña' de
peludos osos blancos. (Soriano 1927: 36)

By now Soriano has decided on 'piel' as a leitmotiv, adding to it the meaning
now of 'leather' (a commodity for which Russia was famed). All is deceptive,
illusory, in this new Russia of marked sexual diversity, and this is part of its
exciting attraction:

Así está Rusia, la soñada Rusia, donde podéis comprar petacas bien olientes
¡hasta de piel de grandes duques! que parece ser hoy aquí la antigua 'piel
de Rusia" tan afamada; donde el libre amor os permite cambiar de novia
como de camisa; donde los cosacos se visten de mujeres: donde tanto se
miente y se fantasea tanto. Porque, naturalmente, caros lectores, ni esa piel
de duque, ni ese libre amor, ni ese cosaco femenino, en fin, ni tantas otras
invenciones, que invento ahora yo como pasatiempo, y por no ser menos
que los demas, fueron, a la postre, más que novelas pagadas y cobradas,
dulces fantasías, que también he de permitirme yo, siquiera por reír una
vez, y para estar de acuerdo con el clima … [sic] Pero distingamos: mis
fantasías y bromas, e invenciones nunca rebasarán este capítulo. ¡Quédese
para otros muchos el llenar con ellas libros y más libros, tartarinadas y
mentiras sobre la Rusia bolchevique! (Soriano 1927: 38)

There is some unevenness of tone and attitude in these writers. It is as
though they cannot decide whether they are going to Russia to discover a
sober truth, and report back on it, or to indulge in fantasy. Some of the
writings suggest the model of a young man's voyage of exploration, in which
ideals of spirituality of women move in and out of vision, alternating with the
prospect of liberated women, and all the sexual variety and availability that
this appears to offer. With the Orient become reality, and the exotic become
accessible, these convergences of hope and experience prove confusing in
practice. Conceivably the fact that Soriano's work was published in Paris,
outside the boundaries of the Spain of Primo de Rivera, can be attributed to
its daring nature, its flirtation with pornographic writing.

What Russia signified for Spain in the world of art, politics and the national
imaginary was a complex amalgam. In terms of content it represented the
human, the concept of man as a creature who existed in real political systems,
who suffers, and whose cause needed to be espoused. As a consequence, it
represented the major challenge to the world of art: how was Art to respond
to the issues of Politics? If this was a question posed by the 1917 revolution
for Russia, it was equally so a question for Spain, not only in 1917, but also

for the following decades. At the same time, Russia's practice in modern art produced a powerful and attractive cocktail. It was at the forefront of the avant-garde (the main angle of Stravinsky's attraction in Spain was his 'modernity' and 'purity'), and yet it was argued that its link with Spain was via the rich roots in the East that the two nations shared.

And as far as national identity was concerned, Russia was crucial to the Spanish imaginary. Edward Said has commented on how the imaginative figuring of the unknown has a distinct effect for the self: 'there is no doubt that imaginative geography and history help the mind to intensify its own sense of itself by dramatising the distance and difference between what is close to it and what is far away' (Said 1978: 55). In Spain's love-affair with Russia there is both identification and differentiation. The former is invoked so that Spain is supported in key features of its national imaginary: deep feeling and responsiveness that go beyond practicality and fit with difficulty into a modern Europe. The latter allows Spain to engage in fantasies of national virility, while dallying on the borders of decadence that might be felt to be truly part of European civilization. When Hidalgo encounters the exotic harlot on the station, and recognizes her for what she is, he is expressing a type of national virility that is simultaneously 'civilized' enough to relish the exotic. It is in the relationship of desire for the eros of the exotic that the travellers declare their modernity and their occupancy of the modern world, at the same time as their contemporaries declare their affiliation to a more antique virility, valued for its longevity and distinguished lineage.

Throughout the period of this love-affair with Russia Spain also engaged with Europe in general, that is, with nations beyond the Pyrenees (effectively Spain's 'elsewhere'). Spain's interest in 'Europe' was a cultural engagement pursued with some vigour by the most established institutions of culture that lay outside mainline state institutions. Yet the bilateral love-affair with Russia encapsulates feelings of longing, desire and the need for a (br)other with whom to identify in a way that goes beyond the belief that there was the life of civilized Europe in which Spain should be encouraged to participate. The voice of sensibility rather than sense, of longing rather than logic, the affair with Russia disarmingly conveys what it set out as its basis, a feeling of 'primitive' similarity to a distant nation that is more comfortable to manage than the less exotic relations with Spain's immediate neighbours.

SPREADING THE WORD

7   Taking the Knowledge to the People

La difusión de la cultura desarrolla hábitos de inteligencia, amplios, anti-partidistas y fatalmente contrarios a los sofismas de clase y a las frases huevas; y, al aproximar en la colaboración científica a clases socialmente apartadas, favorece el mutuo conocimiento y la información exacta de las condiciones en que se dan las dificultades y las habitúa a acercarse a los problemas sociales con un amplio e imparcial espíritu de información y de curiosidad desinteresada, que necesariamente ha de facilitar las soluciones. (Residencia de Estudiantes, pamphlet on the Bibliotecas Populares, 1920)

Inward outreach

Cultural trafficking in Spain was not restricted to the crossing of national borders. This much in a sense is evident throughout the discussions so far, in that the selection of works for publication, whether in book form or through the medium of a journal, implies the crossing of an internal border. But there are more precise internal questions to be explored.

As announced in Chapter 1, the greater part of my emphasis so far has been upon urban activity and upon Madrid, albeit with a consciousness of the significance of activity within the regions, not least in Catalonia. Using the Certeau strategy/tactics model, however, we might speculate that Madrid-based movements could be viewed as strategic, and regionally based (or inspired) movements as tactical, simply because of the location of political power. The greater part of legislation on education, publishing and planning all emanated from Madrid, and thus can be regarded as the strategic frame-work within which cultural trafficking activity could take place.

But there is a further and vital part of this exploration with which a future study might engage, namely the transmission to and within the regions. This chapter and the following one will therefore look at two aspects of that internal transmission, recognizing that what they cover can only be the tip of the iceberg.

A first and central question relates to internal dissemination. Reference in earlier chapters to the publication of books, even in the cheaply avail-able form of novelettes, has assumed a readership. This readership includes two elements: those actually able to read, and those able to secure reading matter. The two are not necessarily coterminous. Yet we neglect at our peril a further and fundamental question of how knowledge was to reach the people otherwise. By 'people' here I mean two groups: the total 'people' of Spain, and the more narrowly (and emotively) conceived 'people' of the *pueblo*, including both urban proletariat and rural peasantry. It is in this area that the two elements of readership come to be significant and interactive.

Most of this study has concentrated on *passeurs* (see Botrel 2005, 2007: 36), the people and bodies who have enabled cultural exchange to take place. These vital intermediaries – publishers, newspaper owners, editors, journalists – all have contributed to dissemination in simple ways, by the provision of material and by the unglamorous but essential function of allowing the material to reach its destination. The fact that in this process there has been a determined selection of material, based on cultural imaginaries (or indeed, on a practical sense of what might sell), has been highlighted in preceding chapters. But the issue of selection becomes particularly acute when the population to which material is directed is culturally disempowered to an almost total degree.

Spain in the early twentieth century had an enormous cultural and intellectual hinterland, or rather, a hinterland to which dissemination of cultural material from outside might be directed. This regional and largely rural hinterland was characterized by two startling features. Firstly, there were levels of extreme poverty that rendered the purchase of reading material not only impossible but irrelevant. Secondly, linked to this poverty there were levels of illiteracy that made such purchases an academic question anyway. The statistics are both dramatic and sobering. The 1860 census, which was the first to provide data on literacy, indicates an illiteracy rate in Spain of 80 per cent (Vilanova Ribas and Moreno Julià 1992: 62). At the start of the twentieth century, of 14 million inhabitants, only 6 million above the age of ten could read (Botrel 2008: 3). By 1910 there would be 7.3 million who could read, and by 1920 some 9.4 million. Put in other terms, contrasting with the 69 per cent of the population that was unable to read in 1900 there would only be 40 per cent unable to read by 1930. Inevitably the rates of illiteracy were significantly higher in rural areas than in urban zones, but there were also regional variations. In the North for example, with the exception of Galicia, literacy was higher than in the South (Botrel 2008: 11; Vilanova Ribas and Moreno Julià 1992). Such marked variation, including the North/ South discrepancy, could with interest be mapped not only on to variations in population and educational provision, but also on to the patterns of the clergy and religious orders observed by Shubert to populate the North more highly than the South (Shubert 1990: 145–53).

Clearly, extending basic education to all would be a key activity if there were to be participation in national life – a national life that had, as has been evidenced, its aspirations to contact with Europe. This would be part of the 'mission' of the Misiones Pedagógicas as set up by the decree that announced them on 29 May 1931. A *pueblo* that was not educated could not participate in the political life of the country. Hence the decree noted the importance of:

> reuniones públicas donde se afirmen los modernos principios democrá-ticos, conferencias y lecturas donde se examinen las cuestiones pertinentes a la estructura del Estado y sus poderes, administración pública y sus orga-nismos, participación ciudadana en ella y en la actividad política.
>
> (Misiones Pedagógicas 1933: 1)

A system of primary schools existed throughout Spain, and yet illiteracy was high. It was evident in the early twentieth century that Spain did not have a reading culture. Some would argue it is also the case in the early twenty-first century. As the Director General del Libro stated in 1997, 'Leer es la asignatura pendiente' (Botrel 2008: 3). Then, as now, the question was not just how to import cultural and intellectual material from outside, but how to make it actually available to people.

The best-known movement that engaged in the internal transmission of culture in Spain in the early twentieth century is that of the Misiones Peda-gógicas, and their activity will be the focus of the next chapter. But signi-ficant though the Misiones were at the time, and continue to be in Spain's cultural memory, they were neither the first nor the only organs of transmis-sion towards Spain's interior. They were preceded and accompanied by other movements and activities and impulses, more overtly political but no less positive or effective, catholic (and occasionally Catholic) in their profile and intention.

For Bourdieu, cultural knowledge and expertise comprise *capital*. Like 'capital' in the other sense, it can be accrued, and is used in barter – in this case social barter (Bourdieu 1991: 230). Usually the emphasis when writing of cultural capital is on the way the individual may own it, and may be seen to own it, thus gaining a greater sense of *distinction*. In the case of the trafficking of knowledge, however, we can think about how capital can be used to convey distinction through the process of being purveyed. That is, for those who are providers of capital there is the possibility of shaping those who will receive it, and at the same time of receiving recognition for the activity of supplying it. What is curious about the type of cultural capital involved in the early decades of the twentieth century in Spain is the degree to which it appears to offer what is canonical, in the form of a recommended list, and the degree to which that canonical collection has strong markings of the extra-national.

In early twentieth-century Spain the purveying of cultural capital to the *pueblos* by the Misiones Pedagógicas (see Chapter 8) stands as an icon. Less well known than the work of the Misiones, but arguably as important, if not more so, is the project of the popular libraries, the Bibliotecas Populares, and related enterprises to set up libraries for the population at large rather than for specialized and highly educated readers. Like the Misiones, the Bibliotecas Populares were brainchildren of the Residencia de Estudiantes, and in like manner we can view the profile of the cultural capital involved in them as representative of the intellectual ideals, canons and forms of distinction of those associated with the Residencia. The libraries constituted a permanent and ongoing part of the project of the Misiones.

The emphasis of this chapter is not on the reception of the project of the Bibliotecas Populares in the *pueblos* that benefited from it. Rather it is to look at the enterprise as set out in its own terms, and as it can be deduced both from its recommendations about the libraries, and the profile of the holdings it suggested for them. In its turn, such readings of the enterprise tell us about the nature of the cultural capital held to be valuable (and hence fit for purveying). At the same it is important to note the setting of the Bibliotecas Populares project within a wider framework of developing a library system for the Spanish population at large, rather than for specialized and highly educated readers (see Díaz y Pérez 1885; Martínez Rus 2001). This broader setting bears eloquent witness to a drive for improving educational facilities for all in which substantially more people than an elite few from the Residencia were involved. It is clear that a major provision of culture came through workers' libraries, such as the Casas del Pueblo, studies of which broadly corroborate the findings of this chapter (see Mainer 1977; Monguió 1975; Luis Martín 1994, 1997; Franco Fernández, Luis Martín and Arias González 1998). There is not space here to go into a further significant activity in the provision of libraries, namely that of the Junta de Intercambio y Adquisición de Libros (JIAL). But it did provide a parallel and supplementary activity of taking knowledge to the people, and its recommended book lists (Martínez Rus 2003: 76–109) are consistent in their broad outlines with that of the Bibliotecas Populares. The extremely detailed and fundamental study of libraries by Martínez Rus (2003: 19–197), coupled with the buoyant and passionate account of Vicéns (1938), is the source of eloquent testimony to the enterprise of taking the knowledge to the people. Both provide examples of inspiring library enterprises. They also both testify, as does María Moliner (2006), to the difficulties of operation of the libraries, difficulties that are as much to do with apathy and obstruction as with the challenge of taking knowledge to those who want it but whose access is problematic.

The Bibliotecas Populares

The Bibliotecas Populares project was set up from within the Residencia de Estudiantes, falling into this active context and tradition of taking education to the rural areas. It should be noted that libraries had, of course, existed in Spain before this project: the detailed studies of García Ejarque (2000) and Martínez Rus (2003) provide ample proof of the myriad enterprises to make reading available to the public. But just as the Residencia has become the shining emblem in public memory of a high point of Spain's culture (while a broader and no less significant history of the encouragement to read exists), so too with the project of the Bibliotecas Populares.

This subset of the Misiones Pedagógicas tends to be recalled from its activities on the early years of the Second Republic, but it had its origins over a decade earlier. Two pamphlets, of 1918 and 1920, set out the project. The first of these contains instructions on how to organize a popular library, and recommends which books should be purchased. The first edition, which sold out immediately, includes a list of recommended purchases for the libraries. The second reports on adult education, and on the libraries set up in Asturias. It is distinctive for its political line, one that will be expressed yet more emphatically in Vicéns's 1938 history of popular libraries.

Clearly a cultural action that worked *de haut en bas*, from an elite to a group that was materially and educationally impoverished, the Bibliotecas Populares were aimed above all at adult education. They come from a context not just of the desire of the Residencia to give support to public access to reading. Their aim to reach isolated populations was significant, but for over ten years there had been concern to encourage reading as an activity. Public libraries already existed in Spain, and a decree of 24 March 1909 extended their opening hours from 5 pm to 9 pm, and a further Real Orden of 23 July 1909 included a two hours' opening on Sundays. On 1 March 1910 there was a further Real Orden stating that public libraries should be set up in cities where there was a superior or elementary school of 'Artes industriales' or similar. In such libraries there should be books selected by those institutions up to a value of 700 pesetas (García Ejarque 2000: 142). Botrel (2008: 41) lists the first popular library in Madrid as the one set up in Cuatro Caminos. By 1918 there would be seventeen libraries serving 375,807 works to 371,631 readers, rising by 1921 to 445,977 works served to 404,935 readers (Fernández Cifuentes 1982: 123).

Into this broader setting the Bibliotecas Populares project of the Residencia was announced as a piece of philanthropy, as a response from the Residentes to the plight of the *pueblo*: it was asserted that since the students of the Residencia came from all regions, they knew of the urgent need for this activity: 'conocen por experiencia propia que apenas hay lugar de España donde se ponga el libro al alcance de las clases populares (para éstas, puede decirse de un modo general, no se ha inventado la imprenta)' (Residencia de Estudiantes 1918: 3). But the libraries were not to be established just anywhere. Rather they were to go where there was already some possibility of their being well received: the capital was to be 'invested', as it were, in areas that showed a better chance of returns. In a pattern that would be followed by Luis Bello in his travels across Castile and León in the mid-1920s, these libraries were destined to go to 'aquellos pueblos, aldeas o ciudades donde su acción personal pueda tener una mayor garantía de éxito' (Residencia de Estudiantes 1918: 3). Luis Bello would thus choose to visit Castilla and León because they were more advanced in educational practice than other regions. León, another location where educational practice was considered advanced, had a 93 per cent attendance rate for its children (Escolano 1995: 40). Zamora, for example, although singled out by the Patronato de Misiones Pedagógicas as sorely in need of help (Misiones 1935: 9–10) and thus in need of more than educational and spiritual succour, was in fact a province where pupils managed to remain in school through their due five years. The route taken by Bello in his inspection of schools, through Soria, Burgos, Palencia and León, with Cantabria, the Rioja and some of the Basque provinces, formed a 'corredor de la alfabetización' (Escolano 1995: 41; 1992: 21ff). The idea of taking education to areas where education was already held in some respect has its point in terms of being demonstrably practicable. In terms of the grand gesture of cultural capital being extended to the most deprived, however, it falls somewhat short.

The 1918 pamphlet on the Bibliotecas Populares reported back on a project in Asturias already under way: the library at Cangas de Onís. Other libraries in the province, at Avilés, Luarca and Bujalance, were well advanced. The tone of the pamphlet is informal, giving a blow-by-blow account of what seem to be *ad hoc* finances, building and provisions. As it observes, 'Puede decirse que un impulso entusiasta, dirigido con inteligencia y tacto, vence todos los obstáculos e inspira lo que sea más conveniente hacer en cada momento' (Residencia de Estudiantes 1918: 4). This movement from an impulse of enthusiasm strikes a note that will become familiar in the Misiones Pedagó-gicas. Notwithstanding the choice of locations that will be in some manner favourable to the enterprise, the pamphlet makes certain recommendations. It advises that the setting up of a library should always be provisional in the first instance, and that those promoting it always ready to be flexible, to establish it elsewhere, for example.

To set up a library, it was not sufficient to place books somewhere, with means of access to them. More was needed. The intentions stated here in the pamphlet are quite lofty, and again prefigure the educational aims of the Misiones:

1ª enseñar a instruirse por medio de los libros, creando en los lectores un sentido crítico; 2ª mantener vivos en los espíritus la curiosidad y el gusto por el conocimiento. (Residencia de Estudiantes 1918: 5)

Quite clearly, the libraries were not seen as simple resources, but as centres of education, places where the desire to learn might be stimulated. Furthermore, one can detect here the trace of principles of English education as perceived and promoted by Castillejo (see Chapter 5), as much as in the idealism of Cossío in setting up the Misiones. But one can also detect a distinctive cultural attitude of superiority: for those who had not had education, firm guidance might be needed, and thus the purveying of capital was to be careful. While an educated man would approach a book in the knowledge that he had already learned other things at an earlier stage, and therefore would easily be able to acquire new knowledge, one could not be certain that it would be so with the uneducated:

> es posible que muchos carezcan de esa base, y como, aun a los que la poseen, la biblioteca supone una ampliación de sus conocimientos, necesitan ir guiados por una mano más segura que no sólo le aconseje en sus lecturas, sino que vaya despertando su sentido crítico, haciéndole comprender que no es cierto todo lo que un libro dice, sino todo lo que prueba.
>
> (Residencia de Estudiantes 1918: 5)

Such hopes of critical learning suggest that the model of the popular libraries that came out of the Residencia was one more fitted to its students than to the population they hoped to target. But it does indicate clearly that in terms of instruction what was intended was not a simple acquisition of the cultural capital of national learning. The vital thing was to acquire the ability to interpret it, which is quite different.

The idea of a firm hand being needed is echoed in the reports of María Moliner on her 1935 visits to libraries in the Valencia region. In particular the issue of what girls should be allowed to read appears to have been a cause for concern. Moliner learned that in the case of the school at Moncada, the woman in charge of the girls had forbidden them to use the library. In her discussions with the man responsible for the running of the library she urged him to separate out those books that children should not have until they were older, 'insinuándole la posibilidad de que la prohibición a las niñas tenga su origen en no haber llevado con cuidado esta separación' (Moliner 2006: 321). It is also possible to detect an irritation that borders on fussiness in her comments on the problems caused in some places by the mingling of 'bibliotecas escolares' and 'bibliotecas rurales'. In such cases it is possible that children are given any book they ask for, which is clearly not to be condoned: 'En muchos casos esto obedece a desconocimiento de la biblioteca misma y de su carácter: no se han fijado en que unos libros llevan la inscripción *lecturas infantiles* y otros no' (Moliner 2006: 323).As the pamphlet gathers enthusiasm for the task of these libraries, more and more we find that there is an implied, but invisible and unnamed, person or persons who will be needed as *animateurs* or facilitators. One can see the philosophy of the Misiones Pedagógicas already sketched out here: the attention of the public needs to be caught opportunely, and boring approaches must be eschewed:

> Un trabajo de vulgarización, en suma, que debe procurar las enseñanzas más variadas, buscar el asunto más interesante, acomodarle a la exigencia o a la curiosidad del momento, orientarle hacia los intereses más vivos; no profesar enseñanzas metódicas y cursos completos, que, sin duda, tienen su aplicación, pero no concretamente para este objeto.
> (Residencia de Estudiantes 1918: 6)

These general aims of enlightenment and enlivening take on a different colour in the 1920 pamphlet, which now clearly thinks in more political terms. Democracy can only succeed if the greatest number of its citizens have the wherewithal of knowledge to ensure the successful running of the community. In a statement prefigured by Ortega's 1914 speech to the Liga de Educación Política Española where he declared 'Para nosotros, por tanto, es lo primero fomentar la organizacion de una minoría encargada de la educación política de las masas' (Ortega 1914: 302), the pamphlet becomes expansive:

> Puede entonces nacer y afirmarse en las sociedades democráticas una conciencia que las lleve a elegir a las aristocracias naturales que haya en su seno, entregando el gobierno a los mejores y ayudando serenamente, con fino y fecundo instinto histórico y constructivo, al encumbramiento de las minorías directoras. (Residencia de Estudiantes 1920: 4)

That the pamphlet is conscious of social unrest at the time of writing is made more evident by its hope that the libraries will make it possible to 'acercarse a los problemas sociales con un amplio e imparcial espíritu de información y de curiosidad desinteresada' (Residencia de Estudiantes 1920: 4). Indeed the Bibliotecas Populares project as presented in this second pamphlet comes over strongly as a project of social education. The success of the project will depend on the creation of a spirit of social co-operation. Clearly the mark of the Residencia as the originating institution is left on the project, with all its ideals:

> Los progresos de la educación de adultos dependen de la existencia de un hábito de cooperación en el estudio y de un temperamento de *lealtad*

corporativa de los estudiantes hacia la clase o institución educativa a que pertenezcan. (Residencia de Estudiantes 1920: 5, emphasis mine)

Discussion in this vein continues for a further five pages in this pamphlet, the source for them acknowledged as what we can recognize as the report of the Adult Education Committee of the British Ministry of Reconstruction (1919). This would seem to have the hand of Castillejo guiding it, given his intense interest in English education, and his admiration for the movement for adult education in particular as he had observed it in his visits. The report itself is not quoted, but its intentions, and even its ideals, shine out of the pamphlet's opening words of summary. Its recommendations are based on a number of propositions. They include a view of the purpose of education as 'to fit a man for life, and therefore in a civilized community to fit him for his place as a member of that community'. The summary of democracy included in these opening remarks provides an illuminating (yet sober) underpinning to the intentions behind the Bibliotecas Populares project:

> That the essence of democracy being not passive but active participation by all in citizenship, education in a democratic country must aim at fitting each individual progressively not only for his personal, domestic and vocational duties, but, above all, for those duties of citizenship for which these earlier stages are training grounds; that is, he must learn (a) what his nation is, and what it stands for in its past history and literature, and what is its place among the other nations of the modern world; (b) what are his duties to it, from the elementary duties of sharing in its defence and submitting to its laws up to the duty of helping to maintain and even to elevate its standards and ideals; (c) the economic, political and international conditions on which his nation's efficiency and well-being depend; its relation to the other constituent parts of the Commonwealth of British nations called the Empire. (Final Report of the Adult Education Committee of the British Ministry of Reconstruction 1919: 4)

This second pamphlet enters into a new phase of life when compared with its predecessor. Thus whereas the 1918 pamphlet seems closely in tune with what will be the enlivening and evangelistic aims (in relation to education) that will mark the Misiones Pedagógicas, the 1920 pamphlet is directed towards what it believes to be a growing adult education movement, and its aims presuppose a higher level of education that can be attained by the readers. The first pamphlet's idea of the simple single room, cleansed weekly, with its fresh flowers in rustic ceramic vases (Residencia de Estudiantes 1918: 6) does not appear to be the venue for the advanced learning that is envisaged by the 1920 pamphlet. The whole is arguably inflected by the more advanced educational culture that provided the background to the 1919 British report.

Books for the people

The 1918 pamphlet on the Bibliotecas Populares makes general recommendations about the books to be acquired, and gives a list of some 958 volumes.
It suggests two principles of selection: liberal or humanist on the one hand,
and utilitarian on the other. Meeting the first, fitting in with the vision of
the library helping people to read critically, there would be 'todas aquellas
producciones ejemplares capaces de formar al hombre moral, de fortalecer
su juicio, de cultivar su energía, de afirmar sus ideas de deber y de justicia'
(Residencia de Estudiantes 1918: 7). The second principle would set out to
meet the immediate practical needs of the reader. These principles might
seem interventionist and part of a track of social engineering, but there was
nonetheless a sense of balance about them. (See http://www.mml.cam.ac.uk/
spanish/research/bibliotecas_populares)

Commenting on the list that follows, the pamphlet observes that it suffers
an excess: it has an abundance of works of the imagination, included because
they feel it necessary 'para atraer más fácilmente al lector y habituarle a la
lectura' (Residencia de Estudiantes 1918: 7). The justification of the works of
the imagination suggests both patronizing and infantilization of the clientele,
but arguably is also there to anticipate a criticism of lack of seriousness.

The first thing that strikes the eye about the list of books is in fact the high
proportion of them that are written by non-Spaniards. The vast majority of
the works are printed in Spain, but the author of origin, particularly in the
cases of general works, encyclopaedias, manuals and the like is frequently
French, German or English. Encyclopaedias and dictionaries are characterized by being multi-purpose, easy to manipulate. Hence the Pal-las *Diccionario enciclopédico manual, en cinco idiomas* (1913). There is the appeal to
the auto-didact, evident in the three works by Doppelhein on how to teach
oneself French, English and German. A volume by Emilio Faguet tells you
how to read (*El arte de leer*), as does one by Ernesto Legouvé. And while
Spanish grammar is explained, not surprisingly, by Andrés Bello, and the
Real Academia, there are contributions also from Hanssen on historical
grammar of Castilian, and Meyer-Lübcke on the study of Romance linguis-
tics. When one reaches this sort of detail, the question arises of just what
reading public is intended: is this even intended to provide enlightenment
for the rural *maestro*?

A sense of foreignness is even more marked in the area of literary history
where a type of double alterity is marked: a history of French literature by
Dowden, of Spanish literature by Fitzmaurice-Kelly, of Italian literature
by Garnet, James Gow's introduction to classical Greek and Latin authors,
adapted by Reinach, Murray's history of Greek literature, and Taine's history
of English literature. Russian literature is served by Waliszewsky.

The list of individual works of literature reveals interesting emphases.

The greater tendency is to nineteenth-century works, with the exception of Greek classics (Sophocles, Aristophanes, Homer), the works of Shakespeare, a strong Goethe section, and Machiavelli's *Prince*. English is somewhat curiously represented: the presence of four works by Dickens is not unusual, though, with the exception of *Casa por alquilar* (Bleak House), lightweight in both number and nature when compared with the Russian items noted below. Otherwise the canon comprises seven works by Scott (no great surprise), six by H G Wells (mainly the fantasy and science fiction) and two by Wilde (*Salomé* and *Una mujer sin importancia*), with two examples from Kipling (*El libro de las tierras vírgenes* and *Cuentos de montaña*). It is a commonplace that what Spain imported from France, in cultural terms, was literature (importing philosophy from Germany). This list bears out such a generalization in part: plenty of Hugo, four works by Balzac, four major works of Flaubert and two by Stendhal, even more works by Zola (a total of eight), with selected pages of Montaigne. (This is not obviously the reading matter for the simple souls envisaged as occupants of the plain white-washed reading room.) The list also reveals a francophone taste in the inclusion of Barbusse and Bourget, and the Residencia taste in literature by the inclusion of four works by Maeterlinck. The presence of the Residencia is also evident in the inclusion of two works by Rabrindanath Tagore, translated by the wife of Juan Ramón Jiménez. But there is also a strong representation of late nineteenth-century Russian, with six works by Dostoiewski, four by Turgenev and eight by Tolstoy, including the 1899 essay *¿Qué es el arte?* that had given rise to a literary *encuesta* in *La Internacional* (Madrid) in 1920. It seems that some of these choices are led by a sense of 'social relevance' as much as being canonical in terms of 'European literature'. Some of the items appear to be 'accessible' by being in the form of short stories, working under that old illusion that if it is short it must be easy, neglecting the possibility that if it is short, it may well be dense. An alternative way of producing a snapshot of (foreign) culture is in the 'selected pages' model, as in the *Páginas eslavas* (Gogol, Pushkin, Gorki etc.), and *Páginas escogidas* of Heinrich Heine. This relatively broad if cautiously canonic selection of foreign works contrasts with what would be recommended in 1922 by Eugenio D'Ors in his *Plan para la instauración de Bibliotecas Populares en España*, where he proposed that books purchased in the first instance should be in Castilian and French (suggesting his belief that French would be generally accessible, but also indicating that he did not consider access to be only through translation). He noted that 'poco a poco pueden introducir obras escritas en otras lenguas, sobre todo el italiano y el portugués' (García Ejarque 2000: 158, 162). Eugenio D'Ors also expressed the interesting belief that the technical staff of libraries should be women and that the training of a librarian would be 'tanto técnica como de cultura general y espiritual, que lo convirtiera en verdadero misionero' (García Ejarque 2000: 156).

As for the Spanish canon included in the book recommendations of the 1918 pamphlet, Cervantes and Calderón have their place, as does Lope (with select theatre), but there is no *Celestina*, no Góngora, and Gracián appears under philosophy. The *Cid* is there, but we also find a surprising four volumes by Rubén Darío, four volumes of poetry by Díez Canedo and poetry by Espronceda. On the basis of this there seems to be the belief that poetry will be either accessible (or conceivably important), and the selection is the poetry of choice of the Residencia. Later, in the activity of the Misiones Pedagógicas, it will be found that that poetry goes down well, but in that case the poetry was – for the most part – popular. Of Valdepeñas de la Sierra (Guadalajara) it is noted that the villagers prefer lyric to narrative, and prefer *romances* 'de sabor villanesco a los heroicos y maravillosos' (Misiones Pedagógicas 1934). At Tamajón, poetry is reported as going down well with all of the villagers, including *canciones primitivas*, *romancillos populares* and the *lírica nueva* of Juan Ramón Jiménez and Antonio Machado. The difference is clear: the Bibliotecas Populares recommend elite modern poetry (with the exception of Espronceda, and Enrique de Mesa's *Cancionero castellano*). By the time of the Misiones, then, there seems to be some recognition or some idea of taking the popular back to the *pueblo*. For Galdós, the choice of the complete works, if possible, is offered, but failing that, the *Episodios nacionales*. (This focus on Galdós as a 'national' novelist can be observed elsewhere. In 1935 the JIAL provided 200 pesetas funding to expand the library at Alájar (Huelva), with a series of suggested purchases, including ten volumes of the second series of the *Episodios*, valued at 52.50 pesetas [Martínez Rus 2003: 159]. This amounted to just over half of the grant, the rest being used for literature, and for technical books relating to local farming specialities.) There is no inclusion in the Bibliotecas Populares list of the major *novelas contemporáneas*, but, instead, the early thesis novels: *Doña Perfecta*, *Marianela* and *Gloria*. Here more than elsewhere, the guiding principle seems to be 'education' but in rather heavy-handed manner. Yet entertainment is offered, six volumes of Palacio Valdés, and more socially committed writing from Blasco Ibáñez (four major works). Compared with the Russian selection, and to some degree with the French selection, the list for Spanish seems a mixture of the lightweight and somewhat eccentric choice.

In the section on philosophy, it is noteworthy that the majority of the items are translations (nearly 70 per cent). The emphases in the subject matter are identifiably those of the Residencia, so that Kant gets a good showing, with the *Crítica de la razón práctica* and *Crítica del juicio*. These are both translated by the Residencia central figure, Manuel Morente, and with Morente's introduction to Kant's philosophy (as well as to that of Bergson).

A broad numerical survey of categories within the list of books shown in Figure 1 indicates the outlines and emphasis of the proposed frame of cultural capital offered in the popular libraries, individual categories here being expressed as a percentage of the whole. From this breakdown of the contents of the list of books we can see that, consistent with the slightly apologetic tone of the first pamphlet, over a third of the books come in the category of 'literature'. The next highest category after literature is that of agriculture, one that includes a broad range of agricultural practice, and about a third of which is in a format suitable for popular self-education. With the miscellaneous practical volumes (from book-keeping to bee-keeping, from the making of *licores* to the making of locks, from tanning to typography), this category, along with agriculture, forms 30.9 per cent of the recommended holdings. A brief conclusion is that the intention of the library is to provide the necessary information for the occupants of the *pueblos*, so that their occupations and crafts are informed by current knowledge, and that they should have literature to entertain them, and to give rein to their fantasies in a supposed leisure period of their lives.

More striking is the high proportion, across the board (and not restricted to literature), of works translated into Spanish. It is difficult to tell with precision from the list just how many of these works are in translation, but a cautious indication is given in Figures 2 and 3. Certain categories are exceptionally high, particularly education, and the volumes on practical matters. Most of the works were actually published in Spain, but as shown by Figure 4, the majority of those that were not were published in France, with the US outstripping England, Germany and Latin America.

It might be observed that the practical occupations covered by the last come fundamentally from a man's world. There is a striking absence of any volumes related to traditionally female occupations (sewing, knitting, cookery, childcare), and an equally striking absence of works on medicine or hygiene. Since the latter was, for example, found to be a major problem in Las Hurdes, it would appear that this area of knowledge is seen to be a separate province, that of doctors (of whom there are few in remote areas). Practical knowledge on health, diet and hygiene is neglected, while mathematics, philosophy and fantasy are well served. This area of neglect of the world of the woman is echoed in the data on the reduction of illiteracy in Spain between 1887 and 1941: with the passage of time, as more men became literate, female illiterates would outnumber their male counterparts to greater and greater degrees. As Vilanova Ribas and Moreno Julià observe,

> a medida que desciende el peso del analfabetismo en el conjunto del cuerpo social, mayor es la diferencia que separa a las mujeres de los hombres, y por tanto mayor es la marginación cultural de la mujer. La sociedad analfabeta parece ser, por lo que a nivel básico de instrucción se refiere, más igualitaria que la sociedad alfabetizada. (1992: 71)

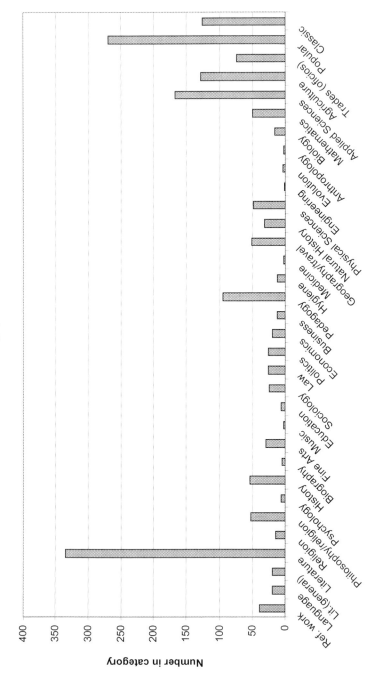

Figure 1. Bibliotecas Populares: Categories of books (according to reading list)

Language

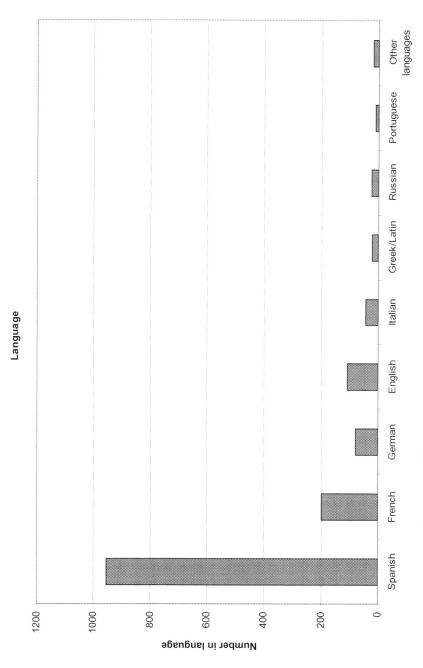

Figure 2. Bibliotecas Populares: Language of published texts in reading list

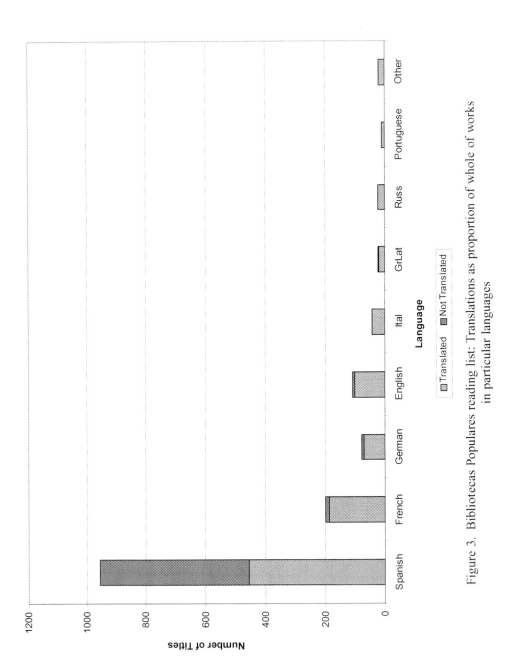

Figure 3. Bibliotecas Populares reading list: Translations as proportion of whole of works in particular languages

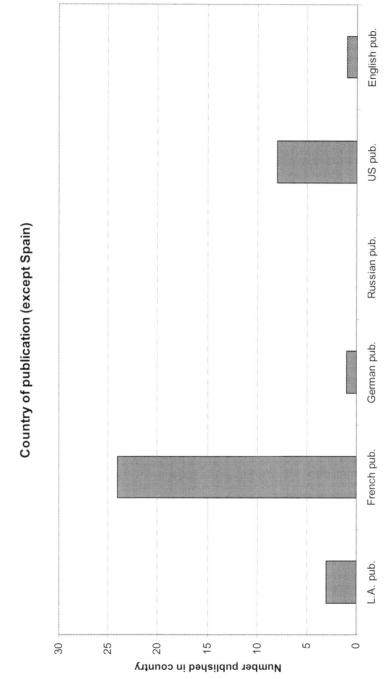

Country of publication (except Spain)

Figure 4.   Bibliotecas Populares: Country of publication (except Spain) of works on reading list: 1

Provision and use

A question posed by the reading list of the Bibliotecas Populares is whether it corresponded with the interests and desires of their public, or whether at the least the shape of library collections corresponded to what would be the use. The resulting loss can be seen in the mismatch between the works catalogued and the works available. Although the Bibliotecas Populares were set up under a different dispensation to that of the JIAL, the analyses offered by Martínez Rus of examples from the latter bear out a structure of use that might plausibly be common to all. Thus, for example, she cites the case of the Biblioteca Municipal de Vallecas, serving a population of 51,767, which in 1934 attracted 22,559 readers, of whom 10,529 were boys, 4,408 were girls, 6,972 were men and 450 were women. Of the 883 books that were borrowed (773 by men and 110 by women) the majority (653) were literary in nature (Martínez Rus 2003: 155). In 1935 the figures of readers using the reading room rose to 23,567, of whom 9,492 were boys, 5,146 girls, 8,125 were men and 804 were women. The relative increase in the readership of girls and women in this case is quite striking. Of the books served, 16,484 were 'infantiles', 6,862 were literary, 1,825 were works of reference, 1,040 works of history, 766 of pure science and 657 of applied science. While some variation between libraries can be observed in the statistical data for municipal libraries for 1934, 1935 and 1936 (Martínez Rus 2003: tables at pp. 433 to 452), the general structure of reading patterns remains strikingly consistent. The decision to include substantial numbers of works of literature in the Bibliotecas Populares list also appears to be justified, since, as Martínez Rus observes, 'Estos datos demuestran que los ciudadanos acudían a la biblioteca para informarse, instruirse y entretenerse' (Martínez Rus 2003: 156). The type of readers reported on by the *bibliotecario* of Vallecas is also of interest. The majority of men were *jornaleros*, *empleados municipales*, *oficinistas* and *tipógrafos*, whereas the majority of women, perhaps unsurprisingly, were *amas de casa*. But the *bibliotecario* also pointed out the sheer range of works consulted, 'y desterró la idea generalizada de que esta biblioteca de tipo popular fuese refugio de personas desocupadas o bien que sólo se leyesen novelas de corte vulgar o de mero pasatiempo' (Martínez Rus 2003: 157).

The financial accounts for the Misiones archived in the AGA record bulk purchases of various volumes that took place between October and December 1933. Some orders, which are composed of single volumes, are clearly for individual *misioneros*. There is for example, the order to the Librería Renacimiento on 25 December 1933, with an emphasis on travel and adventure:

1 Azorín, *Los pueblos*
1 Blasco Ibáñez, *La vuelta al mundo*

1 idem, *Mare Nostrum*
1 idem, *Los cuatro jinetes del Apocalipsis*
1 Marañón, *Amor, eugenesia*
1 Altolaguirre, *Antología romántica*
1 Amumsen [sic], *Cuentos*
1 Dickens, *David Copperfiel* [sic]
1 Lummis, *Exploradores españoles*
1 Cruz Rueda, *Las gestas heróicas*

By contrast, there is the order to the same bookshop of 30 December 1933, which is solely of poetry:

1 Mesa, *Poesías*
1 Gabriel y Galán, *Obras completas* rústica
1 Gabriel y Galán, *Obras completas*, encuadernaciones
1 García Lorca, *Poemas*
1 Manuel Machado, *Alma*
1 Rubén Darío, *Poesías*

The inclusion of Gabriel y Galán is worthy of note. A poet of the province of Salamanca, where he had come to the notice of Unamuno in some *juegos florales* in 1901, he was the subject of a lecture delivered to the Spanish Society of Scotland by the Spanish ambassador on 29 October 1926, subsequently published in the *Bulletin of Spanish Studies* in January 1927, and reprinted almost instantly in *Hispania* in March 1927. Gabriel y Galán's qualities as a 'countryman', claimed by the ambassador in his lecture to be the epitome of Castile, was clearly promoted as emblematic of a type of Spanishness being promoted to the *pueblos*, where men of 'upright, unswerving character, born fearless and inured to hardships' might have been examples of favourable mirrors being offered to the inhabitants of the *pueblos*. In the same number of *Hispania* (10:2 [1927]) there is the note of the growth of Spanish studies in the UK. This earlier promotion of Gabriel y Galán is then re-circulated within Spain back, as it were, to its claimed point of origin.

Other lists refer to bulk purchases, not therefore intended to provide a whole library, these purchases constituting a restricted list of volumes that were thought to be useful for wide distribution. The works are listed according to publisher. The first order, of 16 December 1933, lists the following to be obtained from Biblioteca Nueva:

300 *Ideario* de Costa
300 Juan Valera, *Doña Luz*
300 Azorín, *Los pueblos*
300 Carmen de Burgos, *Riego*

Elsewhere in the lists there are numerous volumes of Pereda (*El sabor de la tierruca*, 1000 copies) and Concha Espina (*La esfinge maragata*, 300 copies and *El metal de los muertos*, 758 copies). This appears to be giving back the world of the *pueblo* to the *pueblo*. But there is also the aim of 'learning about the world', in the form of 400 copies of the four volumes of *Lecturas geográficas*. And there is learning about the world according to political theory: 500 copies of Engels, *Origen de la Familia, de la Propiedad Privada y del Estado*. There is blanket coverage of literature and general knowledge as in the following order submitted to Ramón Sopena, Barcelona, on 7 November 1933:

200 *Grandes Novelas*
200 *Biblioteca Sopena*
300 *Dicc° La Fuente*

Finally, there is a staggering world view suggested by the list sent to Baldomero Merchante of 15 December 1933, in which the heroic, ancient and classical merges with Dostoiewski, with a brief admixture of Blasco Ibáñez.

500 *Iliada Tomo I*
500 *Iliada Tomo II*
400 *Tragedias Tomo I* [i.e. Sophocles]
400 *Tragedias Tomo II*
500 *La Barraca*
500 *Crimen y Castigo Tomo I*
500 *Crimen y Castigo Tomo II*

This snapshot reveals the Misiones' idea of the cultural capital to be taken to the *pueblo*. They would also be offered film, mainly nature films and comedy, in keeping with what is still thought to be traditional fare for children, though in this case the 'children' were the inhabitants of the *pueblos*. But the main emphasis of the books is on literature, with a focus on the canonically classical, and what is deemed to be 'proper' or 'attractive' for the target clientele. The prestige status of Homer's *Iliad* would be confirmed by the *ayuntamiento* of Alájar (Huelva) in April 1936, which included it in an order with works on the rearing of pigs and goats, and Remarque's *Sin novedad en la frente* (Martínez Rus 2003: 159).

By contrast, as shown in Chapter 4, we can see how a very different view of cultural capital at the time emerges from the records of the library held by the Instituto de Reformas Sociales. As an institution it was clearly more political (and left-wing) than the Bibliotecas Populares. But it reveals what was the *choice* of reading at least of *obreros* if not of *campesinos* in this period. Its surveys of borrowing records reveals a clear interest in political and social questions, and its bibliographies offered month by month bring in items from abroad on burning issues for workers. One can query whether this serves as an appropriate measure for contrast with the Bibliotecas Populares, in that the clientele is not the same, and yet perhaps not quite so different. Those assumed to be reading in the Bibliotecas Populares are assumed to desire knowledge and entertainment, but of a certain limited sort. The records published month by month in the *Boletín del Instituto de Reformas Sociales* of the library of the institute suggest a quite distinct panorama. When workers were able to select the cultural capital for themselves, they brought a sharp focus to their working conditions and rights. What is desired is a social and political understanding of the world, with its legislature: man's position in the social system is to the fore. Well behind is any desire to enter a world of fantasy through literature. When during the winter months there was a growth in reading indicated in books borrowed, and books requested in the reading (here we can take as an example the records for 1924) what people chose to take home to read was not literature, but philosophy.

The politics of readership

The provision of public library facilities in Spain was a sharply contested public space. Outreach to distant *pueblos* demonstrably pre-dated the exciting early stages of the Second Republic (evident in the visits to Las Hurdes in 1904, 1913, 1922, 1929 [Sinclair 2004b]), and key figures included Lorenzano Luzuriaga, the educationalist, and Juan Vicéns. Luzuriaga, a beneficiary of JAE funding to study in Germany in 1913, took an early interest in literacy issues (see Luzuriaga 1919). Vicéns, like Castillejo (see Chapter 5), formed part of the sector in the Residencia that was alternative rather than avant-garde in lifestyle. During his time there between 1922 and 1925 he was known for his theosophy, his naturism, his vegetarianism, and – according to Buñuel – as a freemason (Salaberria Lizarazu 2002: 12). Vicéns trained as a librarian and in 1933 became Inspector de las Bibliotecas Públicas Municipales de la Junta de Intercambio y de las Misiones Pedagógicas. The volume he published in French in 1938 under the title *L'Espagne vivante: le people à la conquête de la culture*, and subsequently reprinted as *España viva: el pueblo a la conquista de la cultura* (2002) contains five articles originally printed in a Madrid daily, and reprinted in 1937 in the French review *Archives et Bibliothèques* (Vicéns 1938: 37).

Vicéns is a missionary born, and his perspective from the war years that see the publication of this book is of clear vindication of the library system, and defence of the *pueblo* that he had sought to reach through the activity of the libraries. His view of the uprising of 1936 is that it was a clear attack on the project of taking culture to the people. In his 1935 articles that form the first part of the book he sets up a rearguard action against anti-library action that had been taking place since the 1933 elections. For Vicéns, the *pueblo* did not just need libraries and the facilities they offered: they welcomed them, under whatever conditions. They were eager for what they could find. The almost absurd underprovision constituted by the libraries that could be set up in the years of the Republic, according to the depiction offered by Vicéns, stimulated rather than stultified the desire for knowledge. The *pueblo*, for him, was eager:

> El pueblo, animado de un enorme deseo de cultura, se arroja sobre las bibliotecas. Pero las bibliotecas son pocas, el personal escaso. Muchas de ellas contienen un exceso de viejos libros en latín, sin valor biblio-gráfico, sin actualidad, ilegibles. Su organización, por falta de personal y de medios, no ha podido ponerse a tono con las necesidades actuales; no tienen catálogos de materias, no prestan libros a domicilio; sólo quienes tienen tiempo para permanecer en sus salas de lectura pueden utilizarlas. No importa; el pueblo español se arroja sobre ellas, las invade, hace cola ante sus puertas. (Vicéns 1938: 38)

As a missionary, Vicéns was also at pains to demonstrate that the *pueblo* was not only deserving on the basis of need, but also that it had a natural orderliness that meant that it would be protective and careful of resources. He produces a range of examples to show this. One of the more dramatic is that of Mérida, a *pueblo* of over 10,000 inhabitants in Badajoz:

> A las cinco de la tarde se abre al público y éste se precipita en torrente por la puerta. El bibliotecario distribuye y registra los libros a una velocidad de campeonato mundial. Un cuarto de hora despúes apenas queda un libro y la sala de lectura está atestada de lectores sentados en las ventanas, en el suelo, de pie. (No se ha podido organizar el préstamo a domicilio por falta de volúmenes.) En ese momento el bibliotecario tiene que cerrar la puerta. En la calle queda un nutrido grupo de gente; esperan a pie firme y cuando uno de los afortunados que entraron sale, terminada su lectura, el que está el primero entra, toma el sitio del que salió, y se podría decir el libro del que salió, sea el que sea. En el mejor de los casos, tiene que escoger entre el que dejó el que salió y ocho o diez volúmenes que nadie solicitó. Hay, pues, lectores de estos que esperan un rato largo para entrar, sin saber si les tocará leer una Aritmética o la Historia de España. (Vicéns 1938: 45–6)

While there seems to be some level of improbability in the scenario depicted here, Vicéns's case is for the desire for knowledge. He coupled it with the conviction that the *pueblo* was inclined to orderliness. Thus he cites the case of Villanueva del Rosario (Málaga) of 3,000 inhabitants where 500 books had been placed on open shelves, and there appeared to be a self-righting mechanism:

> Los lectores tomaban libremente los libros y los leían allí o en su casa;
> cuando se desordenaban, siempre surgía un espontáneo que se pasaba un
> par de horas ordenándolos. Un año duró ese régimen sin que faltara un solo
> volumen. (Vicéns 1938: 47)

The care for books, in his account, extended to other forms of heritage, so
that in the early years of the war, a guard was set up at the palace of the
Duque de Alba in Madrid. This was not occupation, but rather protection
and care:

> pronto los milicianos encargados de la vigilancia se ocuparon de encerar
> los parquets, de mantener el palacio con el cuidado más grande, sin olvidar
> a los canarios y a los perros; los criados del duque continuaron viviendo
> allí y en modo alguno fueron maltratados. (Vicéns 1938: 86)

As indicated at the start of the chapter, transferring cultural capital to the
pueblos was an enterprise necessarily fraught with difficulty. It was also one
that was engaged in on a variety of fronts. The success or otherwise of the
diverse enterprise of taking the knowledge to the people deserves a whole
study on its own, one that would integrate the sobering statistical knowledge
we have on illiteracy (Vilanova Ribas and Moreno Julià 1992) with the varied
channels not just for educating the illiterate, but for placing reading matter
at their disposal. Thus a thoroughgoing consideration of the facilities offered
by *ateneos*, *casas de cultura*, *casas de pueblo* and *ateneos obreros* would
embrace not just major urban centres, but the small local centres from which
dissemination was offered. The Bibliotecas Populares venture, emanating as
it did from the Residencia de Estudiantes, was a specific gesture towards
taking cultural capital to the *pueblo*. Well intentioned, idealistic, socially
focused, it could be said to have bordered on the quixotic in terms of what it
tried to do against all odds.

It is worth mentioning, nonetheless, that the project of supplying libraries
for the general population was approved of by publishers. In the context it
would appear that such approval was not solely based upon the prospect
of gain, but rather in a shared desire for general literacy and the taste for
reading. Thus in an interview given to *El Sol* on 25 January 1933 Manuel
Aguilar took the view that in each *pueblo* of 4,000 or 5,000 inhabitants where
the government set up a library, a bookseller would come into being. Ruiz-
Castillo was yet more emphatic in an interview, again for *El Sol*, on 9 April
1934, expressing his belief that the increase of sales of books in Spain in
the Republic could be attributed to the work of the Misiones Pedagógicas
(Martínez Martín and Martínez Rus 2004: 128). This perception from the
point of view of publishers adds a serious and almost sombre note to the
history of the libraries in that it indicates the implications of success or

failure as related also to economic thriving. The shared fate of small libraries in general, characterized by activity and flowering through the early decades of the twentieth century, and suddenly threatened from 1933 onwards with the shift to the right in Republican government, is a window on to private desire and public idealism, tempered and frustrated by circumstance and the sheer enormity of the problems of fuelling an appetite for knowledge, and feeding that appetite once kindled.

8   Travelling with a Mission

en esas reuniones lo que se pretendía era una doble vertiente: valorar lo suyo y mostrarles otro horizonte, pero basándose en la estimación de lo propio. (Gonzalo Menéndez-Pidal, interview with Gonzalo Tapia, Otero Urtaza, *Las Misiones Pedagógicas 1931–1936*, 2006a)

In early twentieth-century Spain the purveying of cultural capital to the *pueblos* by the Misiones Pedagógicas stands as an icon, and the provision of the Bibliotecas Populares a specific example of how they set out to make a lasting difference to the inhabitants of the *pueblos*. An initial figure of 3,506 pueblos that received libraries through this activity (Misiones Pedagógicas 1934: xxi) would grow so that, by June 1936, 5,522 villages had been reached by the libraries (Salaberria Lizarazu 2006: 306), an increase of 57.5 per cent.

The activity of the Misiones Pedagógicas extended well beyond the setting up of libraries, however, and the daring and enterprise involved in their activity of spreading culture to distant *pueblos* has captured the imagination. This is perhaps despite (or because of) the fact that much of the detail has been lost, and most of our information about the reception of the work of the Misiones comes from those who purveyed the capital, not from those who received it. Nonetheless, recent work on the Misiones and the visits to Las Hurdes, particularly that of Mendelson (1996, 2000, 2001, 2002), has thrown light on the complexity, in social and anthropological terms, of cultural outreach to the *pueblo*, and on how Las Hurdes became 'contested territory'. The understanding of the work of the Misiones has been further complicated by the degree to which the project has been retrospectively romanticized. The quixotic venture was breathtaking in its daring, and clearly inspired both its participants and those who have recently re-examined its activities. This is conveyed with particular eloquence by the collection of essays that accompanied the exhibition on the Misiones published by the Sociedad Estatal de Conmemoraciones Culturales and the Residencia de Estudiantes and the range of photographs included, many unknown to the general public (Otero Urtaza 2006a). Yet the excitement provoked by the Misiones is complicated. A sense of loss in relation to the cultural outreach activities of the Republic permeates their reception as does the desire to celebrate the venture: both affect our capacity to assess their nature and impact in their time.

   The Misiones Pedagógicas, by their association with both the Republic
and the Residencia, were automatically part of an outward-looking attitude,
and yet their focus was inward-looking. This *doble vertiente* is a logical
consequence of the processes of change rather than an existential paradox.
The relationship between the Misiones and the cultural trafficking with the
pueblo discussed in preceding chapters hinges on a project of self-definition.
Within this the interest in the *pueblo* (or in the geographical concept of the
pueblos) can be seen as an activity of enlightenment, by which the deprived
poor would be put in touch with a culture that had ignored them. But just
as importantly it can be understood as a project of putting Spain back in
touch with itself, at the same time as it allows for viewing part of that self as
abjected (Sinclair 2004b).
   This chapter sets out to examine the Misiones in two ways. Firstly, in line
with discussions in previous chapters, it sets out to contextualize (and hence
to nuance and partially to demystify) one of the iconic occupants of Spanish
cultural memory by contrasting the visits made by the missionaries with other
types of visitation of the *pueblos*. Secondly, it also considers the question
of self-definition that arises from any journeying, so that Spain's journey
towards its interior is understood as part of its response to its relationship
with the outside world.

Going to the *pueblo* with a mission

The marker I shall take to contextualize the journeys of the Misiones is
formed by journeys associated with the Liga de Campesinos that took place in
Spain in the 1930s. The missions of the two organizations differed in aim: the
objectives of the Misiones Pedagógicas were cultural and educational, while
those of the Liga were primarily political. But the nature of their outreach,
in terms of the places visited, was broadly similar. This similarity extends to
the style that each of the organizations had in reporting back on its journeys
and missionary activities: the writing of their accounts constitutes a cultural
act that simultaneously defines them, their purpose, and – in terms of their
purpose – those that they visit. Between them the two sets of journeys show
the degree to which endeavours to 'know Spain' were highly selective, and
dominated by preconceived views of the unknown to be visited. The narratives are furthermore driven by the intended readership, one that is going to
be informed by these travellers' tales in a way that fits a set of accepted ideas
about the different social components of Spain.
   Few journeys are innocent of agendas, and missions necessarily have
explicit ones. Missionaries are sent, and while a fundamental part of their
activity is to communicate with those they visit, equally fundamental is their
task to report back. By comparing the respective agendas of the journeys of

the Misiones Pedagógicas and the Liga de Campesinos in the 1930s, both missionary in type, but one of them far better known than the other, and specifically by examining their reporting back, it is possible to perceive different levels and nature of purpose. The journeys in question, and the accounts given of them to presumed third parties, are cultural and social acts that ultimately reveal more about the travellers than about the objects they saw on their travels. Thus the unacknowledged purposes of missions and the attitudes from which they derive stand in some tension with their overt and stated objectives. The interface between acknowledged and unacknowledged agendas, between conscious and unconscious motivation, says as much about the missions themselves as the society from which they spring.

Journeys in Spain in the twentieth century do not exist in a vacuum. Feijóo in 1730 and Madoz in 1846 had provided visions of Spain based upon their travels and observations, both considering their writings to be the transmission of objective evidence. A significant part of the context in which they wrote was that of travel writings by foreigners visiting Spain. What they produced was thus inevitably (if not always explicitly) a response, a counter-narrative of Spain as observed by its own people that might contrast with the narrative produced by outsiders. Added to this narrative tradition, the educational framework set up by the ILE was one that privileged hands-on practical discovery, and included excursions and practical observation as prime elements in intellectual development. The Generation of 1898, in its turn heir to the teachings of the ILE, had also produced its travellers and travel writings. The precise tradition of a close contact with nature, beloved of Giner, continued into the 'child' of the ILE, the Residencia de Estudiantes. As Altamira would summarize in his 1915 *Memoria* written in response to the death of Giner, knowledge of the physical world went hand in hand with man's spiritual and moral development. What in Giner was a 'sentido orgánico de la vida humana' (Altamira 1915: 23), elaborated in Giner's essay 'Espíritu y naturaleza' (1897) and linked to a knowledge of the world, and what was the body, was all of a piece.

The tradition of visiting the *pueblos* in the twentieth century thus significantly predates the activity of the Misiones. Besides the generalizaed '98 notion of 'recorrer España para conocerla', there had been other, rather more academic sorties. Visiting internal Spain was as much an occupation for philologists as any other form of academic. Hence Menéndez Pidal and his philological expedition of August 1910 for which he travelled first by donkey and then on horseback (D Castillejo 1998: 191–2). Curiously, the idea of going to the interior of Spain in the early twentieth century was in part impelled by a reaction to a less than successful visit led by Luis Santullano in which he took Spanish teachers to France. On Santullano's return, José Castillejo, temporarily in charge at the Residencia, suggested to him that there could be a change of direction and a type of role-reversal, so that those who had been going to be educated would now become educators:

> Las excursiones de maestros y obreros por países extranjeros se podían convertir en lo contrario: equipos itinerantes que viajarían por España educando a la gente de los pueblos. Aunque no tuvieran nada que ver, conscientemente, una cosa con otra, es una curiosa casualidad que inmediatamente después de organizar tres grupos – de obreros, maestros y extranjeros – se les ocurriera algo parecido para España.

Castillejo reported to Giner on this in a letter of 24 July 1912: 'Tengo con Santullano un cierto plan de una especie de misión que haríamos durante el invierno, él y los expensionados maestros, por esas escuelas de Dios' (D Castillejo 1998: 734). But if Castillejo had this idea, it was not a novelty. Not only was the tradition of travelling abroad to see schools well established, but also the idea of travelling to Spanish ones, as evidenced by the travels of F Martí Alpera and A Llorca (Escolano 1995: 19). Indeed, the report made by Llorca on the schools visited was one habitually exacted by the JAE to those it funded for study trips abroad, and focused as much attention on the rural schools of Spain as on those abroad (Escolano 1995: 18–20).

An example of the heritage of the attitude of enquiry about Spain that embraced real contact with the physical world at large is to be found in the 1926 numbers of *Residencia* in the section of 'Guía de excursiones'. Although these sections were significantly smaller than a corresponding section of 'Guía de Madrid', and although the excursions were patently to be made by car or train, the spirit of internal investigation of the Spanish hinterland beyond Madrid was clearly there, and prominent as an educational activity. The section did not remain, and would be displaced from December 1927 by extensive coverage of anthropological material. This included articles on Mexico (*Residencia* 2 (1), December 1927), the serialization of 'La Guayana desconocida' by A Hamilton Rice (*Residencia* 2 (2), May 1928, December 1931, February, April and May 1932), followed by the report of a lecture by René Gouzy, 'En el cielo africano' (*Residencia* 3 (4) October 1932) on the exploits in 'el Continente negro' of the Swiss aviator Walter Mittelholzer. This series of cultural excursions beyond Spain was then succeeded in the next issue, February 1933, by Santullano's account of the Misiones Pedagógicas, and was followed in turn by a series of sections of internal exploration, 'Por tierras de España' (October–November 1933, December 1933, February 1934, April 1934).

This trajectory, from the known to the exotic, and then back to what was believed to be known, can be understood, as can much of the project of 'knowing Spain', within the structure of Bourdieu's *habitus* and its relationship to change. Always veering towards a conservative retention of what is known, the *habitus* locates us in our own time and place, and in relation to what is external to us. Paradoxically, however, this conservative aspect of *habitus* is coupled with Bourdieu's privileging of nurture over nature. Culture can be acquired, but once acquired, it has to be defended. Arguably the conservative aspect of *habitus* is related to this very openness to change through nurture, and to the subsequent need to defend. The anticipation that change is in the air provokes a response in terms of a felt necessity to defend the existing culture, or in the case of 'knowing Spain', of returning to roots for further self-affirmation. The ventures into the exotic (clearly not Spain) can thus be read as a venture into the world of the Other that is rather more clearly distant from Spain than is the world of Europe with which most of the cultural trafficking of the period is concerned. The exotic or the primitive acts thus as a type of accessible cultural litmus paper, made less problematic by the degree of its difference from the culture of those who observe. This also raises, however, the question of whether – in the excursions to the *pueblos* of Spain, and particularly to the most distant and primitive parts, such as Las Hurdes – there is a type of return to the exotic that allows for the reinforcement of a sense of identity in those who visit and observe.

The concept of the *habitus* can also be used to shed light on the nature of a conflict between two predominant tropes of rural Spain: 'internal' or 'inner' Spain, a concept of national character and tradition, and 'interior Spain', a reality, the geographical interior that could be visited and known in material and scientific terms (Sinclair 2004b). 'Internal' or 'inner' Spain obviously and readily falls within the area of national imaginaries. What is inner is part of the mind, the desire for the future of the nation, and it is undeniably part of the *habitus* of Spain in the early twentieth century. By contrast, 'interior Spain', that of travellers, anthropologists and geographers, is apparently more rational, grounded in systematic and scientific observation, and we could observe that it forms a different subset of *habitus* within Spanish national life. The distinction between the two views is, however, less than clear. Both the 'inner' and the 'interior' are mediated by writers who are inevitably affected by the overall cultural *habitus* of their time. More crucially, perhaps, the two tropes went hand in hand, with the result that searches for 'inner' Spain were often combined with the practical activity of visiting 'interior' Spain. As a result much of the 'objective' writing dealing with 'interior' Spain was driven by visions of the national imaginary as much as was the writing that sought to define national character or 'inner' Spain. As a background, the complexities of the meaning of the *pueblo* in Spain viewed variously as political saviour or as political danger point, as innocent or as ignorant (Fuentes 2002), necessarily underpins the cultural activities of the early twentieth century.

Journeys at this period were not, however, the domain of the elite alone, as the discussion below of the Liga de Campesinos will illustrate. The tradition of workers' movements in Spain in this period is also one of education, involving those who spread it in varying degrees of travel around Spain. Yet one of the striking features of the accounts of these journeys is the apparent lack of mutual awareness on the part of these groups simultaneously involved in travel at this time, frequently over the same terrain.

Dynamics of internal journeys

The inhabitants of rural Spain were fully acknowledged by those engaged in visiting them as belonging to the same nation. It is this commonality that motivated the visits. But the urgency of the journeys was to do with the condition of those in the *pueblos* to be visited. With an overall illiteracy rate in Spain of 31 per cent at the inception of the Republic, and with 57.3 per cent of the population living in rural areas, and with 40 per cent of the population living in settlements smaller than 5,000 inhabitants (Martínez Rus 2003: 19, 29) the need for energetic action was evident. In the case of the Misiones there is a significant chasm between the population to be visited and those making the journeys, a chasm in terms of social condition, culture and expectations, that they were habitually experienced (and reported) as 'other'. Those involved in the activities of the Liga would have seen themselves as closer to those they visited, because of an adduced common condition as *campesinos*, but even here, as with the Misiones, the consequences to which we have been alerted by Said (1978) and others can readily be inferred. There is not the obvious power relationship that obtains between those oppressed by colonialism and their oppressors, and indeed those engaging in the visits of both the Misiones and the Liga would have resisted such an interpretation. Yet almost inevitably the people visited in their rural isolation in Spain and whose way of life was reported back to others were presented in a framework that labelled them both powerless and dispossessed.

Spivak poses the rhetorical question of whether the subaltern can speak (Spivak 1988: 283), and the assumption for those visited in these journeys would appear to be 'no'. Consonant with this, a prime feature of the writings of the Misiones and the Liga is that those who are observed are silent; as in the Victorian adage, within these narratives they are seen but not heard. That is, the intention is that they should be relayed as without a voice. If they speak, it is in gratitude, admiration for what the visitors bring, welcome for the interest they take in them. They are the deserving and grateful poor. Their attitude is expected to be that described by Mancebo in the journal devoted to devotees of Las Hurdes, which had become a centre of tourist attention in the early years of the twentieth century. In an encounter between an octogenarian Hurdana and a French visitor, philanthropy was offered and was delicately and gratefully received, the former declaring that 'se alegraba de haber vivido tanto tiempo, a pesar de sus infinitas privaciones, por tener la fortuna de admirar junto a ella a tan caritativa y cumplida dama' (Mancebo 1904: 197). Mancebo commented on how visitors came to '*admirar la sobriedad* de nuestros hurdanos, a *estudiar sus costumbres* y las bellezas naturales de su suelo, a compadecer y socorrer sus miserias y a *abrirles horizontes de civilización* para alentarles a la vida y hacerles más llevadera su desgracia' (Mancebo 1904: 197, emphasis mine).

How do we know that the observed are silent? We know it because this is how they are shown to us. Indeed, in the accounts we have of the two sets of journeys, to a large degree those visited are frequently edited out. This is with the exception of the photographs printed with the reports, most of which were by José Val de Omar, but some also by Gonzalo Menéndez-Pidal (see Otero Urtaza 2006a; Mendelson 2001, 2002, 2005, 2006). The consequence of this is that the emphasis in the written accounts is not upon those who received the visits, but rather on the energy expended by those who did the travelling. The reason for this balance lies in the fact that these are narratives of journeys, and they presuppose a readership. An example of Said's point that 'cultural discourse and exchange within a culture that what is commonly circulated by it is not "truth" but representations' (1978: 21), these representations contain agendas of intention, identification, awareness of the cultural expectations of the receiver. In the very act of relaying the information to a third party, something curious occurs. Bhabha refers to this phenomenon, in a sense as if it were a type of dialogic complexity, a sort of doubly oriented speech that is not quite made articulate. Those reporting back on the observed do not do so in a vacuum: they do so in the knowledge that their reporting is not for the observed, but for others. Bhabha notes that the 'pact of interpretation is never simply an act of communication between the I and the You designated in the statement', because for him the engagement in interpretation takes place in a Third Space. This permits elements in the interaction to surface, significantly those relating to the performance of those communicating, and which results in an 'ambivalence in the act of interpretation.' Despite the complex dynamic between the travellers of the Misiones and the Liga, they remain, as Bhabha predicts, remarkably unaware of the complexity (Bhabha 1988: 20).

The Misiones figure prominently in the inevitably edited cultural memory of Spain's Second Republic, both enhanced and diminished by selective amnesia. They were officially set up by decree on 29 May 1931, early in the Republic. They had begun unofficially, however, in 1928, with a visit to two villages (Los Ángeles and Las Mestas) in the district of Hervás in Cáceres ('Minutas de órdenes de expedición' (1930), AGA, 31/1302–3). Missionary activity would continue into 1937 (Otero Urtaza 2006a: 56). Much of our contemporary information comes via two memoirs published by the Patronato de Misiones Pedagógicas (1934 and 1935). The maps printed in the first memoir (1934) relate closely to the information of that memoir, showing both the extent and the limitations of missionary activity. In addition there is an article by 'S' (Luis Santullano) accompanied by a set of canonical photographs, which appeared in February 1933 in *Residencia*, the journal of the Residencia de Estudiantes. This provides a number of practical details recorded in the 1934 memoir: who was on the committee, which provinces were visited, the places visited by the theatre and choir. It pointed out that the intention was not just to provide cultural visitations, but to set up other forms of cultural dissemination, the most important of these being the founding of the Bibliotecas Populares. It also revealed a civil or political agenda indicative of its democratic roots, yet illustrative of its structured and hierarchical view of society. It was anticipated that there would be 'reuniones públicas donde se afirmen los modernos principios democráticos, conferencias y lecturas donde se examinen las cuestiones pertinentes a la estructura del Estado y sus poderes, administración pública y sus organismos' (Santullano 1933: 1).

Contrasting with the memoir form in which the journeys of the Misiones were narrated, the Liga produced an ongoing detailed record of its activities for the public domain through its journal *Ciencia y acción*. A Christian foundation that had been in existence since 1923, its primary aims were political and social. It is possible that the records of the Liga have survived to the extent they have (holdings in the Hemeroteca date from 1930) because it had been less lionized than the Misiones and hence was less threatened later. Alternatively, we might speculate that individual periodical publications may be able better to survive than archives associated with particular educational or cultural projects headed up by prominent public figures.

The Liga also had a practical educational aspect, channelled through its journal, and its intended audience was of agricultural labourers. Thus whereas the Misiones placed considerable emphasis on imparting the canonical culture of an elite, 'amazing' the *pueblo* with the richness of a culture they had, and yet had never possessed, the Liga concentrated its efforts on conveying practical information about agriculture and politics. By way of illustration, we could take the issue of *Ciencia y acción* of May 1931. It includes articles on the composition of fertilizer, on the change of regime (and its implications for *campesinos*), an article on how Spain's lack of a middle class has had a negative effect on the development of its agriculture (when compared with other European countries), an article on the market in corn, one on 'Los campos de demostración' (where *campesinos* can see new procedures they can carry out), one on 'Los trigos mejorados' (including advice to *campesinos* that they have to take account of the market). This issue also contains the statutes of the Liga, a question and answer section on disorders of vines, and an article on the advisability of washing wool before sale in order to get a better price for it.

The Misiones had two styles of visit, one that concentrated on a cluster of small settlements, and the other consisting of more ambitious tours that took in major centres of population. The pattern of visiting small clusters of villages was that adopted in Las Hurdes in 1928, then in January, June and September of 1930. In the 1930 visit to Cáceres, partido de Hervás, the Misiones went to Ladrillar, Huerta, Ríomalo de Abajo, Casares, Ríomalo de Arriba, Nuñomoral, Asegur and Rubiaco. All the settlements were in a small area and, while population figures are not available for all, census data from 1930 (http://www.ine.es/inebaseweb/) show the population of Ladrillar as 1,152, Casares as 744 and Nuñomoral as 1,702 (in each case an increase on the figures for 1920). In the mission of 5–11 October 1933, to the province of Valencia, seven villages were visited, in a maximum area of 10 km square: Alpuente, Campo de Arriba, La Carraca, Campo de Abajo, el Chopo, Las Heras and Baldobar (Misiones Pedagógicas 1934: 28). Alpuente, listed first, and as the prime *pueblo* of the visit, had a population of 2,745 in 1920, which fell to 2,493 in 1930. A similar average size can be noted in the visit of 24 to 30 June 1933. In these cases also the population dropped between 1920 and 1930, with Torrebaja falling from 1,016 to 896, Puebla de San Miguel from 399 to 375, and Castielfabib from 2,028 to 1798 in 1930 (Misiones Pedagógicas 1934: 28; http://www.ine.es/inebaseweb/).

When the missions went farther afield, they had the tendency to include significant centres of population, frequently situated on main roads, and at times with considerable distances between them. The accounts in the AGA indicate that there were visits north and west, to Pontevedra (December 1933), and then to a series of northern and western provinces between August and December 1933: La Coruña, Orense (two listings), La Coruña, Lugo (two listings), Oviedo. In the first visit to Orense the mission seems to have visited main centres of population, connected by major roads, with a second visit to El Barco de Baldeorras. In the 1930 census, El Barco had a population of 5,930, and the other *pueblos* in that district were similarly substantial: Carballeda 3,806; Petín 2,887; Rúa 3,224; Rubiana 4,164; La Vega 6,742; Villamartín de Valdeorras 4,190, in all cases save that of Carballeda an increase on the 1920 figures. The mission to La Coruña visited significant settlements spread along the coastal road. The route is such as to suggest that this could have been a pleasant outing. Some large crowds are occasionally recorded. There is a passing mention of a crowd of a thousand in the mission to León and Orense in July 1932 (Misiones Pedagógicas 1934: 19).

The overall claims for the activity of the Misiones, whether in Santullano's article, or in the 1934 memoir, are impressive. In addition, although the financial accounts in the AGA are incomplete, they list activity that is not included in the memoirs, most notably early and late activity. The 1934 memoir lists seventy missions to 298 villages in the provinces of Álava, Almería, Ávila, Badajoz, Burgos, Cáceres, Cádiz, Ciudad Real, Cuenca, Galicia, Granada, Guadalajara, Huesca, León, Lérida, Madrid, Málaga, Murcia, Oviedo, Palencia, Segovia, Soria, Teruel, Toledo, Valencia, Vizcaya and Zamora, and

3,506 libraries sent to as many villages (1934: xxi). From this list the coverage of the Misiones might seem initially to extend to virtually the whole of
Spain, but it is in fact with the exception of nearly the whole of the South,
Catalonia and the Basque country. This limitation of coverage is most marked
in the more adventurous activities of the Misiones. The maps in the 1934
memoirs show that the travelling museum and theatre, courses for primary
school teachers and the travelling choir only reached certain areas. The desti-
nations of the theatre and museum were necessarily limited by the need for
good road access, so that the reality of the cultural contact achieved was that
great swathes of the country were left without visitation. In general the greatest concentration of activity was in the provinces adjacent to Madrid, some
of it to the *pueblos* immediately surrounding Madrid, with further concentra-
tions in León and Asturias, in the Val d'Arán, and the Alpujarras. This pattern
of concentration bears a close resemblance to that of Luis Bello who in his
visits to Spanish schools in 1927 and 1928 had placed his focus, after the
area around Madrid, on Castile and León. Significantly his decision to do so
was because levels of literacy and school attendance in these regions were
already higher than elsewhere, and thus provided a better platform on which
to build educational reform (Escolano 1995: 39–40).

The pattern of the Liga contrasted with the above, in that its typical visit
was in the form of a whistle-stop tour, where speakers would address a crowd,
and then move on to another meeting. The Liga set out on its many journeys
from two centres: Madrid, and Dueñas, a small town between Palencia and
Valladolid that provided a good starting point for some of the journeys to
the north. The distances travelled were easily comparable with those of the
Misiones, and frequently greater. In the financial accounts of the Misiones,
special mention, for example, is made of the November 1933 visit to Segovia,
where it was noted that the museum had gone from Coca to Cuéllar, then
back to Madrid, making a round trip of 344 km. In addition, the journey
around La Coruña between August and December 1933 is singled out for
having covered some 340 km (without counting the initial journey from
Madrid to the area). But the details of the Liga's journeys show distinct
energy in the covering of distance. Thus between 25 and 30 May 1930, some
1,052 km were travelled in a journey over the Sierra de Guadarrama, into
Soria, and then sweeping north-west, and then south ([Hidalgo] 1930: 8–15,
calculations mine). The journey of 11–15 June 1930 towards the provinces of
León and Zamora was of 556 km (Hidalgo 1930b: 10–15). Round trips from
Dueñas were regularly between 100 km and 300 km, with one in October
1931 of 380 km (Hidalgo 1932a: 8–12). The greater part of the settlements
visited had populations of between 500 and 1,500. In sum, although the
overall scope of the visits the Liga made is less than that of the Misiones,
in those regions where it operated it is clearly comparable. This is in terms
of the size and numbers of the villages that were visited, the isolation of the

villages, and the populations with which it made contact. In a number of cases, one could speculate that certain areas, certainly the province of Soria and around Gredos, benefited from a high level of visitation. Centres such as Aguilafuente and Fuentepelayo received missions from both sources, so that their inhabitants would have been able to compare and contrast.

Because the Liga's intention was political, it aimed at reaching a wide audience, and wished to be seen to do so. The information about the meetings given in *Ciencia y acción* indicates a huge work of dissemination. But the actual function of *Ciencia y acción* was also one of social creation, involving consolidation (through print) of its mission activity. It may thus be licit to take a pinch of salt in relation to the estimates of numbers, which – as would be common with political publications – are likely to have erred on the generous side. Consistent with the journal's function of creation, it aimed to establish and communicate a sense of history of the movement of the Liga. As with the Misiones, the actual activities of the Liga pre-dated the formal foundation of the movement. The journal was used not least to recount the history of the movement, and the scope and growth of its activities over time. A report in October 1930 declared that the founder of the Liga, Don Antonio Monedero Marín, had visited Almenar in 1913, and spoken to seven labourers: now there were 'crowds' there, and in the meantime he had given 4,000 lectures ([Hidalgo] 1930: 15). The February 1933 number also referred back to an earlier visit, recording that the Liga had visited Las Nieves and Salvatierras, in Galicia, in 1918 (Hidalgo 1933b: 6–8). In February of 1931, *Ciencia y acción* asserted that Don Antonio had – over the course of the three cycles of the Liga – spoken to some 320,000 workers, adding that in the current cycle he had spoken to 50,000 in sixty-five lectures given over twenty-one days in eleven provinces (Hidalgo 1931a: 11).

Monedero Marín was evidently a figure of some productivity. The Biblioteca Nacional lists seven works by him, revealing his political and agricultural interests: *A los agricultores de Dueñas, ejemplos y enseñanzas agrícolas* (Madrid: Antonio Marzo, 1907), 14 pp; *La Confederación Nacional Católico-Agraria en 1920: Su espíritu. Su organización. Su porvenir* (Madrid: V. Rico, 1921), 200 pp; *El obrero regenerado* (Palencia: Gutiérrez, Liter y Herrero, 1912), 22pp; *Por Dios y por los humildes: Colección de folletos, Conferencias y Artículos de Vulgarización* (Madrid: Vicente Rico, 1920), 163 pp; *El problema de la tierra: Aspecto fiscal. Modificaciones en el régimen fiscal en relación con la capacidad del pequeño y grande propietario rural* (Madrid: Antonio Marzo, 1928), 34 pp; *Siete años de propaganda [para organizar la Confederación Nacional Católico-Agraria] (Crónicas de 'Juan Hidalgo'[seud.])* (Madrid: s.n., 1921), 226 pp; *Vulgarización de la ciencia agrícola moderna: III Los abonos químicos* (Madrid: Antonio Marzo, 1906), 45 pp. At the same time, some of the wording of the titles of his pieces in *Ciencia y acción* convey a paternalistic attitude to his audience, referred to

variously as 'los pequeños' (1930a, 1930b, 1930c, 1931b), echoing his reference to them as 'los humildes' in the 1920 collection of pamphlets.

Writing history

In writing their respective histories, the Misiones and the Liga justified their
existence, but they also communicated a specific yet elusive reality, that of
cultural and social contacts between isolated peoples and visiting missionaries. Clearly one of the major differences between the information about
the Misiones and the Liga is that the former produced retrospective reports,
while the latter produced a running commentary on its activities through
the pages of its journal. But the Liga also, as shown above, was intent upon
constructing its own living history of activity, keeping it in the mind of its
readers, impressing upon them the scope and significance of what it did. The
readership of *Ciencia y acción* is obviously assumed to include – literacy
permitting – those who were addressed in the public meetings. The Misiones,
by contrast, did not write for those they addressed, but rather reported back
to elite peers about their activities and progress. Notwithstanding these differences, and despite the dynamic of the different time frames they had for
their re-presentation of their activities to others, marked similarities can be
discerned between the two groups in the manner of reporting such activity,
and the way in which they viewed those that they visited. The level of similarity in the reporting is more remarkable than the surface differences of the
travels.

The writings about the Misiones convey a flurry of activity in the villages
visited, but underlying their vision of the interaction of the missionaries and
the population there is a decided sense of distance. Partly this derives from
the style of contacts with the populations of the villages. The visits of the
Misiones to villages were habitually for a few days, during which there was a
concentrated timetable of meetings, performances, talks and social exchanges.
There was variation in the style of activity, which included readings, story-
telling, practical work (such as the rehabilitation of school buildings), but the
memoirs convey a quite structured set of social contacts. Major events, such
as the mounting of plays and musical performances, were also so structured
that those taking the cultural information were distinct from those receiving
it. In addition to the interaction, there was also the photographic recording of
the contacts as they happened. While we might conclude that photographing
the natives (at a distance) felt less risky than any real contact with them, and
the act of taking the photograph automatically affirmed a distinction and a
distance, the informal nature of many of the photographs, and the degree to
which the subjects face not into the camera, but focus their gaze elsewhere
avoids the photographic mode associated with early anthropology and its

links with Foucault's 'carceral network' (Green 1984: 33). They fit rather into the frame of anthropological photography, reflecting the degree to which, through the 1920s, such photography evolved, as did anthropology itself, with a prioritization of interest in social and cultural processes rather than anthropometry and racial classification (Green 1984: 35).

The meeting of social worlds in the Misiones was not obviously comfortable for the elite missionaries. The poverty and the unhygienic surroundings of those visited were evident. The memoirs generally avoid extremes of documentation or anecdote, and abstain from offering the shock element Buñuel produced in relation to Las Hurdes in his film *Tierra sin pan* (1933), where a wide spectrum of unsavoury aspects of rural life was presented (Sinclair 2004b). Nor do they convey the warmth of the 1922 visit of the king to Las Hurdes, as conveyed by Carandell, one of whose anecdotes recalls what happened when one of the ministers accompanying the king asked for some milk to go with his coffee. After a pause some milk was brought. Shortly afterwards a man came in and assured them they could drink the milk in all confidence, as it had come from his wife (Carandell 1993: 38). It is evident from the financial accounts, however, that those on the Misiones were venturing into strange territory, and thought to make their immediate working environment safe. One set of accounts dated December 1933 lists in its expenses two rolls of toilet paper, vaseline to remove the make-up of actors in the Teatro del Pueblo, two sets of ink and pens to copy a map of Spain and a packet of nails. This group of missionaries also asks for a number of Michelin maps. The expenses for November 1933 (Segovia) request disinfectant to use on the quarters of the offices of the Patronato de Misiones Pedagógicas. This caution reflects the same attitude to contagion as that displayed in the pamphlet on setting up Bibliotecas Populares, which recommended that the place for a village library should be light and airy, and that it should be whitewashed once a week (Residencia de Estudiantes 1918–19: 6).

At the start of this chapter I referred to Said's comment that in cultural discourse and exchange within a culture what is commonly circulated by it is not 'truth' but representations. We can view the account of the Misiones in *Residencia* as the more extreme example of positive packaging of a cultural event. It would contrast with the two official reports made for the Patronato, particularly the second one (Misiones Pedagógicas 1934; 1935). The two main ways in which we can see representation as a part of cultural exchange are first in the pictorial context in which photographs of the missions appeared, and second in the packaging of the written word that frames them.

The photographic portrayal of villagers visited by the Misiones in *Residencia* contrasts with that attitude of caution revealed in the detail of a need for disinfectant. In particular the photographs selected for publication in *Residencia* in February 1933, are a topic of considerable complexity, not least in their use and appropriation, as analyzed by Mendelson (2005: 106;

2006). Yet fundamentally they are also the acceptable face of poverty. As Mendelson comments,

> It is as if the photographs represented a timeless present that mirrored the Spanish peasant's own timelessness. They provide a nonconfrontational, easy window into rural Spain for urban viewers and readers.
>
> (Mendelson 2005: 95)

With subsequent pieces under the title of 'Por tierras de España', they convey a specific cultural message, presenting aesthetically pleasing and arresting visual images. Most of the subjects look not at the camera, but (supposedly) at the objects brought to them by the Misiones. Thus the first photograph from the Misiones shows two young girls, enthralled by the cinema (albeit with a less enthusiastic older woman at their side) (*Residencia* 4 (1), opp. p. 1). Two pages later a shot of two women, showing a look of intelligent appraisal (apparently at the picture of Santa Isabel de Hungría), with – as the caption notes, *Las hilanderas* by Velázquez in the background – is one that shows fortitude, style, interest, absorption (3). The child and woman looking at *El dragoncillo* by Calderón (5) are rapt, amazed, totally absorbed. Later, a man with pointed beard and sharp features, gazing – we are told – at Goya's painting *Los fusilamientos* displays a demeanour of alert, intelligent appraisal. He is part of an intertextual conversation through the pages of *Residencia*, and represents among other things the relation of man to the work of art, while encapsulated in another work of art (Mendelson 2006: 169). The classical bone-structure and focus of his head have resonances with other images in *Residencia*. It echoes the ascetic lines of a head of Góngora (*Residencia* 3 (4) (May 1932) 97), and foreshadows the profile of a man in a sculpture by Berruguete (*Residencia* 4 (3) (May 1933) 86).

What is significant about these photographs in *Residencia* is that, as briefly indicated in the comments on intertextual resonances above, they do not occur in isolation, since the journal is one in which, as noted above, alien or exotic others have figured prominently. In addition to the articles on Mexico, Guayana and Africa, there were other lengthy pieces on anthropology, on excavations and on explorations, and on 'findings' about exotic peoples and civilizations. These included a report of work on Peking Man (December 1931) and, in December 1932, a lengthy article by Grafton Elliot Smith on 'El hombre prehistórico y la deuda cultural de las islas británicas para con España'. The latter was strikingly illustrated by the artistic reconstruction of the appearance of Peking man by A Forestier (*Residencia* 3 (6) [December 1932] 163). The article's conclusion was – consonant with a colonially inflected imaginary – that the direction of cultural inheritance went from Spain to Britain, and not in the reverse direction, as had previously been believed.

It is into this context in *Residencia* that the illustrations of the 'natives' of the Spanish *pueblos* are inserted: in this selection they are depicted as neither primitive, nor ugly, nor even downtrodden. The contrast, and yet the relationship, between the photographs of the Misiones and other photographs in *Residencia* is striking, and presumably not without intent. Yet as the photographs indicate, the people of the *pueblos* are 'other', and are shown as demonstrating a co-operative otherness in their amazement at the cultural objects brought to them by the people of the missions. It is this beauty and amazement (contrasting with the incomprehension on the unresponsive faces of the natives of Guayana) that is relayed to the readers of *Residencia*. If you are to take your culture to the *pueblo*, and report back to a journal that is essentially an alumni publication for the institution that provided many of the missionaries, the presentation needs to be consonant with the audience and its expectations.

The written packaging for this visual record of the Misiones is carefully confirmed by Salaverría in the following number of *Residencia*. Without self-consciousness and with more than a little condescension, he notes the pictorial curiosity of the people of the villages who appear in the photographs: 'un aire de salud física y *moral* baña sus semblantes rústicos y da una expresión tan *pintoresca* como *graciosa* a sus sorprendidas actitudes' (Salaverría 1933: 74, emphasis mine). The villagers have been looking at reproductions of famous pictures. As noted above, in the inclusion of the photographs there is a strong sense of aesthetic and cultural placing. Salaverría goes further, and leaps to an obvious, and undoubtedly correct conclusion: he doubts that even Russian film-makers could be better at capturing what he refers to as the expression of the 'documento humano en sus momentos de mayor espontaneidad psicológica'. Ingenuously yet disarmingly he reverses the intention of the mission, thinking not of what might be taken to the *pueblos*, but rather of what the mission of the *pueblos* themselves might be. In terms redolent of the traditional Catholic understanding of the function of the poor in society (they are there to inspire us to worthy acts of compassion and charity), Salaverría declares that it is the mission of the villagers to live a hard life, and simultaneously to reveal an essential virtue of humanity:

> El alma entera les sale a los ojos … Almas que revelan la más esencial virtud del humanismo. Vivir para el trabajo y para el deber, en lucha constante dentro de una naturaleza con frecuencia hostil y muy pocas veces pródiga: hé ahí su obscura y, sin embargo, gloriosa misión, que saben cumplirla de un modo que acaso en las grandes ciudades los hombres que lo saben todo no son capaces de imitar .

Their mission is also, as within Unamuno's concept of *intrahistoria*, to last, to withstand the changes and disruptions of life. Should their function in relation to the reader not be clear from this, the final words of the article emphasize their role as cultural fodder. They are not so much recipients as providers, not so much needy as needed – 'Son el depósito en que se conservan las reservas de salud y de ingenuidad destinadas a nutrir las ciudades' – thus counteracting the natural wastage and ensuring a balance in life. No room is left for doubt about the people the selective images of whom have been presented to the readers of *Residencia*. They are the worthy poor, the beautiful poor, and they have a necessary function in society.

The highly selective nature of the photographs that are printed in *Residencia* cannot be overemphasized. It is noticeable that the photographs included in the 1935 *memoria* of the Misiones are less obviously or canonically beautiful, and in general are more clearly 'other', more strikingly foreign, and also more primitive. As a consequence, and in relation also to a text that reports more openly on social difficulties in the *pueblos*, in the reporting of the Misiones we can detect not a single and unvaried attitude, but an evolution in the style of reporting. The Misiones and their self-representation can thus be seen to engage in a conscious (or even self-conscious) self-definition in relation to the rural sites that concerned them.

When we turn to the accounts of the travels of the *Liga*, mostly penned under the Antonio Monedero Marín's pseudonym of Juan Hidalgo, we find they differ from Salaverría's article on the Misiones mainly because they are more direct. They are warm and communicative, a blow-by-blow account of visits as they were made, telling the reader of what Don Antonio has done.

Nonetheless the writing is directed to a desired or implied reader, even if that reader is figured as less distant, more engaged, than the alumnus reader of *Residencia*. This reader is engaged instantly into an emotive atmosphere, Bhabha's 'passage through a Third Space' (1988: 208). In the first journey through Soria, reported on in 1930, an element of cultural recollection is added to the account of the villagers. This is in prose that could have come from the same pen as Machado's *Campos de Castilla*, and enlists the villagers in the history of resistance to external others of high historical profile:

> Al mismo tiempo, estos antiquísimos héroes de la patria que osaron resistir hasta la muerte las legiones romanas y quemaron ciudades y habitantes antes que entregárseles, son gente dura que viven casi sin comer, y de carácter noble y leal. (Anon [Hidalgo] 1930: 14)

This cultural representation is also cultural reconstruction, and situates itself within current myths about race and virility. The journey through Soria is over territory that was formerly Numancia, and Hidalgo recalls 'aquellos héroes primitivos que desde Indíbil y Mandonio supieron hacer frente a todos los invasores y encarnan las raíces de virilidad de nuestra raza' ([Hidalgo] 1930: 15). This reference to the territory of prehistoric glory, frequently revisited in waves of nationalism (Álvarez Junco 2001: 266), confirms a set of expectations about those to be visited consistent with an essentializing and conservative view of the rural villages in Spanish society, and consistent with the reading of the same in *Residencia*. Similarly in the October 1931 account of the journey through Palencia, the echoes of *intrahistoria* are strong: 'Las tempestades humanas pasan y se diluyen como las olas, dejando a través de la historia el doble rastro de purificación y de destrucción, pero Dios no pasa, Dios recoge a la vez que se dá y con ello, una vez más, crea y salva' (Hidalgo 1931b: 11).

Both the Misiones and the Liga had taken to the roads in order to spread their respective versions of the word, and both showed a considerable level of commitment, energy and activity. Both had had some activity prior to the coming of the Second Republic, but in these early years of the 1930s took to outlining their activity in detail.

An initial consideration of the two movements suggests that there were fundamental distinctions between them. Firstly, the Misiones had official support from the Ministry of Education from 1931: their activity, cultural and educational was official and authorized. The Liga had no such institutional backing, and indeed ran against official organizations. Secondly, they differed in their primary and explicit aims. The mission statement of the Misiones reveals the degree to which it was felt necessary to establish them as an apolitical organ of action. According to Santullano, the fact that the missionaries were readily seen to be without a political agenda was a major factor in securing popular positive reception of them. The cultural agenda they took, however, included (in his words) 'aquello que quisiéramos que vosotros supiéseis y que, incorporándose a vuestra inteligencia y a vuestros corazones, os alegrara más la vida' ([S]antullano 1933: 1). While the Liga clearly had a political message, it was one that was intended to bring something positive to its recipients.

Notwithstanding these differences, the nature and operation of both groups visiting outposts of rural Spain had much in common. The major similarity resides in the way in which the inhabitants of the villages were regarded. The illustrations from the article in *Residencia* demonstrate the emphasis of the Misiones on depicting the recipients of their culture: noble savages, innocent, startled, naïve, an emphasis that is elaborated further by the April 1933 article of Salaverría. But the *Liga* was not innocent of this. It is not clear for whom *Ciencia y acción* was written. It was obviously not for illiterate farmworkers, and it seems unlikely that it was intended simply to be read to the unlettered by those of their communities who enjoyed the benefits of literacy. The main complication in assessing the intended readership of *Ciencia y acción* resides in the highly literary style of some of its articles. This presupposes some capacity in the readership to pick up and understand the 1898-style resonances that depicts the peasants as heroic.

It would appear that the coverage of the Misiones in *Residencia* (and the official memoirs) was intended for elite third parties, and it is into this context that the photographic record fits. Yet by July 1932, the options of photography and film have entered the accounts of the Liga. Hidalgo mentions that they might think of taking a photograph of the girls in Paradinas (a small village) (Hidalgo 1932b: 9), as if he had passed to the side of the elite visitors of the Misiones. It is not clear for whom the photographs of the girls would be intended. And in January 1933 we find that the cinema, a medium of communication that had proved to be particularly popular in the Misiones, has been adopted by the Liga as a tool, recognized now as a powerful means for instructing and imparting morality to the *pueblo* (Hidalgo 1933a: 13). By May 1933, technology came to centre in the communication, and Hidalgo's article has a photo of the *campesinos* of the *partido* of Medinaceli who have come to listen to Don Antonio (Hidalgo 1933c).

As we reach the last detailed report (June 1933), it is as if some cultural merger has taken place between the implied reading public of *Residencia* and that of *Ciencia y acción*. The eloquence of the prose nonetheless now evokes the misery rather than the cultural riches of the *pueblo*, and paves the way for the re-visioning of the *pueblo* that would occur in the latter years of the Second Republic (Sinclair 2004b). The written journey, which the reader is invited to follow, is now one that permits contact with a reality perceived as wretched, but no longer distanced through an aestheticizing lens:

> La carretera, llena de curvas y de pendientes, bordea de tarde en tarde en estas soledades míseras algún minúsculo pueblecito de pobres chozas y casas de piedra sin labrar, muchas de ellas sin ventanas, y en cuyo redu-cido espacio viven amontonadas, si vivir puede llamarse a eso, las familias campesinas en la ausencia de las más perentorias comodidades.
>
> (Hidalgo 1933d: 16, dated Madrid 21 May 1933)

RE-GROUPING

9 Wheels within Wheels

> The relationships and concerns of the typical metropolitan resident are so
> manifold and complex that, especially as a result of the agglomeration of
> so many persons with such differentiated interests, their relationships and
> activities intertwine with one another into a many-membered organism.
> (Simmel, 'Metropolis and Mental Life', 1903)

A driving force in writing this book was the conviction that there was a
wealth of intellectual history that risked being lost through a process of
cultural *desmemoria*. It was coupled with another conviction, namely that
if we only looked at the histories of individuals, or those of institutions, we
missed something. The interactive nature of individuals with one another,
and with their institutions, is as significant an element in the trafficking of
knowledge as is any single interaction of either with the outside world.

These interactions are challenging to map, but the preceding chapters have
aimed to capture different areas of a complex landscape. This has varied and
developed along the chronological trajectory from the turn of the century to
the Civil War, but it has also been variable geographically, not least in the
divide between city and country, and most prominently between Madrid and
the rest of Spain. One of the most striking features of the cultural panorama
in Spain through these years is not simply the richness of activity that can
be perceived in some areas of the population, with the undoubted capacity to
reach out, to import and to receive that which is foreign to Spain. Rather it is
the co-existence of these areas of intense and vital activity with a hinterland
whose capacity for trafficking is severely limited. We might imagine the idea
of the *pueblo* as unchanging and eternal to be an imaginary and idealized
view of Spain's population. But to some degree it was in fact a reality, a
backcloth of the unchanging that stood in contrast with the rapidity of change
in the urban centres.

Modern theories of the city have pictured it as a place of anonymity. For
Benjamin, closely engaged with Simmel, the city 'provides the possibility for
total indifference towards one's neighbours' (Frisby 1985: 78). In this sense
the city offers freedom, and it is not fortuitous (economic and industrial conditions aside) that the city, as a social phenomenon, is the locus that provides

for outward-looking desire. It offers the capacity for variation, eccentricity, experimentation, that smaller social units will not provide. Simmel had in his turn enthused Ortega during the latter's stay in Berlin in 1906. It is a sign of the modernity of both Spain and Ortega that to an extent Madrid is appropriately reflected in these more northerly views of the city and its specific mode of social existence. And yet this both is, and is not the case. There are other features of Spain as a country engaged in cultural trafficking.

If we think of Madrid at the start of the twentieth century, it was clearly not a *pueblo*, and it was clearly not provincial. Yet the dimensions of the centre were such as to give a village feel to the place. A perusal of the addresses of members of the Ateneo de Madrid for 1909 or 1914 (the two 'listas de socios' surviving in the Biblioteca Nacional) reveals that most of them lived within twenty minutes' walk of the Ateneo. The Residencia de Estudiantes, housed first in Fortuny, and then in Pinar behind the Museo de Ciencias Naturales, was somewhat further away than this (albeit still within walking distance), no doubt suiting the intentions of providing a type of safe haven for students who had come to Madrid from the provinces. Bumping into someone you knew on the Castellana, or in the Prado, or in one of the central cafés of Madrid, was less a chance than a palpable certainty. There were cross-hatchings of relationship that cut across the freedom and the anonymity of city life, but which also enabled the development and the thriving of Spain's cultural traffic.

It would be impossible to chart the various cross-relations of individuals and institutions in Spain in the early decades of the twentieth century, but this concluding chapter aims at providing some examples. Within these I include professional relations, generations, schooling, family links and other groupings that interacted with and at times enabled intellectual and cultural contacts.

Repeatedly in preceding chapters I have spoken of institutions that were of importance in Spain's cultural and intellectual trafficking of this period: the ILE, the JAE, the Residencia. These institutions, alternative to state agencies or governmental organizations, form an effective backbone structure for a longitudinal debt of influence in Spain. At the same time there is also a latitudinal trajectory of enquiry. When we consider the desire to have cultural contact with Europe and elsewhere in these early years of the twentieth century that desire is located within two frameworks. One of these stretches out sideways, so that institutions with an interest in such contact are able to have interaction with one another, and individuals within or passing through those institutions will have their own contact points. But collectively and individually they operate within a context of intellectual inheritance, one that cannot help but include the inheritance of imaginaries and ideals.

Longitude

For simplicity, let us return once more to that backbone by which a line that arises from Giner de los Ríos gives us the ILE, set up in 1876, and leads to the JAE in 1907, which in its turn produces the Residencia de Estudiantes in 1910. The backbone can also be viewed within the generational structures of those involved in the institutions.

David Castillejo refers to the JAE providing the 'primer puente cultural hacia Europa'. His analysis of the generations involved is a fundamental basis for orientation in thinking about networking and influences in the institutions involved. He outlines how Giner and Gumersindo de Azcárate were senior members of the ILE at the time when the JAE was set up, with Menéndez Pidal, Gómez-Moreno, Castillejo, and Ortega the younger members, while Cossío, Rubio, Altamira and Hinojosa formed a bridge. Taking the ten-year period between 1905 and 1915, he considers the ages of the major players: Giner and Gumersindo de Azcárate went from their mid-sixties to mid-seventies; a second set, including Costa, Ramón y Cajal and Hinojosa went from their early fifties into their sixties; a third set, including Menéndez Pelayo, Cossío, Adolfo Posada, the Conde de Romanones, Sorolla and Unamuno spanned from their forties into the fifties; a fourth set, including Altamira, Menéndez Pidal, Manuel Gómez-Moreno and Asín Palacios were ten years younger. Finally, among those who were in their twenties in 1905 we find the impressive list that contains José Castillejo, Blas Cabrera, Luis de Zulueta, Domingo Barnés, Fernando de los Ríos, Pí y Suñer, María de Maeztu, Alberto Jiménez Fraud, Ortega, José Pijoán, Federico de Onís, Tomás Navarro Tomás, Américo Castro, and Julio Rey Pastor. A telling detail supplied by David Castillejo is on the 'tratamiento' between generations: the older ones addressed one another as 'tú' while the rest 'solían hablar a todos de usted y con apellidos, aunque llegaron a un alto grado de amistad y confianza. El tono constante de fina seriedad, ironía y divertida comprensión fue la clave de todo' (D Castillejo 1997: 17–19). It is clear that a sense of hierarchy reigned, and that courtesy stretched to a sense of recognition of previous generations, if not to entire compliance. What also stands out here is the sense of a group where individualism was subsumed into a collective mode of being. As Ribagorda comments, the ethos of the ILE was such as to lead those associated with it 'a huir de todo protagonismo, para actuar desde un segundo plano, que tuvo en el contacto directo, la influencia personal, la persuasión y la creación de un ambiente cultural, un medio de actuación discreto' (Ribagorda 2008: 3).

There are other, more familial links that have longitudinal implications as well as providing lateral ties. The influence of Giner, for example, is not limited to his mentoring and inspiration. This man of slight stature coupled with tremendous will, integrity and vision fulfilled his mentoring role through example, and through advice that went beyond the purely intellectual. Hence his advice to Castillejo on the importance of physical exercise (D Castillejo 1997: 61). The manner in which Giner acted as much as father as mentor, and indeed would be remembered as such, shows how in the development of the backbone it becomes hard to make a full distinction between family ties and ties that become family. Castillejo follows a type of standard route, being pupil at the ILE, then administrator of the JAE, but also having his influence at the Residencia. Meanwhile Cossío, so central to the Misiones Pedagógicas, takes over the ILE when Giner dies, and it is his daughter Natalia who marries Jiménez Fraud, the youthful director of the Residencia. In addition, Castillejo lists other significant marriages: Isabel Uña with Manuel Varela Radio, Lucila Posada with Antonio Martín Gamero, Irene Claremont with José Castillejo, Mariana Castillejo with Juan López Suárez, Carmen Uña with José María González (Castillejo 1998: 567, note of David Castillejo). In this way marriage is part of a structure for the strengthening and extending ties, possibilities and networks for the transfer of culture. It is also the bond through which loosely cognate but not identical activities come to be grouped. Vicéns, Republican, professional librarian and active campaigner for the spreading of library facilities to the entire population (see Chapter 7), is married to an equally active Republican, María Luisa González. Her activities, however, centre upon the periodical press, and she edits in 1932 the monthly atheist and Leninist *Sin Dios*, in which political radicals including Sediles, Balbontín, Ángel Pestaña, Rodrigo Soriano, Margarita Nelken and Hildegart collaborate (Salaberria Lizarazu 2002: 20; Santonja 2000: 181). In the same year, Augusto Vivero becomes editor of a related series, Biblioteca de los sin dios. Vivero at the same time was the major player in the series La novela proletaria, which included works by Rodrigo Soriano, José Antonio Balbontín, Eduardo Barriobero, along with the infamous *¿Quo vadis burguesía?* of Hildegart, which produced a barely veiled attack upon Alcalá Zamora and Largo Caballero (Sinclair 2007: 75–7).

Family also plays a part in the recording of history. It is thanks to David Castillejo that we have the ample volumes of his father's correspondence. Meanwhile the history of the Instituto Internacional will be written by Carmen Zulueta, daughter of Luis Zulueta who had sent her at the age of nine to the Instituto-Escuela. The head of the primary section was María de Maeztu, sister of Ramiro de Maeztu, head of the Residencia de Señoritas from 1913 and much admired by Castillejo (D Castillejo 1999: 28). It was in the Instituto that Carmen Zulueta was taught philosophy by María Zambrano (Zulueta 1992: 11).

The JAE had its own genealogy of influence, most demonstrably by the level of funding it managed to distribute. In twenty-nine years it received 9,100 applications for funding for 'pensiones' and gave out 1,500 (Zulueta and Moreno, 1993: 32). In its earliest moments, in 1907, Ramón y Cajal and

Simarro were funded to attend a Congreso internacional de psiquiatría in Amsterdam. Simarro was unable to go. Ramón y Cajal reported back, clearly having benefited from the European contact and saying that the best sessions were in the section of neurology and psychiatry, and had included presentations by Janet and Jung on hysteria. In the period before the Civil War the JAE sent 1,594 Spaniards to study abroad, and Zulueta comments that the 'list' of those sent reads like a who's who of the first thirty years of the twentieth century (Zulueta 1992: 190). Those who were sent sent as *pensionados* abroad included Álvarez del Vayo, Domingo Barnés, Julián Besteiro, Manuel Cossío, Antonio Machado, María de Maeztu, Ortega, Pérez de Ayala, Rey Pastor, Fernando de los Ríos Urruti, Gonzalo Rodríguez Lafora and Antonio de Zulueta (D Castillejo 1998: 17–18). The JAE inventory held in the Residencia de Estudiantes names in addition Nicolás Achúcarro, the Duque de Alba, Rafael Alberti, Rafael Altamira, Álvarez del Vayo, Vital Aza, Manuel Azaña, Bernaldo de Quirós (funded to research banditry in Andalucía), Julio Caro Baroja, Díaz Plaja, Froebenius, Francisco García Lorca, Madariaga, Pittaluga, Luis Recaséns Siches, Sacristán, Saldaña and Varela Radio. These names form a list that is by no means comprehensive, but their presence on other lists marks them out as a set of educational siblings launched into outside contact, but simultaneously available for networking from within.

Other types of genealogy existed, which we can see via two other institutions linked to the world of the Residencia: the Instituto-Escuela (mentioned above), set up in 1918, and the American Instituto Internacional, housed in Fortuny in Madrid from 1903 (Zulueta 1992: 137–9). A perusal of those involved with both of these institutions reveals a list of the 'usual suspects', individuals prominent in lists of those funded by the JAE, and/or active in the Residencia: offering lectures, coming to meet visitors and so forth. These institutions are thus independent units, but they fall under the cloak of the parent unit. The Instituto-Escuela educated pupils drawn mainly from the petit bourgeoisie, industrialists and liberal professions. This included the children of doctors: García del Real, Pittaluga, Sánchez Covisa, Lafora, Márquez, Goyanes, Negrín, García Tapia, Calandre, Bastos, Sacristán, Tello (assistant to Ramón y Cajal in histology). They rubbed shoulders with the children of writers, such as Maeztu, Ramón Pérez de Ayala, Ortega, Luis de Zulueta, Américo Castro, Ramón Menéndez Pidal, Eugenio d'Ors and Valle-Inclán. There were, furthermore, the nephews of those who did not have children of their own, such as Azorín and Pío Baroja. There were also grandchildren of scientists or lecturers from the university, so that there were branches of the third generation of the Bolívar family, and the children of Blas Cabrera, the physicist who was a major player in the cultural activities of the Residencia (Ruiz-Castillo 1979: 151). A scrutiny of the records of the activities of the Residencia de Estudiantes in the *Memorias* of the JAE reveals that all of the above writers, with the exception of Pérez de Ayala, were invited to lecture at the Residencia in the first twenty years of its existence. Of the doctors, there was less public involvement with the Residencia other than the activity of Sánchez Covisa, Lafora, Negrín and Sacristán in the laboratory work of the Residencia, and the lively participation of Pittaluga (known as much for his musical activities as for his lectures on aspects of public health and psychiatry). The other evident coincidence is between the list of those who sent their children to the Instituto-Escuela, and those of the youngest generation associated with the JAE, as noted above. That is, those who treated the ILE elders with respect are also those who would be at the forefront of outreach from the Residencia. The creation of the Instituto-Escuela is significant. It simultaneously brings into being an alternative educational institution that will be in close contact with a world beyond Spain, and strategically settles the educational future of enquiry and outreach.

Degrees of latitude

The longitudinal simplification of the line stretching from Giner to the ILE to the JAE and to the Residencia indicates the routes along which not just knowledge, but structures of thinking and enquiry were able to be passed down through the generations. But the examples cited briefly above also indicate the lateral reach of generational groups, clusters of contemporaries who rubbed shoulders with one another, or who might have eased the path for one another. Such clusters are not necessarily simple institutions, nor single self-contained units. They may be, in functional terms, sub-units of a larger whole. In the case of the Residencia, for example, there is a Trojan horse in the shape of the Comité Hispano-Inglés, which lodges a bit of England (apparently to the delight of all parties) within the Residencia. As outlined in Chapter 5, the CHI plays a major part in running lectures, organizing exchanges, and a significant part in the publication of *Residencia*, the house-journal that is effectively an alumni publication. The CHI also has certain connexions with another body within the Residencia, namely the Sociedad de Cursos y Conferencias (SCC). In fact, although we can see that they operated with separate arrangements, with separate subscriptions and invited their own lecturers, there was some overlap between them in the form of their clientèle.

If we then think of the outreach of these two circles, in terms of their links with the outside world, they have quite particular limitations. The CHI reaches out to England, but it is to the England of the Spanish ambassador in London, Alfonso de Merry del Val, and it does so via the Duque de Alba, known in the CHI correspondence in the Palacio de Liria as 'Jimmy'. This England is generally quite different from the England that Giner encouraged his disciples to reach out to. When he writes to Castillejo about his travels, he encourages him to visit London, certainly, but also the North, and the universities of Leeds, Liverpool and Sheffield figure on his routes.

Meanwhile, the membership of the SCC has a distinctly aristocratic flavour, linked to Madrid aristocracy. At its founding, they declare that the intention is to invite lecturers 'entre los que figuran relevantes personalidades de las Artes, las Ciencias, el Profesorado y la aristocracia española' (JAE 1929: 346). Despite this declared limitation, however, they also mount the lectures for which the Residencia gained its reputation, including Janet and Marinetti, and in 1928/9 Ravel and Ferenczi, in 1929/30 Poulenc and Keyserling (JAE 1931: 387, 391).

We can return to Collini's pithy comment that 'Professions, like clubs, are about excluding people' (1991: 237). Whether or not clubs are more exclusive and self-limiting than other institutions I have discussed is unclear, but as cultural phenomena they are significant, and what they offer as nodal points in cultural trafficking is a mixture of the random and the structured. Spain has for a long time had a hierarchy of social structures that control admission. We could view Ateneos are more excluding than casinos (and with more elevated intellectual aims: if most small towns could boast a casino, not all could rise to an Ateneo). The tradition of café *tertulias*, meanwhile, hallowed in the history of artistic movements rather than political ones, is one of looser margins. Co-existing with all of these in a remarkable range of locations we find, for example, a network of the lodges of freemasonry (a network in the most intentional sense of promoting universal brotherhood and transcending local and national boundaries) (Ferrer Benimeli 1980: 4).

The Ateneo de Madrid, like the Residencia, can be seen as a type of small and enclosed world, at the same time as it offered movement, outreach and breadth of intellectual contact. Perhaps more than any other example here it could be considered to be the epitome of the closed institution, in that to join it you had to be proposed and seconded. Just like a club, in fact. But its membership has traditionally been more catholic than was the membership of the Residencia, most notably with the inclusion of lawyers, *periodistas* and those associated with the military (Villacorta Baños 1980: 38–42, 248–9). This is partly to do with a different constitution and intention, although educational intention was central. Commenting specifically on the foundation of the Ateneo de Madrid in 1836, Villacorta Baños observes that its aim, *inter alia*, was to make good what was properly the function of the university. If the university covered routine education, the Ateneo would work on the dissemination of modern thought (Villacorta Baños 1985: xv). And if we regard Ateneos in the broad sense as meeting places for intellectuals, and transitional spaces that might facilitate contacts with 'elsewhere', the base of the Ateneo is not dissimilar to the Residencia. But there are distinctions. In terms of openness and variety, we could generalize that that the Ateneo of Madrid is to the Residencia what casinos were to Ateneos, and in their turn café *tertulias* compared similarly to casinos. All of these meeting places can be thought of in terms of local populations that over the years reached significant numbers: between 1835 and 1899 some 7,030 members were admitted to the Ateneo of Madrid (Guereña 1999: 35).

A survey of the lectures given in the Ateneo in 1910–11 reveals that a range of them were on international/European issues, albeit constituting no more than five percent of the total. But the Ateneo in general was concerned, among other things, with the spread of information and the fostering of debate. To this end it had its Escuela de Estudios Superiores, and lectures were arranged not as single events, but in the form of series or courses (see Villacorta Baños 1980: 77–8, 130; 1985: 39–41, 97–111). Its participants included: Ramón y Cajal, Azcárate, Ortí y Lara, Menéndez Pelayo, Cossío, Pardo Bazán, Labra, Simarro, Echegaray, Pedrell, Alas, San Martín, Salillas, Riaño, Antón, Menéndez Pidal, Torres Campos, Mélida, Sales y Ferré, Posada, Lampérez, Pittaluga, Barcia, Flores de Lemus, Silvela, Bonilla y San Martín, Marvá, Rodríguez Carracido, Rodríguez Mourelo and Cejador, and more than half of them were ILE products. What they spoke on were all the big questions of the day. In the publicity they were not billed as being international (that is, directly concerned with 'elsewhere'). But by their nature they inevitably were, and it is possible that they were so in more integrative manner than visiting lecturers who were big names from abroad. Their topics included Darwinism, general anthropology and criminology, literary and artistic history, neurology, neo-Thomism, *positivismo jurídico*, mathematics, physics and chemistry (Villacorta-Baños 1980: 77–8). When we think of the Residencia as the main centre of cultural exoticism in Madrid in these years, we neglect the Ateneo at our peril.

Perhaps more important than all this is the way in which the Ateneo also functioned as a significant meeting place for those who would be central in other institutions. The membership list for 1909 includes many who would have Residencia connexions. If we assume that they did not relinquish Ateneo membership on becoming associated with the Residencia, the majority could be understood as meeting twice over, including Cossío, García Morente, Castillejo, Ortega, Baeza, Menéndez Pelayo, Ramón y Cajal, Azcárate, Costa, Alfonso de Borbón, Díez Canedo, Jiménez Fraud, Madinaveitia, Martínez Sierra, Pittaluga, Sebastián Recasens, Lafora and Simarro. By 1914, some other names appear, as secretaries of sections and who would figure in cultural and intellectual networking, including: Madariaga (who would enter the stage of European diplomacy), Salinas (who would figure among those lecturing in the Residencia, and in the Universidad Internacional Menéndez Pelayo at Santander in the early 1930s) and Otaola y Richter (who would be prominent in the Spanish chapter of the World League for Sexual Reform).

The Ateneo was not neutral in its outlook, and became distinctly pro-Ally in the course of the First World War (Villacorta Baños 1980: 130). One could speculate that this was either reflected or could have been predicted by the profile of its journal holdings. From their records we find that in 1909 there were seventy-three French titles, plus four from Belgium, compared with sixty-four titles in Spanish and nineteen in English, of which four were from the US, and eight from Germany.

Just as in the Residencia there were subsets and clusters, including the CHI and the Sociedad de Cursos y Conferencias, there were other groupings that cut across the boundaries. These ranged from the highly organized, but secretive membership of Masonic lodges to the diffuse and wide-ranging interest in theosophy, spiritualism and naturism. Freemasonry in Spain, documented by the numerous studies of Ferrer Benimeli, was a force to be reckoned with. Its social mix was broad, arguably more so than that of the Ateneo. Of 1,059 members of the Gran Logia Regional del Mediodía de España in 1926, 455 belonged to the 'clases burguesas' (comerciantes, industriales, propietarios, abogados, catedráticos, médicos), and 604 were in salaried professions and occupations (Ferrer Benimeli 1980: 61). Numerically it was important: in 1931, there were 167 lodges in Spain with numbers close to 5,000 (Ferrer Benimeli 1980: 68). The presence of theosophy is harder to chart, but it was, for example, a perceptible presence in the Residencia, and one associated with Vicéns. Responding to Max Aub's comment that he had had his 'época vegetariana de rábanos y lechugas', Buñuel responded

> Sí, es verdad, fue la influencia de Vicéns, por el 19 o el 20. Vicéns era vegetariano, masón y teósofo. Una vez quiso hacerme ingresar en una logia. A mí me parece muy bien. A mí todas esas cosas de tipo romántico me entusiasman. Era una logia que se llamaba *Fuerza Numantina*.
>
> (Salaberria 2002: 13)

Networking and association brought benefits, but they were not without a more sinister resonance. Two examples illustrate this, one concerning membership of a club, the other an example of how a history of networking came to be disowned.

For the first of these we can see how a small but significant institution, the Lyceum Club, a women-only club, was perceived as dangerous, and socially threatening. Founded in 1929, the Lyceum had María de Maeztu as its president. The vice-presidents were Beatriz Galindo and Victoria Kent, the secretary was Zenobia Camprubí, the wife of Juan Ramón Jiménez, a lynch pin of the Residencia in the mid-1920s, and the vice-secretary was Helen Phipps, a teacher at the Instituto Internacional. Other women associated with it included the wives of Pérez de Ayala, Araquistaín, Álvarez del Vayo, Ucelay, Besterio, González Martínez, Ortega y Gasset, Fabra Ribas, Mesa, Maeztu, Gutiérrez (Juan de la Encina), Diez Canedo, Caro Raggio, Baeza, Elorrieta and Marañón (Zulueta 1992: 208). The Lyceum Club was the counterpart of similar women's clubs in the US and Europe, but in some circles at least in Spain was perceived as a network that spelled danger. The Junta Central de la Unión de Damas Españolas had sent a protest in August 1927 to *ABC* against certain 'centros de recreo'. In terms that could well have been found in mid-nineteenth-century attacks on liberalism, the Unión clearly links networking and the dissemination of knowledge with the undermining of Catholic family life:

> Existen en España centros de recreo y de cultura femeninos *neutros*, que significa abiertos a todas las creencias, y por lo tanto, que admiten a todo el que llegue aportando su cuota, y le facilitan *todo género* de lecturas, desde el *Corán* hasta el *Ripalda*.
> En esos centros, bajo el antifaz de obras culturales, económicas, benéficas y sociales, se ocultan los trabajos demoledores contra la sociedad y la familia católica apostólica romana.

A nerve is touched here: knowledge, and the freedom to read without restriction, and with no guidance or control, is a social danger. It echoes that suspiciousness reported in reaction to the Bibliotecas Populares project and to 'improper' reading matter being made available to particular sections of the population that was encountered by María Moliner on her visits of inspection. The suspicion frequently turned on the question of what children, but girls in particular, might be allowed to read (Moliner 2006: 323). If we are inclined to believe that city life was always and necessarily more sophisticated than rural life in matters of education and knowledge, this statement of the Unión acts as a corrective reminder. Its implication is that a grouping of women is dangerous because of the facilitation of access to reading, as though this group might need to be protected, but also because lack of protection would undermine society and the family. The clear gendered marking of attitudes towards literacy that would leave women more marginalized than men (Vilanova Ribas and Moreno Juliá 1992: 70–1) extends to the provision of more sophisticated levels of knowledge.

A sadly salutory lesson can be observed in relation to the Lyceum Club. The wife of the Duque de Alba was a member, and one of the members wrote to him in 1927 to ask for his support in the light of the letter from the Unión. The Duque's reply was cautious, diplomatic, and – writing from his summer residence in Santander – indicated that little if anything could be done, responding clearly in the hope that things would blow over. The coming of the Republic brought renewed attack on this quarter, and a letter of 3 April 1931 from María Díaz to the Duquesa de Alba pulled no punches:

> Muy Sra. mía: Parece mentira que perteneciendo Ud a la aristocracia más linajuda de España, y además persona de ideales religiosos, pertenezca Ud

a un club Femenino de ideas republicanas, comunistas y revolucionarias, ayudando con su dinero a un centro donde la mayoría de sus socias y especialmente las que componen la Junta Directiva son mujeres enemigas de las normas de la Iglesia y de ideas contrarias a la monarquía.

En Palacio y en círculos que Ud frecuenta se ha comentado no se haya dado Ud de baja, al hacerse público el homenaje que en dicho centro se ha celebrado en honor de la abogada Sra Kent y de los revolucionarios que tan injustamente están en la calle.

Indudablemente Ud es una de las muchas engañadas que con fines culturales han sabido conquistar (Liria).

On 28 April 1931 the Duquesa cancelled her subscription to the Lyceum. Whatever the impulse towards liberal cultural exchange that might have been lodged in the club, outside pressures and perceptions cast it into a mould that rendered participants dangerous by association. The example also illustrates the degree to which cultural developments in Spain continued to be vitiated by traditional beliefs that perceived activities along lines that were both gendered and confessional, and kicked into operation in a manner that hardened the lines of difference between left and right.

Related to this, and similarly indicative of the problematic atmosphere in which those involved in cultural activity perennially found themselves there is Diego Hidalgo's disavowal of a past association. As outlined in Chapter 6, he was one of those who had visited Soviet Russia in the 1920s and had been linked with the left-wing publishing house Cénit in the 1920s (Santonja 1989: 42–3). Later, however, in a heightened political climate he was to be defensive about his relationship to Cénit, referring in Parliamentary session to his initial dealings with it, which were financial, he states, rather than anything else, and lasted up to 1931: 'Desde esa época yo no he vuelto a tener con la Editorial Cénit otras relaciones que las que se derivan del cobro de intereses de ese préstamo y de la amortización del mismo' (D Hidalgo 1934: 20–2).

The WLSR and networking

The population in Spain involved in the trafficking of knowledge is remarkably diverse, albeit existing within frameworks that are varying in their degrees of formality. In this last section I would like to take the example of an organization that was actively involved in taking in knowledge from countries outside Europe, and in disseminating it to others. Through it we can see the myriad clusters of contact that were able to exist, and that allowed for a series of complex interrelations.

My example comes from an organization that, like freemasonry, did not have its roots in Spain. The World League for Sexual Reform was officially

founded in 1928, although some relevant activities were included in its development retrospectively (Dose 2003). Membership of the WLSR would reach
190,000 (Dose 2003: 3). In Spain a small group of individuals met to set up
the Spanish chapter of the WLSR in March 1932. Unlike the institutions
discussed elsewhere in this book, the WLSR itself and its Spanish chapter
were not long-lived, but it does provide an example of highly effective
networking for cultural and intellectual trafficking.

The founding group of the Spanish chapter of the WLSR had forty-one
members based in Madrid, and there were a further ten in the provinces. In a
mix that partially echoes that of the Ateneo, but also of the Cortes of 1931,
twenty-eight belonged to the field of medicine, eight were lawyers, and the
rest were associated with other areas of public life, including journalism and
education (Sinclair 2007: 91).

A feature that is prominent in the group is their internationalism, in both
contacts and publications, including the works for which they wrote prefaces.
In this international category we find Barrio de Medina, Julio Bravo,
Cansinos Assens, Cifuentes Díaz, Cossío, González Blanco, Haro, Jiménez
de Asua, Lafora, Marañón, Morata, Nóvoa Santos, Pittaluga, Ramón y Cajal,
Recasens, Rocamora, Ruiz Funes, Sacristán, Saldaña and Zozaya. This is a
mixture that includes doctors, lawyers, men of literature and proponents of
social hygiene.

To both indicate and simplify the sense of their overlapping affiliations
and points of contact Figure 5 indicates the founding members in broad
terms. It will be evident by this stage that a considerable number were associated with the institutions that have figured prominently in this study. Some
were in the Ateneo together (but not, on the whole, in the Residencia or the
JAE together). There are others in this initial founding group of the Spanish
WLSR who are present in the major organs, such as Cossío (so prominent
in connexion with the Residencia and the Misiones Pedagógicas), and they
stand out as not having other defining attributes of the group, such as being
a doctor or hygienist, or dealing with sexuality or venereal disease.

The individuals in the group are notable for their polyvalency and catholicity of activity, arguably something that cut across the possibly stultifying
enclosure of individual units. By belonging to several places and professions,
not to mention having different levels and styles of output, both professional
and popular, they are able to operate as organic, with their own trajectory.
They do not belong to a set pattern. It is striking to see how many published
at a popular level as well as for elite consumption. This is perhaps not
surprising given the common aim of the WLSR to communicate hygiene
to the broad public. But in their activity, several on this list mix literature
and medicine, high and low, theology and sexology. We find them together
in the lists of popular novels. César Juarros Ortega, a neuropathologist, is
particularly notable for the number of popular novelettes he wrote, as well

as propaganda (such as *Los engaños de la morfina*, Madrid 1929, in the Libro del pueblo series). Quintiliano Saldaña is a lawyer and sexologist, who also writes a novel entitled *Las corridas: novela de pasión y entendimiento*, Madrid 1914. Julio Bravo is a doctor and hygienist with international contacts, who also writes lyrics for the popular theatre, and plays of his own. Edmundo González Blanco is a novelist, prolific writer, also preface writer, and illustrator, writing on current politics, art, the history of journalism, but also popular novels. They move fluidly outside their given professional areas. Jaime Torrubiano Ripoll is a writer of philosophy and theology who also writes on matters of sexual and moral nature. He contributes repeatedly in 1925 to a section on 'Teología sexual' in the review *Sexualidad*. Luis Jiménez de Asúa is a lawyer, producing solid legal writing on an international scale, but also writes on eugenics and euthanasia.

We can take Gustavo Pittaluga as an example of multi-faceted activity that moves across borders both national and disciplinary. He is a doctor and ardent hygienist but he operates also as a musician in the Residencia. He speaks on the Balkans and Russia in the Residencia in 1925 (in the same year as Álvarez del Vayo does it). In so doing, alongside Baeza, Ortega and Marañón, he is with a crowd of international stars, and what he has to speak about ('La sangre' in 1926/7, and in 1929/30, 'La vida doméstica y la formación de la personalidad') is delivered into an international context. Musically he also moves across borders. Having conducted a concert of the Madrid Philharmonic in 1932/3 he goes on in 1933/4 to conduct Poulenc with the same orchestra. Pittaluga is also noticeable in the Ateneo. Having taught in the session 1903/4, and 1907/8, and having given lectures in 1905/6, he could be said to have 'trained' in the Ateneo before moving to the Residencia.

Finally, we can look at the other places in which they met. In the case of the hygienists there were the Sunday meetings of the Campaña Sanitaria where Hildegart from 1926 would be in company with many who would form part of the Spanish WLSR. They also 'met' in the pages of *Sexualidad*, and contributors included Jiménez de Asúa, Juarros, Macau, Marañón, Pittaluga, Saldaña, Recaséns and Jaime Torrubiano Ripoll (Sinclair 2007: 45–7). There seems to be a real possibility of both networking and mentoring here. There were links in other areas of publishing. In some cases the link is just what one would expect, as in the pages of *La Gaceta Médica*, where leading lights such as Lafora and Sacristán wrote. But about a third of the founding members of the Spanish WLSR published with Morata, as did a similar proportion of those interested in the organization who came from the provinces. The link between Mario Sánchez Taboada and the group is less obvious, but must come from the fact that he was *gerente* of the *Archivos de Higiene y Sanidad Pública*. In this journal, published through 1925, Pittaluga, Navarro Fernández and Julio Bravo (among others) are contributors, and there is a markedly international character to the topics covered and the books under review.

Figure 5. Affiliations of founding members of WLSR in Spain

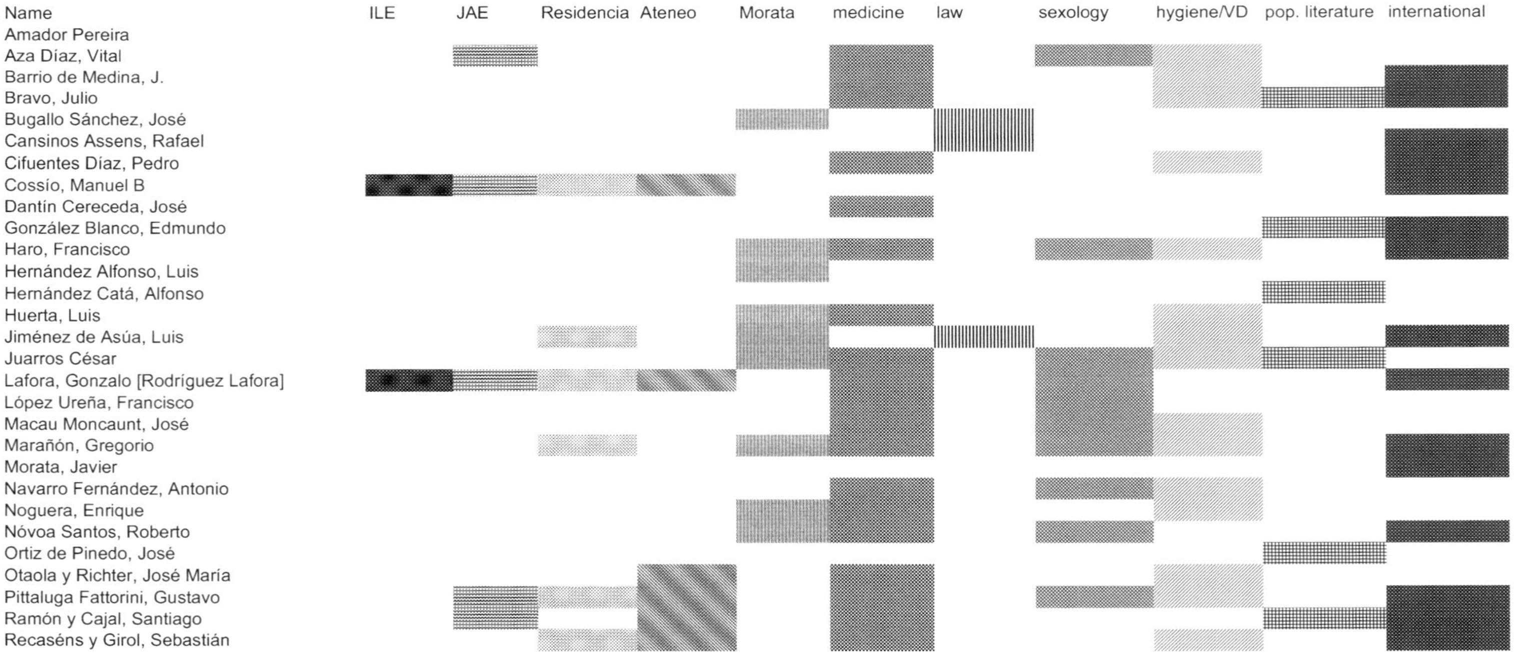

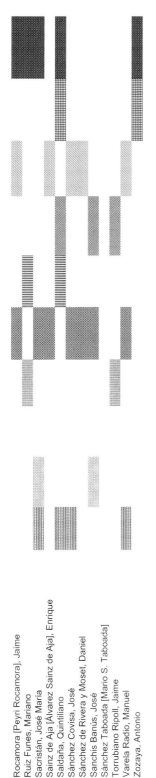

Rocamora [Peyri Rocamora], Jaime
Ruiz Funes, Mariano
Sacristán, José María
Sainz de Aja [Álvarez Sainz de Aja], Enrique
Saldaña, Quintiliano
Sánchez Covisa, José
Sánchez de Rivera y Moset, Daniel
Sanchis Banús, José
Sánchez Taboada [Mario S. Taboada]
Torrubiano Ripoll, Jaime
Varela Radio, Manuel
Zozaya, Antonio

Two members of this group do not appear with any affiliations. Amador Pereira has proved impossible to trace, although he may have been in the legal profession. Sánchez Taboada was manager of the *Archivos de Higiene y Sanidad* and listed as medical correspondent in this journal and for *El Liberal* (1925)

Dissolution or invisibility?

It is not actually clear that the WLSR in Spain came to an end with the death of Hildegart at the hands of her mother in 1933, but there seems little doubt that this tragic event contributed to its invisibility (Sinclair 2007: 157–8). We could speculate that the structures for the networks of the WLSR, insofar as they were based in professional activity, or membership of various circles, continued to exist. What happened, arguably, was a disappearance from public view, a re-grouping in silence, perhaps from which other paths were followed, other developments pursued. Spain was not lacking in experience of such disappearances. The closure of the Ateneo de Madrid in 1924 by Primo de Rivera's regime is a case in point, and the management of the Residencia in the Primo years demonstrates the careful handling of public life in order to permit a private (institutional) life of exploration and creativity.

There is no doubt of the tremendous loss to Spain's cultural trafficking that was brought about by and at the conclusion of the Civil War. The intention of this study, among others, has been to demonstrate the extent and the nature of that loss, one that consisted not only in material realities, but also in dreams of the imaginary. Vicéns, glossing an article that appeared in *Unidad* in the war years, paints a picture that is scathing in its adoption of dismissive discourse:

> Un poco más de seriedad señores; éste no es el momento de perder el tiempo en congresos de enseñanza y otras sandeces; es necesario que se sepa de una vez por todas que el tiempo de las Misiones Pedagógicas y otras empresas de Cultura Popular está completamente acabado y nosotros no toleraremos que estas comedias recomiencen. (Vicéns 1938: 97–8)

Vilanova Ribas, in a commentary that contests the implications of this view, simultaneously indicates how some could be considered to have been immune to the cultural losses entailed by the war, because of their lack of literacy. Thus while he asserts that the effect of Francoism was a *noche oscura* for culture, there was a type of grim escape, so that the Francoist victory of 1939

> puede interpretarse como el sacrificio a gran escala de las élites obreras militantes y alfabetizadas, mientras que a las masas, en gran parte analfabetas, les obligó a través de la condena reiterada y vociferante de la República y de la Guerra y, a través del silencio que les impuso, a interiorizarse para sobrevivir. La reacción de la población analfabeta ante la represión fue variada, sutil y sabia. En cierta medida su propia marginalidad del poder y de la cultura escrita les ahorró la decapitación física que sufrieron los militantes alfabetizados. Paradójicamente la ausencia de escolaridad y alfabetización que les impidió una integración más completa en el sistema, les permitió defenderse de los avatares de la guerra, la revolución y la represión. (Vilanova Ribas and Moreno Juliá 1992: 64)

The implied Pyrrhic victory of a lack of letters that might have defended against the impact of the Nationalist years has its attractions, but also its limitation. Becoming open to the world of letters, and particularly to the cultural worlds outside Spain, had without doubt enriched the life of many in Spain, even if, in terms of the general cultural level of the population, such enrichment was not to be total. The loss, however, would be for all. The horizons of the imaginary, whether those of the intellectual or those that the idealists of the Republic endeavoured to make available to the wider population, were necessarily fragile, not always well-based, but grounded in desire. The forward-seeking movement of curiosity and openness that fuelled so much of Spain's cultural trafficking of the early twentieth century was to be a loss not just in terms of its objects of desire, but in terms of the desire itself, and as such a central part of Spain's cultural heritage.

BIBLIOGRAPHY

Ahearne, J (1995). *Michel de Certeau: Interpretation and its Other*. Cambridge: Polity

Alberich, J (1966). *Los ingleses y otros temas de Pío Baroja*. Madrid: Alfaguara

Altamira, R (1915). *Giner de los Ríos: educador*. Valencia: Prometeo

Álvarez del Vayo , J (1926). *La nueva Rusia; En camión por la estepa; Las dos revoluciones; Siluetas: Lenin, Trotzki, Stalin, Chicherin, Dzerchinski, Zinovieff, Radek; Moscú; Leningrado...* Madrid: Espasa Calpe

Álvarez del Vayo, J (1950). *The Last Optimist*. London: Putnam

Álvarez, J T, *et al.* (1989a). *Historia de los medios de comunicación en España: Periodismo, imagen y publicidad (1900–1990)*. Barcelona: Ariel

Álvarez, J T (1989b). 'Los frustrados intentos de regeneración informativa', in *Historia de los medios de comunicación en España: Periodismo, imagen y publicidad (1900–1990)*, ed. J T Álvarez. Barcelona: Ariel, pp. 83–103

Álvarez Junco, J (1993). 'Los intelectuales: anticlericalismo y republicanismo', in *Los orígenes culturales de la II República*, ed. J L García Delgado. Madrid: Siglo XXI, pp. 101–26

Álvarez Junco, J (1996). 'Redes locales, lealtades tradicionales y nuevas identidades colectivas en la España del siglo XX', in *Política en penumbra: Patronazgo y clientelismo políticos en la España contemporánea*, ed. A Robles Egea. Madrid: Siglo XXI, pp. 71–94

Álvarez Junco, J (2001). *Mater dolorosa: la idea de España en el siglo XIX*. Madrid: Taurus

Álvarez Peláez, R (1987). 'Herencia, sexo y eugenesia', in *Perspectivas Psiquiátricas*, ed. R Huertas, A I Romero and R Álvarez Peláez. Madrid: CSIC, pp. 203–18

Álvarez Peláez, R (1988). 'Origen y desarrollo de la eugenesia en España', in *Ciencia y sociedad en España. De la Ilustración a la Guerra Civil*, ed. J M Sánchez Ron. Madrid: CSIC, pp. 179–204

Anderson, B (1983). *Imagined Communities: Reflections on the Origin and Spread of Nationalism*. London: Verso

Anon (1904). 'Al lector', *Boletín del Instituto de Reformas Sociales* I (1): 1–2

Anon (1920). 'Conferencia de Marcelino Domingo', *La Voz*: 7

Anon (1925). 'Oradores que han tomado parte en los mitines de propaganda sanitaria', *Sexualidad* 1 (22): 12–16

Araquistain, L (1915). 'Que España quiere vivir', *España* 1 (4): 3

Arroyo Reyes, C (2003). 'José Carlos Mariátegui, *Amauta* y la literatura rusa de la revolución', *La Hoja Latinoamericana* (84): 19–40

Balbontín, J A (1932). *Una pedrada a la Virgen*. Madrid: Ediciones Libertad

Balcells, A (ed.) (1977). *Teoría y práctica del movimiento obrero español (1900–1936)*. Valencia: Fernando Torres Editor

Baroja, P. (1917). 'Europeización', in *Nuevo tablado de Arlequín*. Madrid: Caro Raggio, pp.47-51.

Baeza, R. (1922). 'Hombres y rusos'. *El Sol*, 31 March 1922, p 5.

Bécarud, J and E López Campillo (1978). *Los intelectuales españoles durante la II República*. Madrid: Siglo XXI de España

Bernaldo de Quirós, C and J Llanas de Aguilaniedo (1901). *La mala vida en Madrid*. Madrid: Rodríguez Serra

Bhabha, H (1988). 'Cultural Diversity and Cultural Differences' in *The Postcolonial Studies Reader*, edited by Bill Ashcroft, Gareth Griffiths and Helen Tiffin. London and New York: Routledge, 1995), (reprinted from 'The Commitment to Theory, *New Formations* 5, 1988), pp. 206–9

Borrow, G (1843). *The Bible in Spain, or, the Journeys, Adventures and Imprisonments of an Englishman, in an Attempt to Circulate the Scriptures in the Peninsula*. London: Murray

Borrow, G (1921). *La Biblia en España*. Madrid: Imp. Clásica Española

Botrel, J-F. 'Passeurs culturels en Espagne (1875–1914)', in: D. Cooper-Richet, J-Y. Mollier, A. Silem (dir.), *Passeurs culturels dans le monde des médias et de l'édition en Europe (XIXe et XXe siècles)*, Villeurbanne, Presses de l'enssib, 2005, pp. 209–228

Botrel, J-F (2007). 'Cosmopolitismo y mediación cultural en la España del siglo XIX', *Península. Revista de Estudos Ibéricos*, 4, pp. 35–44

Botrel, J-F (2008). *Libros y lectores en la España del siglo XX*. Rennes: Jean-François Botrel

Bourdieu, P (1991). *Language and Symbolic Power*. Cambridge: Polity

Bourdieu, P (1992). *The Logic of Practice*. Oxford: Polity

Brenan, G (1943). *The Spanish Labyrinth: An Account of the Social and Political Background of the Spanish Civil War*. Cambridge: Cambridge University Press

Brenan, G (1950). *The Face of Spain*. London: Turnstile

Brenan, G (1951). *The Literature of the Spanish People: From Roman Times to the Present Day*. Cambridge: Cambridge University Press

Brenan, G (1957). *South from Granada*. London: Hamish Hamilton

Brenan, G (1974). *Personal Record: 1920–1972*. London: Jonathan Cape

British Ministry of Reconstruction, A E C (1919). *Adult Education Committee: Final Report (Chaired by Arthur L. Smith)*. London: HMSO

Buñuel, L (1994). *My Last Breath*. London: Vintage [orig. edn 1982]

Cacho Viu, V (1962). *La Institución Libre de Enseñanza I. Orígenes y etapa universitaria (1860–1881)*. Madrid: Rialp

Calpe (1923). *Catálogo general*. Madrid

Calvo Sotelo, J (1916). 'Noches del Real: Bailes Rusos IV: Los remedios. – La cultura', *El Debate* 5 June 1916, 1

Carandell, L (1993). 'Crónica de las crónicas', in *Viaje a Las Hurdes: el manuscrito inédito de Gregorio Marañón y las fotografías de la visita de Alfonso XII*, ed. Madrid: El País-Aguilar/Fundación Gregorio Marañón, pp. 21–48

Castellano, P (2000). *Enciclopedia Espasa: historia de una aventura editorial*. Madrid: Espasa

Castillejo, D (1997). *El epistolario de José Castillejo. I. Un puente hacia Europa 1896–1909. Cartas reunidas por David Castillejo*. Madrid: Castalia

Castillejo, D (1998). *Epistolarios de José Castillejo y de Manuel Gómez-Moreno. II. El espíritu de una época 1910–1912*. Madrid: Castalia

Castillejo, D (1999). *Epistolario de José Castillejo. III. Fatalidad y porvenir 1913–1937. Cartas reunidas y enlazadas por David Castillejo*. Madrid: Castalia

Castillejo, I C d (1967). *I Married a Stranger. Life with One of Spain's Enigmatic Men* [mimeographed]

Castillejo, J (1919). *La educación en Inglaterra*. Madrid [La Lectura]

Castillejo, J (1930). *La educación en Inglaterra. Sus ideales, su historia y su organización nacional*. Madrid [La Lectura]

Chacel, R (1931). 'Esquema de los problemas prácticos y actuales del amor', *Revista de Occidente* 9 (92): 129–80

Chaves Nogales [1929]. *La vuelta a Europa en avión. Un pequeño burgués en la Rusia Roja*. Madrid: Editorial Latino

Chaves Nogales (1931). *Lo que ha quedado del imperio de los zares*. Madrid: Editorial Estampa

Cleminson, R (2000). *Anarchism, Science and Sex: Eugenics in Eastern Spain, 1900–1937*. Oxford: Peter Lang

Cleminson, R (2003). '"Science and Sympathy" or "Sexual Subversion on a Human Basis"? Anarchists in Spain and the World League for Sexual Reform', *Journal of the History of Sexuality* 12 (1): 110–21

Collini, S (1991). *Public Moralists: Political Thought and Intellectual Life in Britain*. Oxford: Clarendon Press

Collini, S (2006). *Absent Minds*. Oxford: Oxford University Press

Costa, J (1981). 'Reconstitución y europeización de España: Mensaje y programa de la Cámara agrícola del Alto-Aragón [1898]', in *Reconstitución de europeización de España y otros escritos*, ed. S Martín-Retortillo y Baquer. Madrid: Instituto de Estudios de Administración Local, pp. 3–42

Crispin, J (1981). *Oxford and Cambridge in Madrid*. Santander: Isla de los Ratones

Cruz, M (1988). '"Sois un honor para España" asegura el Rey en Las Hurdes', *El Mundo*, 15 April

Davies, R (2000). *'La España Moderna' and 'Regeneración': a Cultural Review in Restoration Spain, 1889–1914*. Manchester: Manchester University Press

Davis, S (1999). 'The Hispanic Canon'. Birmingham: University of Birmingham (MPhil thesis)

Davis, S (2001). 'In Defence of an Institution: Approaches to the Peninsular Spanish Canon', *Journal of Iberian and Latin American Studies* 7 (2): 129–42

de Certeau, M (1984). *The Practice of Everyday Life*. Berkeley: University of California Press

de Certeau, M (1988). *The Writing of History*. New York and Oxford: University of Columbia Press

de los Ríos, F (1921). *Mi viaje a la Rusia soviética*. Madrid: Imp. de Caro Raggio

Díaz Plaja, F (1973). *Francófilos y germanófilos: Los españoles en la guerra europea*. Barcelona: Dopesa

Díaz y Pérez, N (1885). *Las bibliotecas de España en sus relaciones con la educación popular y la instrucción pública*. Madrid: Manuel G Hernández

Díaz-Retg (1931). *En Rusia, la revolución empieza ahora: Informaciones y estudios objetivos llevados a cabo en Rusia, en plena ejecución del Plan Quinquenal, hasta enero de 1932*. Madrid: Prensa Moderna [Zeus Sociedad Anónima Editorial]

Dobson, A (1989). *An Introduction to the Politics and Philosophy of J. Ortega y Gasset*. Cambridge: Cambridge University Press

Dose, R (2003). 'The World League for Sexual Reform: Some Possible Approaches', *Journal of the History of Sexuality* 12 (1): 1–15

Dougherty, D (1982). *Un Valle-Inclán olvidado*. Madrid: Taurus

Ellis, H H (1908). *The Soul of Spain*. London: Constable

Escolano, A, ed. (1992). *Leer y escribir en España: Doscientos años de alfabetización*. Madrid: Pirámide-Fundación G S Ruipérez

Escolano, A (1995). *Luis Bello: Viaje por las escuelas de Castilla y León*. Valladolid: Ámbito

Espasa Calpe (1926). *Catálogo general*. Madrid

Espectador (1928). 'Pro Cultura Sanitaria', *Sexualidad* 5 (140): 3–5

Espina, A. (1926). 'Varios libros acerca de la nueva Rusia de Álvarez del Vayo, Béraud, Chklovski'. *Revista de Occidente* 4 (36): 372–80

Estudiantes, Residencia de (1918). *Bibliotecas populares (Instrucciones para su organización y catálogo de libros)*. Madrid: Residencia de Estudiantes

Estudiantes, Residencia de (1920). *Bibliotecas populares (Educación de adultos. Bibliotecas asturianas)*. Madrid: Residencia de Estudiantes

Feijóo y Montenegro, P B J (1730 (repr. 1961)). 'Fábulas de las Batuecas y países imaginarios', in *Teatro crítico IV*, ed. Madrid: Biblioteca de Autores Españoles 142, pp. 85–901

Fernández Cifuentes, L (1982). *Teoría y mercado de la novela en España: del 98 a la República*. Madrid: Gredos

Fernández Sebastián, J and J F Fuentes, eds (2002). *Diccionario político y social del siglo XIX español*. Madrid: Alianza

Ferrer Benimeli, J A (1980 (expanded 1987)). *Masonería española contemporánea I 1800–1868; II Desde 1868 hasta nuestros días*. Madrid: Siglo XXI

Ford, R (1845). *A Hand-book for Travellers in Spain and Readers at Home,*

Describing the Countries and Cities, the Natives and their Manners, the Antiquities, Religion, Legends, Fine Arts, Literature ... with Notices on Spanish History. London: Murray

Forgacs, D, ed. (1988). *A Gramsci Reader.* London: Lawrence & Wishart

Fox, E I (1976). *La crisis intelectual del 98.* Madrid: Edicusa

Fox, E I, ed. (1977). *Ramiro de Maeztu: artículos desconocidos 1897–1904.* Madrid: Castalia

Franco Fernández, N, Francisco de Luis Martín and Luis Arias González (1998). *Catálogo de la Biblioteca de la Casa del Pueblo de Madrid, 1908/1939.* Madrid: Conserjería de Educación

Frank, W (1929). 'Europa destruída: la acción como decadencia', *Revista de Occidente* 7 (72): 354–79

Frisby, D (1985). *Fragments of Modernity: Theories of Modernity in the Work of Simmel, Kracauer and Benjamin.* Cambridge: Polity

Fuentes, J F (2002). 'Pueblo', in *Diccionario político y social del siglo XIX español*, ed. J Fernández Sebastián and J F Fuentes. Madrid: Alianza, pp. 586–93

Garcia Ejarque, L (2000). *Historia de la lectura pública en España.* Gijón: Trea

García Morente, M (1914). 'La universidad', *Boletín de la Institución Libre de Enseñanza* 38: 161–8

García Morente, M. G. (1925). 'G. Popoff: Tscheka. Der Staat im Staate (Cheka. El Estado en el Estado)'. *Revista de Occidente* 3 (22): 126–34

Garitaonandía, C (1989). 'Las palabras como armas: la propaganda en la república', in *Historia de los medios de comunicación en España: Periodismo, imagen y publicidad (1900–1990)*, ed. J T Álvarez. Barcelona: Ariel, pp. 159–67

Gastardi, E (1930). *El sol.* Madrid: Cia Ibero-Americana

Gathorne-Hardy, J (1992). *The Interior Castle: a Life of Gerald Brenan.* London: Sinclair-Stevenson

Gautier, T (1883). *Voyage en Espagne: (tra los montes).* Paris: Charpentier

Gautier, T (1920). *Viaje por Espana.* Madrid: Espasa Calpe

Gibson, I (1997). *The Shameful Life of Salvador Dalí.* London: Faber & Faber

Giménez Caballero, E (1932). *Genio de España.* Madrid: La Gaceta Literaria

Giner, F (1897). 'Espíritu y naturaleza', *Boletín de la Institución Libre de Enseñanza* 21: 165–9

Giner, F (1926). *En el cincuentenario de la Institución Libre de Enseñanza.* Madrid: Archivos

Glick, T F (1982). 'The Naked Science: Psychoanalysis in Spain, 1914–1948', *Comparative Studies in Society and History* 24: 533–71

Glick, T F (1987). 'Cultural Issues in the Reception of Relativity', in *The Comparative Reception of Relativity*, ed. T F Glick. Dordrecht: D Reidel, pp. 381–400

Glick, T (1988). *Einstein in Spain: Relativity and the Recovery of Science.* Princeton: Princeton University Press

Golinski, J (1998). *Making Natural Knowledge: Constructivism and the History of Science*. Cambridge: Cambridge University Press

Gómez, M (2002). 'Bringing Home the Truth about the Revolution: Spanish Travellers to the Soviet Union in the 1930s', in *Cultural Encounters: European Travel Writing in the 1930s*, ed. Charles Burdett and Derek Duncan. New York/Oxford: Berghahn, pp. 65–83

Gómez Aparicio, P (1974). *Historia del periodismo español: de las guerras coloniales a la Dictadura*. Madrid: Editora Nacional

González, J. V. (1924). 'Lenín'. *Revista de Filosofía* 10 (4): 81–91

Gramsci, A (1973). *Cultura y literatura*. Barcelona: Península.

Gramsci, A (1988). *A Gramsci Reader* (ed David Forgacs). London: Lawrence & Wishart

Grayson, S (2001). *The Spanish Attraction: The British Presence in Spain from 1830 to 1965*. Malaga: Santana

Green, D (1984). 'Classified Subjects: Photography and Anthropology: the Technology of Power', *Ten.8* 14: 30–7

Greenwood, A (1920). *The Education of the Citizen: a Summary of the Proposals of the Adult Education Committee*. London: Workers' Educational Association

Gubern, Román (1999). *Proyector de luna*. Barcelona: Anagrama

Guereña, J-L, I Sánchez Sánchez, and R Villena Espinosa, (coordinators) (coordinators) (1999). *Sociabilidad fin de siglo: espacios asociativos en torno a 1898*. Cuenca: Ediciones de la Universidad de Castilla-La Mancha

Hess, C A (2001). *Manuel de Falla and Modernism in Spain, 1898–1936*. Chicago: University of Chicago Press

Hidalgo D. (1929). *Un notario español en Rusia*. Madrid: Alianza

Hidalgo, D (1934). *¿Por qué fui lanzado del Ministerio de la Guerra? Diez Meses de actuación ministerial*. Madrid: Espasa Calpe

Hidalgo, A (1930a). 'Hacia la unión de todos los pequeños: Caminando entre espinas, pero ¡siempre adelante!' *Ciencia y acción* 7 (74): 8–15

Hidalgo, J (1930b). 'Hacia la unión de todos los pequeños: El clamor de los débiles', *Ciencia y acción* 7 (75): 10–15

Hidalgo, J (1930c). 'Hacia la unión de todos los pequeños: El labrador, ¿tiene derechos?' *Ciencia y acción* 7 (76): 10–15

Hidalgo, J (1931a). 'Hacia la unión de todos los pequeños: El labrador, ¿tiene derechos? (continuación)', *Ciencia y accion* 8 (78): 11–15

Hidalgo, J (1931b). 'De propaganda: por tierras de Palencia', *Ciencia y accion* 8 (86): 8–11

Hidalgo, J (1932a). 'De propaganda. Por tierras zamoranas y leonesas. Peregrinando por tierras de miseria', *Ciencia y acción* 9 (90): 8–12

Hidalgo, J (1932b). 'De propaganda. En busca de la vida más barata', *Ciencia y acción* 9 (95): 9–12

Hidalgo, J (1933a). 'El "Cine" en las Ligas', *Ciencia y accion* 10 (101): 13–16

Hidalgo, J (1933b). 'Hace ya muchos años. Por tierras gallegas. Mítines en Las Nieves y Salvatierra', *Ciencia y accion* 10 (102): 6–8

Hidalgo, J. (1933c). 'De propaganda. Por tierras de Soria'. *Ciencia y acción*. 10 (105): 12–16

Hidalgo, J. (1933d). 'De propaganda. Por tierras de Guadalajara. Miseria y miseria y miseria …' *Ciencia y acción*. 10 (106): 14–16

Hildegart (1931). *Sexo y amor*. Valencia: Rip. P. Quiles

Holroyd M. (1971). *Lytton Strachey: a Biography*. Harmondsworth: Penguin

Hoyos Cascón (1933). *El meridiano de Moscú*. Madrid: Cénit

Infantes, V, F López and J-F Botrel (2003). *Historia de la edición y de la lectura 1472–1914*. Madrid: Fundación S Ruipérez

JAE (n.d.) *Archivo de la Secretaría de la Junta para Ampliación de Estudios (1907–1939): cuadro de clasificación* [inventory of grant-holders]

JAE (1929). *Memoria correspondiente a los años 1926–1927 y 1927–1928*. Madrid: Fortanet

JAE (1931). *Memoria correspondiente a los años 1928–1929, y 1929–30*. Madrid: Fortanet

Jiménez Fraud, A (1972). *La Residencia de Estudiantes: Visita a Maquiavelo*. Barcelona: Ariel

Jiménez Fraud, A (1989). *Residentes: Semblanzas y recuerdos*. Madrid: Alianza

Jiménez-Landí Martínez, A (1973). *La Institución Libre de Enseñanza y su ambiente: I Los orígenes*. Madrid: Taurus

Jiménez-Landí Martínez, A (1987a). *La Institución Libre de Enseñanza y su ambiente: II Período parauniversitario 1*. Madrid: Taurus

Jiménez-Landí Martínez, A (1987b). *La Institución Libre de Enseñanza y su ambiente: III Período parauniversitario 2*. Madrid: Taurus

Juarros, C (1925). 'La higiene del alcohol', *Sexualidad* 1 (15): 12–13

Juarros, C (1927). 'Esterilización de los antisociales', *Sexualidad* 4 (113): 2

Juarros, C (1929). *Los engaños de la morfina*. Madrid: Cia Ibero-Americana de publicaciones

Juliá, S (2005). *Historias de las dos Españas*. Madrid: Taurus

Juliá, S (1998). 'La aparición de "los intelectuales" en España'. *Claves de razón práctica* 86: 2–10

Jung, C G (1925). 'Tipos psicológicos', *Revista de Occidente* 3 (29): 161–83

Jung, C G (1931). 'El hombre arcaico', *Revista de Occidente* 9 (94): 1–36

Key, E (1926). 'El amor libre', *Sexualidad* 2 (62): 4–6

Keyserling, C H (1926). 'España y Europa', *Revista de Occidente* 4 (35): 129–44

Knighton, T K (2009 forthcoming). 'Perspectivas del hispanismo musical británico en el siglo XX: el caso de John Brande Trend (1887-1958)', in (ed.) Juan José Carreras, /La musicología en la Edad de Plata/ (Zarazgoa: Institución Fernando el Católico, 2009)

Labanyi, J (1994). 'Nation, Narration, Naturalization: A Barthesian Critique of the 1898 Generation', in *New Hispanisms: Literature, Culture, Theory*, ed. M I Millington and Paul Julian Smith. Ottawa: Dovehouse Editions Canada, pp. 127–49

Labanyi, J (1999). 'Gramsci and Spanish Cultural Studies', *Paragraph* 22 (1): 95–113

Labanyi, J (2010 forthcoming). 'Political Readings of Don Juan and Romantic Love in Spain from the 1920s to the 1940s', in *New Dangerous Liaisons*, ed. L Passerini, L Ellena and A Geppert. London: Berghahn

Lafora, G R (1920a). 'Psicópatas como jefes revolucionarios', *El Sol*, 3 February

Lafora, G R (1920b). 'Crítica de la Facultad Central de Medicina', *El Sol*, 2 March

Lafora, G R (1920c). 'Crítica de la Facultad de Medicina', *El Sol*, 6 April

Lafora, G R (1920d). 'La organización de los hospitales en Londres', *El Sol*, 14 September

Lauter, C A N (1991). *Canon and Contexts*. Oxford: Oxford University Press

Lefèvre, E [P de la Cerda] (1931). *El sol de los Soviets. La III internacional social de Moscú frente a la internacional armada del capitalismo*. Valladolid: Imp. Castellana

Llopis, R (1929). *Cómo se forja un pueblo (La Rusia que yo he visto)*. Madrid: Yagües

López Campillo, E (1972). *La Revista de Occidente y la formación de minorías (1923–1936)*. Madrid: Taurus

López Campillo, E (1978). *Los intelectuales españoles durante la II República*. Madrid: Siglo XXI

Luis Martín, F (1994). *Cincuenta años de cultura obrera en España, 1890–1940*. Madrid, Pablo Iglesias

Luis Martín, F (1997). *Las Casas del Pueblo socialistas en España: 1900–1936: Estudio social y arquitectónico*. Barcelona, Ariel

Luzuriaga, L (1919). *El analfabetismo en España*. Madrid: Cosano

Luzuriaga, L (1928). 'Algunos aspectos de la educación nueva', *Conferencias dadas en el centro de intercambio intelectual germano-español XIX*. Madrid: n.p.

Madarasz, E (1932). *La lucha del soldado rojo*. Madrid: Ediciones Libertad

Madariaga, S (1931). *España: ensayo de historia contemporánea*. Madrid: Ibero-Americana

Madariaga, S (1980). *Carácter y destino en Europa: Ingleses, franceses, españoles; Bosquejo de Europa; Arceval y los ingleses*. Madrid: Espasa Calpe

Madariaga de la Campa, B and C Valbuena Morán (1999). *La universidad internacional de verano de Santander (1932–1936)*. Santander: Universidad Internacional Menéndez Pelayo

Madoz, P (1846). *Diccionario geográfico-estadístico-histórico de España*. Madrid: Est. lit.-tip. de P Madoz y L Sagasti

Madrid, Universidad de (1933). *Anuario 1932–1933*. Madrid: Gráfica Universal

Maeztu, R de (1899). *Hacia otra España*. Bilbao: Imp. y Enc. de Andrés Cardenal, 1899

Maeztu, R de (1901a). 'El ideal anarquista en España', *El Imparcial*, 28 November

Maeztu, R de (1901b). 'El propaganda por el hecho y la huelga general', *El Imparcial*, 6 December

Maeztu, R de (1901c). 'Los remedios – la fuerza', *El Imparcial*, 16 December

Maeztu, R de (1901d). 'Los remedios – la cultura', *El Imparcial*, 24 December

Maeztu, R de (1902). 'Cómo muere un superhombre', *La Correspondencia de España*, 19 January

Maeztu, R de (1915). 'England and Germany: Two Types of Culture', *New Age* 16 (12): 303

Maeztu, R de (1916). *Authority, Liberty and Function in the Light of the War: a Critique of authority and liberty as the foundations of the modern state and an attempt to base societies on the principle of function.* London and New York: George Allen and Unwin

Magre, R (1932). *Un periodista.* Madrid: Ediciones Libertad

Mainer, C (1972). *Literatura y pequeña burguesía en España (notas 1890–1950).* Madrid: Edicusa

Mainer, C (1977). 'Notas sobre la lectura obrera en España (1890–1930)', in *Teoría y práctica del movimiento obrero español (1900–1936)*, ed. A Balcells. Valencia: Fernando Torres Editor, pp. 173–240

Maistre, J d ([1919–1943]). *La joven siberiana. Novela.* Madrid: Espasa Calpe

Mancebo, J (1904). 'Las Hurdes en la historia (III)', *Las Hurdes* 1 (9): 194–8

Mannheim, K (1956 (repr. 1997)). *Essays on the Sociology of Culture: Collected Works*, vol. 7. London: Routledge

Marañón, G (1925). 'La acción como carácter sexual', *Sexualidad: revista ilustrada de higiene social (dir. Dr Navarro Fernández)* 1 (1): 12–13

Marañón, G (1926). 'El trabajo y la maternidad', *Sexualidad* 2 (59): 10–11

Marañón, G (1929). *El problema social de la infeccion.* Madrid: Cia Ibero-Americana de publicaciones

Marías, J (1961). *El método histórico de las generaciones.* Madrid: Revista de Occidente

Mariátegui, J C (1927). '*Caminantes*, por Lidia Seifulina', *Variedades* [Lima], 15 January

Marichalar, A (1928). 'Las "vidas" de Lytton Strachey', *Revista de Occidente* 6 (57): 343–58

Marichalar, A (1929). 'Nueva dimensión', *Revista de Occidente* 7 (72): 380–3

Martí Alpera, F (1904). *Por las escuelas de Europa.* Valencia: Sempere

Martínez Martín, J (2001). *Historia de la edición en España (1836–1936).* Madrid: Marcial Pons

Martínez Martín, J A, A Martínez Rus, *et al.* (2004). *Los patronos del libro: las asociaciones corporativas de editores y libreros, 1900–1936.* Gijón: Trea

Martínez Rus, A (2001). 'Las bibliotecas y la lectura: de la biblioteca popular a la biblioteca pública', in *Historia de la edición en España (1836–1936)*, ed. J Martínez Martín. Madrid: Marcial Pons, pp. 431–54

Martínez Rus, A (2003). *La política del libro durante la Segunda República: socialización de la lectura*. Gijón: Trea

Mazumdar, P M H (1992). *Eugenics, Human Genetics and Human Failings:The Eugenics Society, its Sources and its Critics in Britain*. London/New York: Routledge

Mendelson, J (1996). 'Contested Territory: The Politics of Geography in Luis Buñuel's *Las Hurdes: Tierra sin pan*', *Locus amoenus (Universitat Autónoma de Barcelona*) 2: 229–42

Mendelson, J (2000). 'Centennial Revisions: Luis Buñuel's *Las Hurdes: Tierra sin pan*', *Journal of Spanish Cultural Studies* 1 (2): 215–23

Mendelson, J (2001). 'Las Misiones Pedagógicas en la prensa de 1935 a 1938', *Boletín Institución Libre de Enseñanza* 40–1: 61–79

Mendelson, J (2002). 'La imagen de España en la década de 1930: paradoja del documental e impulso etnográfico en la obra de José Val del Omar y Luis Buñuel', in *Galaxia Val del Omar/The Galaxy of Val de Omar*, ed. G Sáenz de Buruaga. Madrid: Instituto Cervantes, pp. 19–57

Mendelson, J (2005). *Documenting Spain: Artists, Exhibition Culture, and the Modern Nation, 1929–1939*. Pennsylvania: Penn State University Press

Mendelson, J (2006). 'Archivos colectivos y autoría individual: la fotografía y las Misiones Pedagógicas', in *Las Misiones Pedagógicas 1931–1936*, ed. E Otero Urtaza. Madrid: Sociedad Estatal de Conmemoraciones Culturales/Residencia de Estudiantes, pp. 158–71

Mendelson, J (2007). *Magazines and War 1936–1939/Revistas y guerra 1936–1939*. Madrid: MNCARS

Misiones Pedagógicas, Patronato de (1933). 'Patronato de Misiones Pedagógicas', *Residencia* 4 (1): 1–21

Misiones Pedagógicas, Patronato de (1934). *Patronato de Misiones Pedagógicas: Septiembre de 1931 Diciembre de 1933*. Madrid: Patronato de Misiones Pedagógicas

Misiones Pedagógicas, Patronato de (1935). *Memoria de la Misión Pedagógico-Social en Sanabria (Zamora): Résumen de trabajos realizados en el año 1934*. Madrid: Patronato de Misiones Pedagógicas

Moliner, M (2006). 'Apuntes de María Moliner sobre las bibliotecas de Misiones', in *Las Misiones Pedagógicas: 1931–1936*, ed. E Otero Urtaza. Madrid: Sociedad Estatal de Conmemoraciones Culturales/Residencia de Estudiantes, pp. 318–25

Monguió, L (1975). 'Una biblioteca obrera madrileña en 1912–13', *Bulletin Hispanique* 77 (1975): 154–73

Morris, J (1993 [repr. 1997]). *Travels with Virginia Woolf*. London: Pimlico

Murphy, K (2002). 'Intertexts in the City: Edwardian London in Pío Baroja's *La ciudad de la niebla* and Six English Novels', *Modern Language Review* 97 (1): 149–63

Nash, M (1992). 'Social Eugenics and Nationalist Race Hygiene in Early Twentieth Century Spain', *History of European Ideas* 15 (4–6): 741–8

Nazarli, G (1932). *El traidor*. Madrid: Ediciones Libertad

Nelken, M (1926). 'Enseñanza maternal', *Sexualidad* 2 (69): 11–14

Nordau, M (1892–3). *Degeneration*. London: Heinemann

Orringer, N R (1979). *Ortega y sus fuentes germánicas*. Madrid: Gredos

Ortega y Gasset, J (1908a). 'Las dos Alemanias', *Obras completas*. Madrid: Revista de Occidente. 10, pp. 22–25

Ortega y Gasset, J (1908b). 'Asamblea para el progreso de las ciencias', *Obras completas*. Madrid: Revista de Occidente. 1, pp. 99–104

Ortega y Gasset, J (1909a). 'Los problemas nacionales y la juventud', *Obras completas*. Madrid: Revista de Occidente. 10, pp. 105–18. [Lecture of October 1909]

Ortega y Gasset, J (1909b). 'Unamuno y Europa, fábula', *Obras completas*. Madrid: Revista de Occidente. 1, pp. 128–32. [Originally in *El Imparcial* September 1909]

Ortega y Gasset, J (1910a). 'La pedagogía social como programa político', in *Obras completas*, Madrid: Revista de Occidente 1 (1957), pp. 503–21

Ortega y Gasset, J (1910b). 'Nueva revista', in *Obras completas*, Madrid: Revista de Occidente 1 (1957), pp. 142–5

Ortega y Gasset, J (1914). 'Vieja y nueva política', in *Obras completas*, Madrid: Revista de Occidente 1 (1957), pp. 265–308

Ortega y Gasset, J. (1923a) 'Propósitos', *Revista de Occidente* 1 (1): 1–3

Ortega y Gasset, J (1923b). 'La poesía de Ana de Noailles', *Revista de Occidente* 1 (1): 29–41

Ortega y Gasset, J (1923c). 'Para una topografía de la soberbia española', *Revista de Occidente* 1 (3): 65–280

Ortega y Gasset, J (1925a). 'La deshumanización del arte', in *Obras completas*, Madrid: Revista de Occidente 3 (1957), pp. 353–86

Ortega y Gasset, J (1925b). 'Ideas sobre la novela', in *Obras completas*, Madrid: Revista de Occidente, 1961 3 (1957), pp. 387–449

Ortega y Gasset, J (1930). 'La rebelión de las masas', in *Obras completas*, Madrid: Revista de Occidente 4 (1957), pp. 113–310

Ortega y Gasset, J (1942). 'En torno a Galileo: Esquema de las crisis y otros ensayos', in *Obras completas*, Madrid: Revista de Occidente 5 (1961), pp. 13–164

Ortega y Gasset, J (1974). 'Los problemas nacionales y la juventud', in *Discursos políticos*, Madrid: Alianza Editorial, pp. 11–28

Otero Urtaza, E (1982). *Las misiones pedagógicas: una experiencia de educación popular*. La Coruña: Do Castro

Otero Urtaza, E, ed. (2006a). *Las Misiones Pedagógicas: 1931–1936*. Madrid: Sociedad Estatal de Conmemoraciones Culturales/Residencia de Estudiantes

Otero Urtaza, E (2006b). 'Los marineros del entusiasmo en las Misiones Pedagógicas', in *Las Misiones Pedagógicas: 1931–1936*, ed. E Otero Urtaza. Madrid: Sociedad Estatal de Conmemoraciones Culturales/Residencia de Estudiantes, pp. 65–113

Ouimette, V. (1997) (ed.). *Miguel de Unamuno: De patriotismo espiritual: Artículos en "La Nación" de Buenos Aires 1901–1914*. Salamanca: Ediciones Universidad

Paris VIII, Grupo de investigación de la Universidad de (1986). *Ideología y texto en El cuento semanal*. Madrid: Ediciones de la Torre

Passerini, L (1999). *Europe in Love, Love in Europe: Imagination and Politics in Britain between the Wars*. London/New York: Tauris

Pestaña, Á (1924). *70 días en Rusia*. Barcelona [Tipografía Cosmos]

Pestaña, A (1932). *La caída del dictador*. Madrid: Ediciones Libertad

Pestaña, A (1933). *Lo que aprendí en la vida*. Madrid: Aguilar; repr. 1971, Madrid: Zero

Pestaña, Á (1968). *Informe sobre mi estancia en la URRS*. Madrid: ZYX

Pick, D (1989). *Faces of Degeneration: A European Disorder, c.1848–c.1918*. Cambridge: Cambridge University Press

Pritchett, V S (1971). *Midnight Oil*. London: Chatto & Windus

Rendueles Olmedo, G (1989). *El manuscrito encontrado en Ciempozuelos: análisis de la historia clínica de Aurora Rodríguez*. Madrid: Ediciones de la Piqueta

[Residencia de Estudiantes] (ed.) (1984). *Poesía: Revista Ilustrada de Información poética, nos 18–19*. Madrid [Residencia]

Revel, J (1991). 'Michel de Certeau historien: l'institution et son contraire', in *Histoire, mystique et politique*, ed. L Giard, H Martin and J Revel. Grenoble: Millon, pp. 109–27

Ribagorda, Á (2006). 'La revista *Residencia*: entre el boletín y la alta divulgación', *Boletín de la Institución Libre de Enseñanza* 63–4 (December): 311–36

Ribagorda, Á (2007). 'Las publicaciones de la Residencia de Estudiantes', *Iberoamericana* 7 (25): 43–64

Ribagorda, Á (2008). *La Residencia de Estudiantes: Pedagogía, cultura y proyecto social*. Seminario de Investigación del Departamento de Historia Contemporánea (UCM)

Ribbans, G. (1991). "Unamuno in England: Four Unpublished Articles (1909). Part I." *Bulletin of Hispanic Studies* 68: 383–94

Richards, M (2004). 'Spanish Psychiatry c.1900–1945: Constitutional Theory, Eugenics, and the Nation', in *Bulletin of Spanish Studies. Special Number: Alternative Discourses in Early Twentieth-century Spain: Intellectuals, Dissent and Sub-cultures of Mind and Body*, ed. A Sinclair and R Cleminson. 81, pp. 823–48

Roberts, S (2007). *Miguel de Unamuno o la creación del intelectual español moderno*. Salamanca: Editorial Universidad de Salamanca

Romero Salvadó, F J (1996). 'The Failure of the Liberal Project of the Spanish Nation-State, 1909–1938', in *Nationalism and the Nation in the Iberian Peninsula: Competing and Conflicting Identities*, ed. C Mar-Molinaro and Á Smith. Oxford/Washington: Berg, pp. 119–32

Ruiz-Castillo, J (1979). *El apasionante mundo del libro*. Madrid: Biblioteca Nueva

Russell, B (1930). 'Lugar del amor en la vida humana', *Revista de Occidente* 8 (79): 1–10

S [L Santullano] (1933). 'Patronato de Misiones Pedagógicas', *Residencia* 4 (1): 1–21

Sáenz de la Calzada, M (1986). *La Residencia de Estudiantes 1910–1936*. Madrid: CSIC

Said, E. (1978, repr. 1992 with afterword). *Orientalism: Western Conceptions of the Orient*. Harmondsworth: Penguin

Sainz de Robles, F C (1975). *La promoción de 'El cuento semanal' 1907–1925*. Madrid: Espasa Calpe

Salaberria Lizarazu, R (2002). 'La larga marcha de Juan Vicéns', in *Juan Vicéns, España viva: el pueblo a la conquista de la cultura: las bibliotecas populares en la segunda república*. Madrid: VOSA/Asociación Educación y Bibliotecas, pp. 7–30

Salaberria Lizarazu, R (2006). 'Las bibliotecas de Misiones Pedagógicas: medio millón de libros a las aldeas más olvidadas', in *Las Misiones Pedagógicas*, ed. E Otero Urtaza. Madrid: Sociedad Estatal de Conmemoraciones Culturales/Residencia de Estudiantes, pp. 302–17

Salaverría, J M (1933). 'Actualidades y recuerdos', *Residencia* 4 (2): 74

Sánchez Ron, J M (1988). *1907–1987, La Junta para Ampliación de Estudios e investigaciones científicas 80 años despúes*. Madrid: CSIC

Santonja, G (1989). *La República de los libros: el nuevo libro popular de la II República*. Barcelona: Anthropos

Santonja, G (1994). *Las novelas rojas: estudio y antología*. Madrid: Ediciones de la Torre

Santonja, G (2000). *La insurrección literaria: la novela revolucionaria de quiosco, 1905–1939*. Madrid: SIAL

Sender, R (1934). *Madrid-Moscú. Carta de Moscú sobre el amor (1933–4)*. Madrid: Imp. de Juan Pueyo

Serrano, C (ed.) (2000). *El nacimiento de los intelectuales en España*. Madrid: Ayer

Shubert, A (1990). *A Social History of Modern Spain*. London: Unwin Hyman

Simmel, J (1923a). 'Filosofía de la moda', *Revista de Occidente* 1 (2): 211–30

Simmel, J (1923b). 'Filosofía de la moda', *Revista de Occidente* 1 (1): 43–66

Simmel, J (1923c). 'Lo masculino y lo femenino. Para una psicología de los sexos', *Revista de Occidente* 1 (5): 218–36

Simmel, J (1923d). 'Lo masculino y lo femenino. Para una psicología de los sexos (Conclusión)', *Revista de Occidente* 1 (6): 336–63

Sinclair, A (2001). *Uncovering the Mind: Unamuno, the Unknown and the Vicissitudes of Self*. Manchester: Manchester University Press

Sinclair, A (2004a). '"Telling it like it was?" The "Residencia de Estudiantes" and its Image', *Bulletin of Spanish Studies* 81 (6): 739–63

Sinclair, A (2004b). 'Interior and Internal Spain: Visions of the Primitive at the Cultural Interface', *Romance Studies* 22 (3): 209–21

Sinclair, A (2007). *Sex and Society in Early Twentieth-Century Spain: Hildegart Rodríguez and the World League for Sexual Reform*. Cardiff: University of Wales Press

Sinclair, A (2010 forthcoming). 'Love, again: Crisis and the Search for

Consolation: The *Revista de Occidente* and the Creation of a Culture', in *New Dangerous Liaisons*, ed. L Passerini, L Ellena and A Geppert. London: Berghahn

Smith, P J (2000). *The Moderns: Time, Space, and Subjectivity in Contemporary Spanish Culture*. Oxford: Oxford University Press

Soriano, R [1927]. *San Lenín. (Viaje a Rusia)*. Paris: Agencia Mundial de Librería

Soriano, R. (1932). *La bomba*. Madrid: Ediciones Libertad

Spivak, G C (1988). 'Can the Subaltern Speak?', in *Marxism and the Interpretation of Culture*, ed. C Nelson and L Grossberg. London: Macmillan, pp. 271–313

Starkie, W (1926). 'El teatro inglés contemporáneo', *Residencia* 1 (1): 42–54

Starkie, W (1982). *Aventuras de un irlandés en España*. Madrid: Espasa

Strachey, L (1928a). 'La muerte del general Gordon', *Revista de Occidente* 6 (57): 359–78

Strachey, L (1928b). 'La muerte del general Gordon (Continuación)', *Revista de Occidente* 6 (58): 57–85

Strachey, L (1928c). 'La muerte del general Gordon (Conclusión)', *Revista de Occidente* 6 (59): 194–230

Torrubiano Ripoll, J (1925). 'Títulos de nuestra audacia: fuentes de nuestros estudios', *Sexualidad* 1 (31): 2–3

Townsend, J (1791). *A Journey through Spain in the Years 1786 and 1787; with Particular Attention to the Agriculture, Manufactures, Commerce, Population, Taxes, and Revenue of that Country*. London: Dilly

Trend, J B (1921). *A Picture of Modern Spain: Men and Music*. London: Constable

Trend, J B (1934). *The Origins of Modern Spain*. Cambridge: Cambridge University Press

Trillas, E (1987). 'Foreword to facsimile reproduction', *Residencia*, ed. Madrid: CSIC, pp. vii–viii

Tuñón de Lara, M (1993). 'Grandes corrientes culturales', in *Los orígenes culturales de la II República*, ed. J L García Delgado. Madrid: Siglo XXI, pp. 1–24

Unamuno, M de (1902a). *En torno al casticismo*. Madrid: Escelicer

Unamuno, M de (1902b). 'España y los españoles', in *Obras completas*, ed. M García Blanco. Madrid: Escelicer 3, pp. 718–29

Unamuno, M de (1906). 'Sobre la europeización', in *Obras completas*, ed. M García Blanco. Madrid: Escelicer 3, pp. 925–38

Unamuno, M. de (1909). *The Spirit of Spain (I and II)*. The Englishwoman. 4: 80–93

Valéry, P (1927). 'Notas sobre la grandeza y la decadencia de Europa', *Revista de Occidente* 5 (46): 1–14

Vallejo, C (1978). *Rusia en 1931: Reflexiones al pie del Kremlin*. Lima: Ediciones Ulises

Varela, J (1999). *La novela de España. Los intelectuales y el problema español*. Madrid: Taurus

Vicéns, J (1938). *España viva: el pueblo a la conquista de la cultura*. Madrid: Ediciones VOSA SL y Asociación Educación y Bibliotecas [2002]

Vilanova Ribas, M and X Moreno Julià (1992). *Atlas de la evolución del analfabetismo en España de 1887 a 1981*. Madrid: Ministerio de Educación y Ciencia

Villacorta Baños, F (1980). *Burguesía y cultura: los intelectuales españoles en la sociedad liberal, 1808–1931*. Madrid: Siglo XXI

Villacorta Baños, F (1985). *El Ateneo científico, literario y artístico de Madrid (1885–1912)*. Madrid: Centro de Estudios Históricos, CSIC

Vivero, A (1932). *A tiro limpio*. Madrid: Ediciones Libertad

Wickberg, D (2001). 'Intellectual History vs. the Social History of Intellectuals', *Rethinking History* 5 (3): 383–95

Winnicott, D W (1971). *Playing and Reality*. New York: Basic Books

Witz, A (2001). 'Georg Simmel and the Masculinity of Modernity', *Journal of Classical Sociology* 1 (3): 353–72

Zugazagoitia, J (1932). *Rusia al día*. Madrid: Editorial España

Zulueta, C d (1988). *Misioneras, feministas, educadoras: Historia del Instituto Internacional*. Madrid: Castalia

Zulueta, C d (1992). *Cien anos de educación de la mujer española: Historia del Instituto Internacional*. Madrid: Castalia

Zulueta, C d and A Moreno (1993). *Ni convento ni college: La Residencia de Señoritas*. Madrid: CSIC

Zulueta, L d (1916). 'Los doce mejores libros', *España* (2): 4–5

INDEX